REEDS
SEA TRANSPORT
OPERATION AND ECONOMICS

Other titles of interest from Reeds

REEDS MARINE DISTANCE TABLES
9TH EDITION
R. W. CANEY AND J. E. REYNOLDS
ISBN 0-7136-6805-9

These tables provide the perfect ready-reckoner for any navigator wanting a quick and accurate distance reference between all the regularly used ports around the world.

The book is divided into key 'market areas', and includes a pull-out map for area identification and chartlets for easy port reference.

Reeds Marine Distance Tables are an invaluable reference for ship owners, operators, brokers and navigators for voyage estimating, enabling the user to calculate the shortest or most economical distance between almost 500 major ports worldwide.

REEDS ENGINEERING KNOWLEDGE
INSTRUMENTS AND CONTROL SYSTEMS FOR DECK OFFICERS
5TH EDITION
W. EMBLETON AND T. MORTON
ISBN 0-901281-158

This book presents the principles covered by the DoT examination papers in Engineering Knowledge, Instruments and Control Systems for Masters (foreign-going). It also briefly revises the General Physics for the Second Mate syllabus which is included in the Master's examination.

REEDS
SEA TRANSPORT
OPERATION AND ECONOMICS

FIFTH EDITION

PATRICK M ALDERTON
M Phil, Extra Master, Dip Maths, MCIT

ADLARD COLES NAUTICAL
LONDON

Published by Adlard Coles Nautical
an imprint of A & C Black Publishers Ltd
37 Soho Square, London W1D 3QZ
www.adlardcoles.com

First published by Thomas Reed Publications 1973
Second edition 1980
Third edition 1984
Fourth edition 1995
Fifth edition published by Adlard Coles Nautical 2004

ISBN 0-7136-6944-6
ISBN 978-0-7136-6944-2

A CIP catalogue record for this book is available from the British Library.

A & C Black uses paper produced with elemental chlorine-free pulp,
harvested from managed sustainable forests.

Designed by Dave Saunders
Typeset in 10pt Bliss by Tradespools, Frome, Somerset
Printed and bound in Spain by GraphyCems

Note: While all reasonable care has been taken in the publication of this book,
the publisher takes no responsibility for the use of the methods or products
described in the book.

Contents

Acknowledgements

I would like to thank my former colleagues and students of the World Maritime University in Malmö, and also those at what was the London Guildhall University, now the London Metropolitan University, who have helped in so many ways. I must particularly thank Professor T Sampson for his expert section on safety and environmental issues in Chapter 13. Many of my past students, a considerable number now in exalted positions in the industry, have helped specifically with information and photographs. In this edition I am particularly indebted to Dr Heather Leggate (the Head of the Centre for International Transport Management at the London Metropolitan University) for her valuable chapter on ship-financing.

I am also grateful to Adlard Coles Nautical, the publishers of this fifth edition of *Sea Transport*, who have taken over the publication from Thomas Reed Publications, and in particular to Janet Murphy, a director of Adlard Coles, for her help and suggestions during the preparation of this edition.

Preface

The aim of this book is to give an all-round presentation of the essential elements of maritime transport; and as shipping is one of the oldest forms of commercial activities that has remained in continuous use, it is necessary to consider, at least briefly, the industry's historic development in order to understand its current state of activity.

This book therefore sets out to give a complete picture of the maritime transport industry so that those involved with shipping can see their own specific field of interest in perspective and understand how the basic model of this mode of transport works. Maritime transport is a rapidly changing industry and, in particular since the Second World War, it is not enough to try to learn one's business simply by 'sitting next to Nellie'. Modern transport professionals must be able to adapt to, and anticipate, the implications of changes in the industry. Perhaps one of the most important aspects of modern management is the ability to manage change, and I hope that this book will give an insight as to how management has coped with this over the last century. Such an approach has become an integral part of most of the professional and academic courses that are concerned with shipping, ports and transport. The structure and content of this book are based on the lectures given to, and the interaction I have had with, students in London and at the World Maritime University in Malmö over the last 25 years.

I have tried to avoid the unnecessary use of jargon in this book and hope that the text will be readily understandable to those with little knowledge of sea transport, but also have sufficient depth to be of interest and value to those professionally engaged in the industry.

Where possible, I have quoted actual figures and statistics, as I have noticed that it is easier for students to grasp the relative merits of the size, importance and value of a thing or concept by giving actual data.

However, students will know that even the highest authorities on a subject will not always agree on statistics, as in their collection and selection different assumptions may be possible, and the precise control of the laboratory is not usually available in the actual commercial situation.

I do not anticipate that this book will answer all the reader's questions on sea transport, but I hope that it will at least stimulate curiosity concerning the subject. I have also found that disagreement on a subject can provide as valuable an educational insight as agreement.

When discussing various aspects of those *persons* engaged in ports and shipping, I have tended to use the pronouns 'he' and 'him' rather than 'she' or 'her'. This is not meant to be sexist, but is merely my attempt not to be verbally tedious. Although the world of ports and shipping has tended to be a male-dominated business, women do now occupy many of the highest positions in the shipping industry, and so the terms 'he' and 'she' can in nearly all cases be considered interchangeable.

Patrick Alderton

1 THE SHIP

The function of sea transport, like that of any other form of transport, is to move things; and its success lies in finding people who have things that need moving, then transporting these things safely and efficiently.

Logically one should start with what needs moving, where it needs to be moved to, and how much of it there is. However, before we can make any really useful analysis it is probably better to examine what vehicles and hardware are at our disposal, and then to understand the basic jargon that has inevitably grown up around what must surely be the oldest form of transport.

The number and classification of ships

In the seventeenth century much of the business of the port of London was conducted in the various coffee houses in the city. One such coffee house, much frequented by people concerned with the shipping business, especially underwriters, was run by a man called Edward Lloyd. Anxious to please his clientele, Lloyd produced ships' lists, which gave some account of the various vessels likely to be offered for insurance. Lloyd's Register is a descendant of these lists, and in three large volumes it contains details of all the merchant ships in the world of over 100 tons gross. In 2001, this total was well over 87,500 ships and, as is shown in Chapter 2, is made up of a large variety of types, shapes and sizes.

Ships can be categorised not only by their specialist functions -- ie tankers, general cargo, containers, etc -- but also as to how they are operated.

There are two basic modes of operation. A ship can be employed as a *liner* -- ie it runs on a regular line between two ports or series of ports. It has a regular schedule of sailings and an agreed list of tariffs or prices. Alternatively, a ship can be employed as a *tramp*. This means that the ship is chartered or hired out at the best price the owner can obtain. Such a ship may go anywhere with anything on board. There is in fact a third possibility. This is where merchants or organisations who have a lot of cargo to move, such as oil companies, operate their own ships.

A further tradition is to distinguish, for a variety of reasons, between ships that go a short distance, referred to variously as *coasters, home-traders* or *short sea traders*, and those that venture farther afield and are known as *foreign-going ships* (this will be dealt with in greater detail in Chapter 4).

Design and Classification Societies

Ships are designed by naval architects and they are bound by various constraints, such as the cost of different designs, what is technically possible, what cargoes the vessels are most likely to carry, environmental safety factors, and which ports they are most likely to trade between. The whole problem of planning is made more difficult by the fact that the design, ordering and building of a ship may take two or three years, and also that the expected working life of a ship is still in the region of fifteen to twenty years. Obviously in today's world much can change during this lapse of time.

Many shipowners have their own particular preferences and style, and because few ship types are mass-produced there is considerable room for manoeuvre here on superficial appearance factors such as the shape of the superstructure and funnel. In contrast, under water, the shape of the hull is critical and cannot be left to someone's artistic whims. So in order to prove vessels' viability in this respect, wax models are made and tested in special testing tanks. Being wax, their shape can be easily altered and re-tested and eventually an optimum shape is evolved for that size of ship, its speed and the anticipated sea conditions.

But of course the ship must not only be efficiently designed, it must also be soundly built; and the certificate of an independent body as to quality of design and construction may help a shipowner to convince an insurance underwriter that his ship is seaworthy. Such independent bodies are known as *Classification Societies*. There are numerous societies -- but the oldest, largest and perhaps most famous is Lloyd's Register. (Edward Lloyd made comments on the state of the ship in his original circulars.) An International Association of Classification Societies was founded in 1968 (IACS) and IACS members classify 42,000 ships -- which is more than half the world fleet -- or around 95 per cent of the world's gross tonnage. There are about 40 small Classification Societies, which are not all IACS members. Some notable Classification Societies are given in Table 1.1.

In its original state, when the Register was started in 1760, it was known as the 'green book' and it was for the exclusive use of underwriters. Some years later a rival register was started by shipowners, but in 1834 the two registers were completely reconstituted to form an independent society. As a result, a definite system of classification was started, based on a book of rules. In its early days there were many classes (A1, representing the highest class, first appeared in 1775), but now there is only one class for all types of ocean-going vessel, ie 100 A1. (There are, however, four classes of ice-strengthening in the rules -- vessels that are required to navigate in ice need to be strengthened accordingly, particularly round the bows and stern, which are obviously the most vulnerable areas when battering their way through ice. The degree of strengthening depends on the severity of ice anticipated, and charterers and operators need to know not only these rules, but also the expected weather.)

Table 1.1	Some notable Classification Societies			
Name	Symbol	Date founded	Nationality	Comments
American Bureau	AB	1862	American	
Bureau Veritas	BV	1828	French	The rules of this Society admit two classes, excellent and seaworthy
Germanischer Lloyd	GL	1867	German	
Det Norske Veritas	NV	1864	Norwegian	
Nippon Kaiji Kyokai	NK	1899	Japanese	
Registro Italiano Navale	RL	1861	Italian	Also makes provision for two classes

To obtain Lloyd's class of ✠ 100 A1 the vessel must be built under the scrutiny of the Society's surveyors (the significance of the Maltese cross) and its strength and construction must satisfy the Society's rules. Similar conditions apply to the machinery of the vessel.

In order to *maintain* class, a vessel must undergo periodic surveys. These include annual surveys afloat, dry-docking (with a maximum interval of 24 months), and a special survey at four-yearly intervals (or a five-year continuous survey cycle), which becomes more rigorous as the vessel ages. Engines, machinery parts, boilers, screwshafts and a variety of specific items -- depending on the type of ship -- are also subject to periodic surveys in accordance with the Society's rules.

We must add that, in the UK at least, classification is voluntary -- but in reality few shipowners would or could operate without it. It is not only the underwriters that the shipowners have to convince of the ship's seaworthiness, but also the charterers, shippers, financiers, various cargo interests and the port state authorities of the countries that the ship will visit.

Finally, Lloyd's Register includes all ships over 100 tons gross whether classed with Lloyd's or not, so is often referred to as the 'shipping man's bible'. For this reason, it is obviously important for us to be familiar with its format and content. The key shown at the top of the specimen page (page 4) has been inserted to help identify the data, but in the actual volumes the key is printed on an attached plastic bookmark. The Register of Ships is now also available on a CD-ROM.

EXTRACT FROM LLOYDS REGISTER OF SHIPS

FINNJET

1	2	3	4	5	6	7
LR No Call Sign Official No Fishing No Navigational aids AMVER	SHIP'S NAME Former names Owners Managers Port of Registry SatCom Id	TONNAGE Gross Net *Deadwt Gross Net *Deadwt *(tonnes) Flag	CLASSIFICATION Special Survey Hull Machinery Refrigerated cargo installation Equipment Letter Fee Numeral	HULL Date of Build Shipbuilders - Place of Build Yard Number Length overall (m) Length B.P. (m) Breadth extreme (m) Breadth moulded (m) Draught maximum (m) Depth moulded (m) Keel (mm) Superstructures (m) Decks Riveted/Welded Rise of Floor (m) Additional tanker dimensions Alterations Conversions	SHIP TYPE/CARGO FACILITIES Propulsion Shiptype Shelter deck Passengers Ro-Ro facilities Holds & lengths (m) Cargo tanks & types Grain/Liquid Bale Insulated Heating spaces (m³) coils Containers & lengths (ft) Hatchways & sizes (m) Winches Cargo handling gear (SWL tonnes) Cargo discharge pumps	MACHINERY Design Designation No & Type of engines Bore x Stroke (mm) Power Engine builders Where manufactured Boilers Pressures Heating Surface Furnaces Aux. electrical generating plant & output Special propellers Fuel bunkers (tonnes) Speed
7359632 OIHH 1576 Df Esd Gc RTm/h/v	FINNJET Effôa 1 Oy Oy Silja Line Ab Mariehamn	25 042 10 360 2825 Finland	NV	1977 Oy Wärtsilä Ab–Helsinki/Helsingfors (407) 212,81 196,32 24,44 6,700 14,81 4 dks rf 800	TGT or D-E Passenger/RoRo Cargo/ Ferry 548cbn 1544bth 288dk P Ice strengthened Bow door & ramp L 9,00 W 4,20 Stern door & ramp L 5,25 W 4,80 Lane Length 1750 Cargo Width 4,80 Clear height 4,20 Cars 380 TEU 116 C.116/20'	Wärtsilä 18V32 2 Vee Oil 4SA each 18Cy. 320 X 350 15 5000bhp (11 401kW) driving 2 gen each 5300kW connected to 2 elec. motors each 7205 shp (5300kW) & dr geared to sc. shafts NE(Diesel) added 12/81 (Diesel) Oy Wartsila Ab Vaasa/Vasa 2 Gas Turb tr geared to sc. shafts (Turbine) Turbo Power & Marine Systems Farmington Ct Pratt & Whitney 75000 shp Gen 5 X 1360kW 380V 50 Hz a.c. 2 Controllable pitch propellers 2 Thw. thrust propellers fwd 30.5kn
7608588 YLFI 0624 Df Esd Gc Pfd Rdr RTv	PABAZI ex Sergey Lyulin-92 Riga Trawling & Refrigeration Fleet Base (Rigas Traleru & Refrizeratoru Flotes Baze) Riga	3017 1245 2063 Latvia	RS	1975 VEB - Volkswerft Stralsund-Stralsund (454) 5,650 101,83 (BB) 91,90 15,22 15,19 9,71 2 dks	M Factory Fishing Fish-factory Stern Trawler Ref Ice strengthened 2 Ho In.1 858 2 Ha (each 2.2 X 2.2) Der 2(5) 4(3)	MAN 8ZD72/48 Oil 2SA 8Cy. 480 X 720 3 880bhp (2 854kW) VEB Dieselmotorenwerk (DMR) Rostock Controllable pitch propeller 16.25kn
7719088 3FWD 12048-82 Df Esd Gc Pfd Rdr Rt	PACHITEA Launched as Transatlantico –Monfalcone Woodmere Enterprises Inc. Compania Peruana de Vapores S.A. (CPV) Panama Panama	8281 5003 15 984 Panama	(RI) + Classed LR until 20/9/89	Lch. 1975 Cmpl. 1982-1 Italcantieri S.pA. 9,051 154,24 (BB) 140,01 22,89 22,86 16,21 P 33,0 F 12,8 2 dks rf nil	M RoRo Cargo (4364) Quarter stern door/ramp (s) L 21,75 W 8,00 SWL 80 Lane Length 1300 3 Ho 13,1DTp 13,1DTs 17,6 35,2 33.2 1 TwD C.27 419 B.25 199 TEU 600 C.Dk 600/20 incl. 24' ref C. 8 Ha (stl) (5,4p&s X 4,2) (16,4p&s 31,2p&s 31,2p&s X 8,4) ER Cr 2(35) 2(25) 2(16)	GMT 8550.8L Oil 4SA 8Cy. 550 X 590 with flexible couplings & sr geared to sc. shaft 11 200bhp (8238kw) Grandi Motori Trieste Trieste Gen 3 X 635kW 450V 60Hz a.c. Controllable pitch propeller 16kn

Courtesy of Lloyd's Register.

4

Parts of the ship

Figs 1.1 and 1.2 are typical of the general cargo ships built during the 1960s. However, it is useful to include them in this section on definitions as they contain most of the basic elements found in modern ships. Many ship 'definitions' used in legal documents -- as, say, for charter parties -- may well be decades out of date!

Although the drawings are labelled 'general cargo ship', ships, like cars and houses, vary within certain very wide limits in their design and layout. Even the methods of construction can vary considerably from the traditional floor, frame and beam construction shown in Fig 1.1. Ships used to be built upwards and outwards from the keel, but in most yards they are now built in huge prefabricated sections that are subsequently joined together.

Anchors These are very important and compulsory items of equipment, and the usual arrangement is to have two bow anchors and one spare. They are raised and lowered by a special winch known as the windlass, or perhaps by a

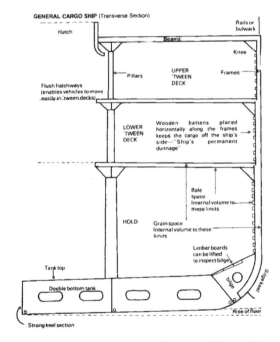

Fig 1.1   Internal structure of a general cargo ship.

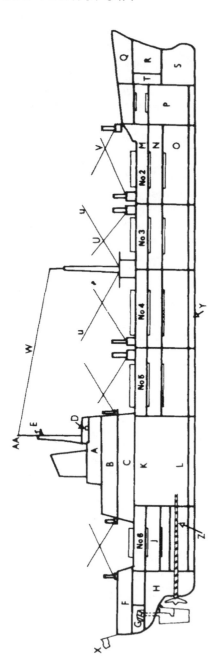

GENERAL CARGO SHIP (longitudinal section)

| AA Flag of country in (courtesy ensign) | Company's house flag | Signal flags and lights |

A	Captain and passengers	K	Refrig machy	T	Chain locker
B	Officer's accommodation	L	Engine room	U	Derricks
C	Crew accommodation	M	No 2 upper 'tween deck	V	Crane
D	Wheelhouse and chart room	N	No 2 lower 'tween deck	W	Radio aerial
E	Radar scanner	O	No 2 lower hold	X	National flag
F	Cargo space	P	Deep tank	Y	Double bottom
G	Steering gear	Q	Store	Z	Propeller shaft
H	Aft peak tank	R	Bosun's store		
J	Ref cargo	S	Fore peak tank		

Fig 1.2   Longitudinal section of a general cargo ship.

capstan on very large ships. The cable drops down off the windlass into the chain locker. A few ships have stern anchors.

When considering an anchorage for a ship, the depth of water, the nature of the bottom and prevailing winds should be known.

On long salvage tows, the ship's anchor cable is often used as part of the towing line.

Ballast This is weight loaded to make the ship seaworthy when she has to go to sea without cargo. Originally this could have been anything – and was often just sand and stones from the beach. However, modern ships use sea water in the double bottom tanks, peak tanks, and also specially constructed ballast tanks.

Bilges These are virtually ditches at each side of the hold where all the condensation, sweat and leaking liquids can drain and be pumped out. Before any loading, particularly of foodstuffs, the bilges must be cleaned out and inspected.

On some ships the double bottoms are carried out to the sides so there will be no bilges. When this occurs, a 'well' or drain is made in an isolated section in the double bottom which then serves the same purpose.

Bulkheads These are vertical partitions or walls, and all ships must have a specified number of bulkheads depending on their length. By dividing the ship into watertight divisions they reduce the danger of sinking if one compartment is holed. They also reduce the risk of fire spreading.

The for'd bulkhead, called the collision bulkhead, is made particularly strong as it has to withstand considerable buffeting if the ship steams to a repair yard having had her bows severely damaged in a collision. Had the *Titanic* hit the iceberg head-on instead of swerving and ripping a long gash down her side, she would almost certainly have made New York safely under her own power instead of being the most terrible maritime casualty of all time. One of the problems of Ro/Ro ferries has been the large undivided car deck spaces, which makes them very vulnerable to flooding and to the subsequent loss of stability. (Note the comments made later concerning 'slack tanks'.)

Decks The number of decks depends entirely on the trade and cargo for which the ship is designed. On some liner trades she may have three or four, and passenger ships may have many more. Ships designed to carry cars may have several portable decks. On the other hand, tramp vessels carrying bulk cargoes may only have one deck.

Deep tanks These are holds with facilities such as wash plates, pipelines and oil-tight hatches so that they can be used for the carriage of liquid cargoes or water ballast.

Derricks or cranes These are used on general cargo ships to lift the cargo on and off. They are usually capable of lifting between 5 and 10 tons, but the

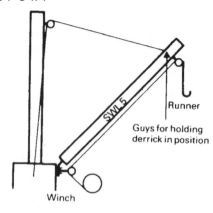

Fig 1.3 A derrick.

ship may be fitted with one or more heavy-lift derricks ('Jumbo') to cope with the heavier items of cargo. Derricks are usually used in pairs, with one being fixed over the hold and the other over the quay. The two runners are then joined together and the cargo lifted out of the hold by the ship derrick. It is moved over the ship's rail by slacking on the ship derrick and heaving on the over-side derrick, and the over-side derrick then lowers the cargo onto the quay. This is known as the *union purchase* method. This has the advantage of rugged simplicity and universal acceptance by stevedores. The shipboard crane is initially more expensive, but it requires fewer stevedores. It can pick up and put down the cargo over a much wider area (it has better 'spotting' facilities) and it is quicker.

Lifting-gear   This is subject to the Merchant Shipping Notice number M 1347 concerning safety and it must be clearly marked with its *SWL* (safe working load). M 1347 gives information on 'The Merchant Shipping (Hatches and Lifting Plant) Regulations 1988', which came into force on 1 January 1989. These regulations form part of a package with the new Docks Regulations prepared by the Health and Safety Commission, and bring the UK into line with the ILO convention 152 concerning safety and health in dock work.

Double bottom tanks   This is a double skin along the bottom of the ship. (From a ship safety point of view, these were not necessary in tankers with their smaller divided cargo spaces; however, from an environmental safety consideration, the American OPA 90 legislation is causing the new generation of tankers to have double skins.) Its purpose is to provide a safeguard in the event of grounding, which happens to about two ships a day. This space is used for water ballast, fresh water or bunkers.

Dunnage   These are bits of wood, sacking, inflatable rubber bags -- in fact, anything that is used to prevent damage to the cargo.

8

Flare This word means the outward curve on the bows. It gives two advantages: (1) it makes a larger fo'c's'le head; (2) it deflects the water when pitching into a seaway, and thus the vessel ships less water. This is very noticeable on container ships.

Hatchway This is the hole through which the cargo is loaded into the ship. Traditionally this hole has been a source of weakness in the structure, but modern technology has provided large steel hatchcovers that can slide back into place at the flick of a lever. Ships with these are allowed to load deeper than the older types covered only by the wooden boards and canvas (see Fig 1.4). There are many different types and designs of steel hatchcovers. The first seems to have appeared around 1937, and 1949 saw the introduction of the 'single pull' hatchcover which by 1955 had established itself as the standard hatchway for most new general cargo tonnage. The year 1952 saw the introduction of flush fitting hatchways in 'tween decks and in 1959 side rolling covers were introduced for bulk carriers.

Because of these developments the hatchway can be made much larger and this means the cargo can be dropped into position. If the hatchway is small, the cargo has to be carried or dragged into position at the sides of the ship. This takes time and costs money. It could be argued that the large 'open' hatchway is the basis of virtually all the major developments in improving ship productivity since the Second World War.

Some modern ships have large hydraulically operated doors in their sides through which fork-lift trucks can drive and stow the cargo directly.

Lock-up space Many breakbulk cargo ships have large rooms or lockers in some of the holds where valuable cargo can be locked up.

Peak tanks These are known as fore-peak and after-peak tanks, and are situated at the ends of the ship. They are usually used for ballast to 'trim' the ship — ie to keep it level or at the angle required.

Reefer space Most liner ships have facilities for carrying refrigerated cargo.

Shaft tunnel If the propeller shaft has to pass through any holds, it has of course to be enclosed in a tunnel that must allow enough room for an engineer to walk along to inspect the shaft. This tunnel takes up considerable space in any hold, which is one argument for putting the engines right aft. Another is that it leaves the middle of the ship, with its large square holds, available for cargo. (Holds at the ends of the ship tend to be V-shaped.)

There were two traditional reasons for having engines amidships. It was essential when ships were fitted with paddle-wheels, and it also meant that vessels with the weight in the middle were on an even keel when completely empty, and thus the minimum of ballast was required. With modern ships, adequate ballast is seldom a problem, as sea water can easily be pumped in as needed.

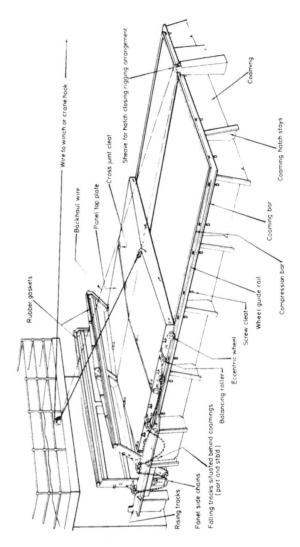

Fig 1.4 Hatchcovers.

Wire to winch or crane hook

Backhaul wire

Panel top plate

Cross joint cleat

Sheave for hatch closing rigging arrangement

Coaming

Coaming hatch stays

Coaming bar

Compression bar

Wheel guide rail

Screw cleat

Eccentric wheel

Balancing roller

Falling tracks situated behind coamings (port and stbd)

Panel side chains

Rising tracks

Rubber gaskets

Ship stresses and stability

Hogging and sagging

On long ships, such as very large tankers and bulk carriers, those responsible for loading the ship have to take care to avoid straining the vessel's hull. If too much weight is placed amidships, the vessel will sag (see Fig 1.5). As the vessel cannot submerge her loadline mark amidships, she will not be able to load her full cargo.

If excess weight is placed at the ends of the ship and not enough in the middle, the vessel may hog. If a vessel in such a condition were loaded with a full deadweight (dwt) cargo, her loadline marks amidships would indicate she could carry more cargo. In the 'bad old days' it is said that this was done deliberately.

With large modern vessels this distortion can be feet rather than inches, and apart from the obvious strain on the hull and the problems already mentioned, it may also increase the draft -- which is often critical for large ships getting in and out of port.

Ships are fairly flexible structures and the bending may not do much permanent harm. If bent severely, however, the ship may become permanently distorted -- which is obviously undesirable from many points of view.

To help ship's officers and those responsible for making the necessary calculations to avoid this bending, they must of course be supplied with the necessary information, gadgets and calculators. Any such longitudinal stresses will be aggravated by the vessel *pitching* when end-on to the waves.

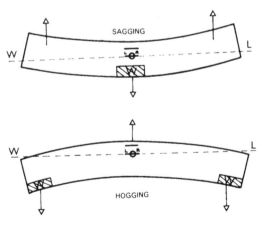

Fig 1.5   Sagging and hogging.

Stability

With smaller general cargo ships the problem of hogging and sagging is not so likely to be serious, but that of stability can well be.

Ship stability can be defined as the ability of the ship to return to the upright when slightly inclined, and instability can result from too much top weight -- or, conversely, too little bottom weight. For the sake of argument, consider all the weight of the ship and cargo to act at a single point G (the centre of gravity) (see Fig 1.6) and the upward force of buoyancy to act at a single point B (the centre of buoyancy). Unless the cargo shifts, the point G will be fixed as the vessel rolls. The point B, on the other hand, will move out to the side as the vessel heels over. The point where the upward force of buoyancy cuts the centre line of the ship is known as M, the metacentre. M can be considered stationary for small angles of heel.

Without going into the mechanics of the situation, it can be seen that as long as M is above G, the vessel is stable, ie returns to the upright. Were the cargo loaded or bottom weight (such as bunkers) used so that G moves up above M, it can be seen that the ship becomes unstable. Should by chance G and M coincide, the vessel's stability is neutral and the ship just *lolls* over at any angle she is moved to.

The ship's GM, known as the *metacentric height*, is therefore a measure of the ship's stability.

The completion of loading of the ship with a safe GM is a prime consideration to the ship's officer and others responsible for stowing the cargo. With large modern container ships, the loading plan of which the stability is part will often form part of the terminal service.

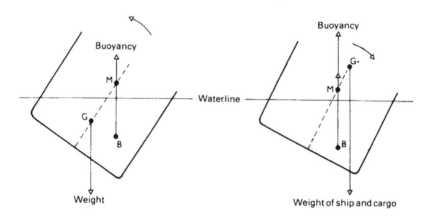

Fig 1.6   Stability of a ship.

12

An empirical formula connecting GM and the ship's period of roll T (T is the time it takes to roll from starboard to port and back to starboard again) is:

$$GM = (0.8 \text{ Beam}/T)^2 \text{ or } T = 0.8 \text{ Beam}/(GM)^{.5}$$

From this it can be seen that if GM is small, the period of roll becomes large and the vessel is said to be *tender*.

As GM becomes larger the period of roll becomes smaller, and the vessel is eventually said to be *stiff* − ie the period of roll becomes excessively fast.

With fast vicious rolling the cargo is more likely to shift, the ship to strain herself, and the crew to be extremely uncomfortable. (The 1986 IUMI Conference noted the dangers of deck cargoes of logs shifting if the GM was too large.) There is also a greater possibility of 'isonchronous' rolling − ie the ship's rolling getting into phase with the passing waves and resulting in increased rolling amplitude.

Example: Assume a vessel of 23 metres beam with a GM of .08 metres, 0.6 metres and 5 metres respectively:

$$T = (.08 \times 23)/(.08)^{.5} = 65 \text{ seconds}$$
$$T = (.08 \times 23)/(0.6)^{.5} = 23.8 \text{ seconds (about right)}$$
$$T = (.08 \times 23)/(5)^{.5} = 8.2 \text{ seconds (too fast)}$$

It can be seen that in this case a GM of about 0.6 metres would be a good level of stability to aim for when loading the cargo, as 65 seconds would indicate that the vessel is verging on instability, and at 8.5 seconds the 'accelerations' would be dangerous.

To reduce the amplitude of rolling there are various expensive devices, such as fins, that can be projected out of the side of the ship under water. They are automatically tilted as the sea tries to push the vessel over and thus the vessel remains upright. Another method is to use liquid in tanks and cause it to flow quickly from one side of the ship to the other, thus cancelling out the tendency to roll caused by the sea.

Another danger to stability is 'slack tanks' − in other words, if liquids are allowed to surge from side to side across the vessel while it is rolling. This causes a virtual rise of G with a consequent reduction in stability. In tanks designed to take liquids, wash plates and bulkheads are constructed to reduce this hazard, but it can be overlooked at such times (eg in firefighting) when water is free to move across the decks.

Should G move off the centre line of the ship due to an excess weight on one side of the ship, the ship is said to *list* (as opposed to *heeling* and *lolling*).

Markings on the ship

The name

This is marked clearly on each bow and across the stern.

Draft marks

These are printed on each side of the bow and stern, and sometimes also amidships. The draft marks are each 10 centimetres high with a gap of 10 centimetres between each mark -- ie draft is shown in decimetres for ships registered after January 1974. Marks should be clearly painted using lines 2 centimetres thick. All measurements are taken from the top edge of the load line marks, but the bottom edge of the draft marks (see Fig 1.7).

Empirical formula to give an approximation for loaded draft:

$$\text{Draft(in metres)} = (\text{dwt}/1,000)^{.5} + 5$$

Load line marks

T Tropical

S Summer

W Winter

F Fresh water mark

TF Tropical fresh water mark

FWA Fresh water allowance (this is simply the difference between the summer and fresh water marks)

LR Lloyd's Register, or the abbreviation for the Society that the vessel is classed with.

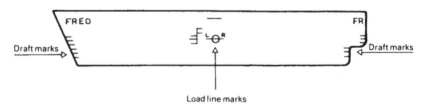

Fig 1.7   Markings on the ship.

Notes on markings

- The summer freeboard and the FWA are not marked as such on the vessel, but are shown in Fig 1.8 to clarify this point.
- As can be seen from Fig 1.8, the freeboard is the distance between the uppermost continuous deck, marked by the deck line, and the waterline. The larger it is, the more reserve buoyancy the vessel has and the less chance there is of waves breaking over the deck.
- The load line marks show the minimum freeboard allowed in certain seasonal areas, ie in a winter zone the vessel has to have a larger freeboard to enable her to cope with the worst weather that can be expected. A chart showing where and when these zones are to be observed is published by the Admiralty.
- There is also a mark and zone for winter North Atlantic (WNA), which must be marked on and used by ships up to and including 100 metres in length.
- The fresh water allowance is for use when the vessel is loading in fresh water, which has not the same buoyancy as sea water (assumed to have a density of 1,025 oz per ft^3). So, if loaded down to F in fresh water, the vessel would rise to S by the time it reaches the open sea. The person responsible for loading the vessel therefore must know the density of the water at the loading berth.
- If the vessel has a TPC of 60 tons and uses 30 tons of fuel and water a day, then it will reduce its draft by half a centimetre a day. (TPC = tons per centimetre, ie the number of tons required to sink the vessel 1 centimetre.)

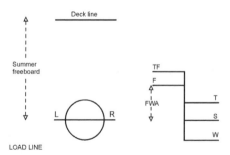

Fig 1.8 Calculating loaded draft.

A brief history of load lines

Although load lines were used by the Italian Republics right back in the Middle Ages, the first record of an assigned freeboard in England is an entry in Lloyd's Register in 1774.

In about 1835, the Committee of Lloyd's proposed that a freeboard of 3 inches per foot depth of hold should be used for safe loading, and this was known as *Lloyd's Rule*.

Samuel Plimsoll brought in legislation concerning freeboard in 1876, but his rules had many loopholes and it was not until 1890 that the Load Line Act came into force. This made it compulsory for sea-going ships to be marked with a load line in a manner decided by the Department of Trade. However, such legislation was not universal, and American ships did not have obligatory load lines until 1917. The 1930 International Load Line Conference instigated an internationally accepted method for calculating load lines.

The latest International Load Line Conference was held in London in March 1966 and the substance of this conference came into being in the UK when the Merchant Shipping (Load Line) Rules 1968 came into force on 21 July of that year.

Tonnage

This word derives from the fact that a 'tun' was a barrel that held 252 gallons of wine -- hence 'ton' in shipping can denote both weight and capacity. We can break down 'tonnage' into 'ship tons' and 'cargo tons' (Fig 1.9).

Ship tons

- *Loaded displacement tonnage* is the actual weight of the ship and cargo.
- *Light displacement tonnage* is the actual weight of the ship. The difference between the loaded *displacement* and the light *displacement* is the weight that the ship can actually carry and is known as the *deadweight* (dwt) tonnage.
- *Gross tonnage (GT)* is, very simply, a measure of the total enclosed volume of the ship in cubic metres multiplied by a constant.
- *Net tonnage (NT)* (or register tonnage) is the total enclosed volume available for cargo in cubic metres multiplied by a constant.

Displacement tonnage has little or no commercial use, and the size of tankers is usually expressed in dwt tonnage -- ie a 250,000 ton dwt tanker means it can carry 250,000 tons of oil, bunkers and stores at its summer draft. It is more convenient when transporting liquids to charge for the ton weight carried -- not only because it is a relatively heavy cargo, but the

Fig 1.9   Ship tonnage.

volume of 250,000 tons of oil can appreciably change with, say, a 10° variation in temperature.

Most general cargo ships, though, are usually full before they are down to their marks, so a shipowner is usually concerned with selling space and he is more interested in the volume of his ship rather than the weight it can carry. Hence one always talks of a cargo ship of, for example, 9,000 gross tonnage (9,000 GT).

Until the introduction of the Universal Tonnage (UT) measurement in 1982, the whole question of GT and NT had been a complicated one from the point of view of a precise definition because port dues, canal dues and various government dues are often levied on these measurement tonnages. So shipowners, who were naturally anxious to keep the dues they paid down to a minimum, instructed their naval architects to study the rules carefully so as to build a ship of a certain capacity with the smallest GT possible.

In order to encourage safety, governments would offer various exempted spaces as an inducement to good building practices -- ie the double bottom was exempted from GT if it was used only for water ballast. Therefore, by this time the precise definitions of measurement tonnage had become long, detailed and fairly complex.

To add to this seeming confusion, different countries had developed different rules for making these measurements. Prior to 1982 there were about five basic systems in use -- ie British, American, most other maritime nations, the Suez Canal Authority and the Panama Canal Authority. However, up until 18 July 1994, ships built before 1982 were allowed to retain their original GRT (gross registered tonnage) and NRT (net registered tonnage) if the owners so wished.

A brief history of ship tonnage

It is generally believed that the Chinese were the first people to see the potential of levying tax on ship tonnage, but that Henry V was the first Englishman to think of it. Throughout the ages, there have been many variations as to how tonnage might be estimated. Often the term 'Tons Burthen' is used, which can be considered a crude estimate for dwt. The following are some significant dates in relation to tonnage:

- In 1694, the Thames Tonnage Measurement was first used.

- In 1849, a Royal Commission originated the basic concept that assessment of dues should be based on the vessel's potential earning capacity. This was known as the 'Moorsom system' after the secretary of the Commission, George Moorsom. This came into force in 1854.
- In 1873, an International Tonnage Commission was held at Constantinople. However, its findings were only followed by the authorities of the newly opened Suez Canal.
- In 1930, the League of Nations tried to get universal agreement on tonnage. The principles proposed were not followed by either the British or Americans, though they were adopted by most other countries.
- In 1967, the Merchant Shipping (Tonnage) Regulations were passed.
- In 1969, the UN Agency, the *IMO* (the *International Maritime Organisation*), held an International Convention on Tonnage Measurement of ships. This convention at long last brought in a universally accepted system of GT and NT on 18 July 1982.
- As these tonnages are independent of the nationality of the ship, they no longer need to be linked to the registration of the ship, so their official title is gross tonnage (GT) instead of gross registered tonnage (GRT). Likewise, since 1982 *net tonnage* is abbreviated to NT instead of NRT (net registered tonnage).
- When initially measured, ships are issued with an *International Tonnage Certificate* (1969).

Tonnage definitions and abbreviations

$GT = K_1 V$ where V is the total volume of all enclosed spaces in cubic metres

$K_1 = 0.2 + .02 \log_{10} V$

$NT = K_2 V_c (4/3 \times d/D)^2$ where V_c = volume of cargo spaces in cubic metres

d = Summer draft of the ship

D = Depth of the ship

$K_2 = 0.2 + .02 \log_{10} V_c$

- The smaller d is in relation to D, then the smaller the NT will be. This allows a similar benefit to the shipowner as the now out-of-date tonnage marks and shelter deck ships did in their era, in that a shipowner knowing that he is going to carry light bulky cargo could declare a small d (draft). NT can only be changed once a year.

- The purpose of the multipliers K_1 and K_2 is to ensure that the new tonnages are similar numerically to the previous tonnages, though some ship types, such as Ro/Ros, have found their measurement tonnages increased.
- For passenger ships the formula for NT becomes more complex.
- Phrases such as tonnage deck, exempted space, alternative tonnage, modified tonnage or tonnage mark no longer apply under these rules.

There is no direct mathematical relationship between these tonnages, whereby with the aid of multipliers you can convert one to the other. However, Appendix A does contain some empirical conversion formulae arrived at by statistical analysis. These will give approximate solutions for typical ships. For example:

The relationship between NT, GT and dwt for a typical traditional cargo ship is such that if NT were one unit, its GT might be 1.5 units and the dwt 2–2.5 units. We need to note, though, that with different ship types and sizes these relationships vary. Some examples are given in Table 1.2.

Although GT and NT are measures of capacity, those actually concerned with shipping space prefer to use the *grain space* and *bale space* figure (see Fig 1.1) as these give the actual volumes available for cargo.

- *Grain space* is the space available for a liquid-type cargo such as bulk grain which can flow into every corner.
- *Bale space* is the space available for solid cargo. Bale space is usually about 7–10 per cent less than grain space.

Paragraph ships   Various government regulations concerning manning, safety appliances etc are determined by the vessel's tonnage; ie a vessel of 499 GT may be a lot cheaper to run than one of 501 GT.

Ships built to take advantage of such limits are known as *paragraph ships*. They are usually of the small coasting or short sea trade variety, but *Aframax* tankers could also be considered a type of paragraph vessel.

British tonnage measurement before 1982   Although this is now largely a matter of history, this system does illustrate the inventive nature of shipowners and designers in their constant attempt to find 'loopholes' in the system and the administrations' endeavours to maintain safety and raise taxes and revenue.

Gross registered tonnage (GRT) was the total internal capacity below the uppermost continuous deck (the 'tonnage' deck for most ships), plus all permanent enclosed spaces above this deck, less exempted spaces. Examples of exempted spaces were double bottom tanks if used only for water ballast, and crew ablution rooms above the upper deck.

Net registered tonnage (NRT) was the GT less deducted spaces. Examples of deducted spaces were machinery spaces, crew accommodation, chart room, radio room, etc.

Tonnages	General cargo	Container	Bulk carrier	Tanker	Tanker
Net (NT)	5,000	8,000	25,000	73,000	7,500
Gross (GT)	7,500	15,600	36,000	85,000	13,000
Deadweight (dwt)	12,500	17,000	54,000	190,000	20,000
Displacement	18,000	23,000	72,000	220,000	27,000

Table 1.2   Examples of types of tonnage for different vessels

We have to note that the expressions 'upper continuous deck' and 'permanent means of closing' gave the naval architect certain scope. If the shipowner built a 'shelter' deck over his uppermost continuous deck and left a small 'tonnage' opening, he had greatly increased his cargo-carrying capacity but not the ship's GT. Such a ship was known as a *shelter deck* ship. The uppermost continuous deck was the deck from which the freeboard was measured in both cases.

However, the shelter deck ship was not as structurally sound as a vessel of equal carrying capacity where the top deck was the uppermost continuous deck, so in the interests of safety the pre-1982 British rules allowed ships to have *two* GT and *two* NT. A ship that had been so measured indicated it by the tonnage mark.

If any part of the tonnage mark was submerged, the vessel used the larger GT. If it was not covered, it used the smaller. This allowed the shipowner to have all the advantages of the shelter deck ship with the safest possible construction. It also allowed him to carry a greater dwt of cargo so the ship was more versatile.

Cargo tons

- Long tons are tons of 2,240 pounds.
- Short tons are tons of 2,000 pounds.
- Metric tons or tonnes are 1,000 kilos.
- Bill of lading (B/L) tons are the tons on which the revenue is earned for shipment. If the cargo is more than 40 cubic feet per ton (or 1 cubic metre per tonne), shipment is charged on measurement -- ie every 40 cubic feet is charged as 1 ton. This is known as a *measurement ton*. If it is less than 40 cubic feet per ton, the shipper is charged on weight. For example, a typical liner ship with 9,802 bill of lading tons on board had in fact only 3,857 tons of 2,240 pounds.

Operational problems relating to dwt and load lines

Let us assume that we have a tanker due to load in Italy and sail for the UK on 20 March. While permitted to load to her summer marks in the Mediterranean, the ship has to pass through Zone 2 (these seasonal zones are part of the International Load Line agreement) on her voyage, and here winter marks are stipulated between 1 November and 31 March. Unless the weight of bunkers, water and stores used in the five-day passage from Italy to the north of Spain (where the winter zone starts) is at least equal to the difference between the summer and winter dwts, the ship cannot load to her summer marks. In such a case, the tanker would have to load to her winter marks plus the weight of bunkers, etc, estimated to be consumed before reaching the restrictive zone. This weight estimation is known as the *zone allowance*.

Deductions from total dwt

Bunkers (13 days at 30 tons per day)	390 tons
Bunker safety margin of 5 extra days	150 tons
Domestic and boiler water	200 tons
Stores	100 tons
TOTAL	**840 tons**

This means that of the total dwt sailing from Italy, 840 tons will not be cargo.

Zone allowance

Bunker consumption per day	30 tons
Water consumption per day	8 tons
TOTAL	**38 tons**

The time to reach the winter zone is five days. Therefore zone allowance is $5 \times 38 = 190$ tons.

Cargo dwt to load

dwt winter marks	19,560 tons
Zone allowance	190 tons
dwt leaving Italy	19,750 tons
Total deductions	840 tons
CARGO TO LOAD	**18,910 tons**

Deadweight scale The deadweight scale can be very useful in estimating the weight of cargo loaded or discharged (see Fig 1.10). For instance, if:

Draft before loading = 14ft 6in
Draft after loading = 29ft 0in

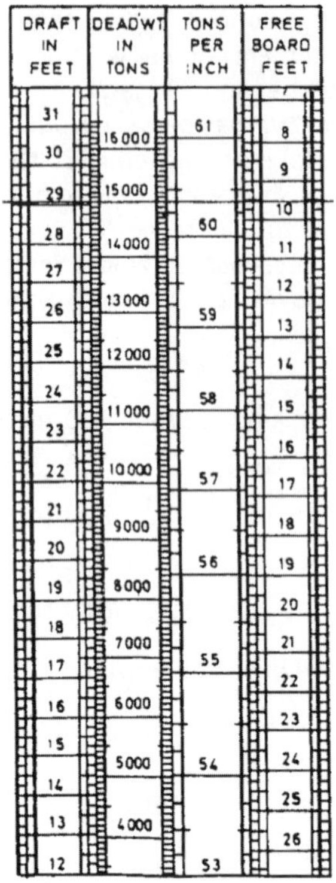

DRAFT IN FEET	DEADWT IN TONS	TONS PER INCH	FREE BOARD FEET
31		61	
	16 000		8
30			9
29	15 000		10
28	14 000	60	11
27			12
26	13 000	59	13
25	12 000		14
24	11 000	58	15
23			16
22	10 000	57	17
21	9 000		18
20		56	19
19	8 000		20
18	7 000		21
17		55	22
16	6 000		23
15			24
14	5 000	54	25
13	4 000		26
12		53	

Fig 1.10   The deadweight scale.

You can see from the scale that the dwt has increased from 5,000 to about 15,000 tons, or 10,000 tons has been loaded. Of course, the density of the water, any stores or bunkers loaded, list and any hogging or sagging would have to be taken into account.

Furthermore, if this method of assessing cargo dwt loaded is to form the basis of a freight payment or claim, then it will need to be done by an independent draft surveyor.

We must note that the tons per inch immersion (TPI) is the number of tons that must be loaded or discharged at that draft to alter the draft by 1 inch. (*Note*: TPC (tons per centimetre) $= 0.4 \times$ TPI.) Assuming that you can only read the draft accurately to within 1 inch, the TPI gives an indication of the accuracy of the draft survey.

You might feel that this book should be consistent in the use of imperial and metric units, but that just illustrates one of the problems you are likely to meet in an international business such as shipping!

2 TYPES OF SHIPS

Fig 2.1 gives a diagrammatic breakdown of the main types of ships. However, the sector we are concerned with in this book is 'ships that carry things', so we will take a detailed look at each of these types in turn. (The *commercial* aspects of the 'main' types will be further discussed in later chapters.) For the 'minor' types of vessel, only specific commercial points of significance will be covered in this chapter. (In 2000, there were 87,546 merchant vessels over 100 GT, but of these only 46,205 (53 per cent) can be considered cargo-carrying ships.)

Passenger ships

Before the Second World War and in the years immediately following it, travel by sea was the usual mode of international passenger travel. Passenger liners were profitable to operate, and the more famous ones became

The cruise liner Carnival Spirit *alongside Vancouver's dedicated cruise terminal.*

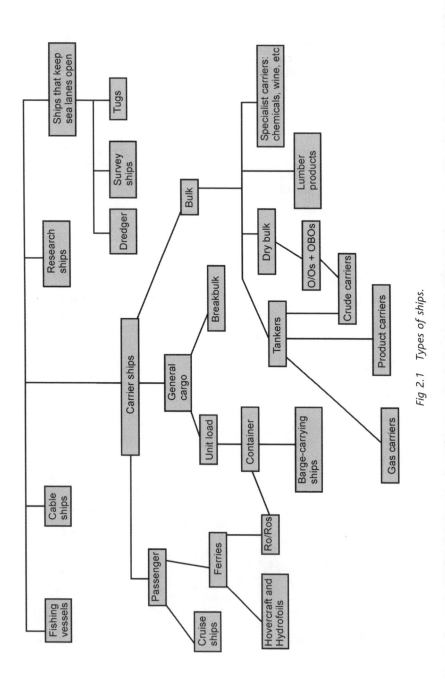

Fig 2.1 Types of ships.

household names. To command one of these liners was considered to be the pinnacle of the seafaring profession.

That there has been a change in the preferred means of travelling is self-evident. On the North Atlantic, where once a fleet of ships ferried the rich and famous on regular services throughout the year, there are now just a few summer sailings run as cruises. The reason for this change is very obvious – the introduction of cheap, fast air flights.

The North Atlantic sea-passenger trade has not of course been the only area to suffer – it simply pre-dated the problems on the other routes by five years or so. The last regular passenger line service out of the UK was in November 1977 when the *Australis* (owned by Chandris) sailed for Australia, and the famous Union Castle Service to South Africa had made its last sailing a few months previously.

Apart from abundant and ever-cheaper flights, there has also been the fact that passenger ships are very labour-intensive, and that their operating and running costs have been greatly increased by spiralling wage costs.

Added to this, until the late 1960s governments looked favourably upon, and encouraged financially, the growth of large fast passenger ships because of their potential use as troop carriers in the event of war. Winston Churchill even referred to the *Queen Mary* and *Queen Elizabeth* as 'war-winning weapons'. Now, though, troops, like passengers, are largely carried by air.

The effect of all this has been to bring about great changes in the number, type, design, size and operation of passenger ships, and as the UK had traditionally been the doyen of the passenger liner trade it has been much involved in these changes. From operating over a hundred such liners, there are now just a fleet of luxurious ferries and a handful of cruise ships under the British flag.

The question of design also raises what is the initial deterrent facing the passenger ship operator – ie the astronomical cost of building a new ship. The new *Queen Mary 2* has been estimated as costing around $800 (USD) million to build. This is obviously a huge sum of money to speculate, and investors in such schemes need to have great faith in the future use of such passenger ships.

As can be seen from Table 2.1, the only countries that expanded their passenger fleet significantly during the period 1972–83, following the ending of the traditional passenger liner trade, were the USSR and Greece. For the USSR, who could meet virtually all its costs in roubles, offering cruises to foreigners became an efficient way of earning foreign currency. And, for a state-run ship, profit need not be a primary motive.

In recent years the analysis of passenger fleets by flag, as in most forms of shipping, becomes less significant as a result of the use of *open registers*. For instance, in 2002 over 27 per cent of passenger GT was under the flag of the Bahamas, with a further 30 per cent split between the Panamanian and Liberian flags. For this reason, it is perhaps more useful to consider the major industry groupings (see Table 2.2). In mid-2003, P&O combined with

Table 2.1 Passenger fleets in 1972, 1983 and 1998

Country	No of ships in 1972	No of ships in 1983	No of ships in 1998
UK	26	9	9
Italy	26	6	4
France	9	0	1
USSR	10	27	7 (Russia)
Norway	13	18	14
Greece	10	29	13
Panama	7	13	36
Liberia	5	6	42
Bahamas			53
Total			226

Carnival, making the new group the market leader by far, and controlling some 40 per cent of GT.

Pure passenger ships as a form of sea transport over long distances have therefore largely disappeared, though large luxury Ro/Ro ferries do move millions of passengers and millions of tons of cargo over relatively short distances on high-density traffic routes – particularly in north-western Europe, the Mediterranean and in Japanese waters.

Table 2.2 Passenger fleets: major industry groupings

Group	Fleet size (Ships)	No of berths (as at mid-2002)	Percentage of GT
Carnival	47	68,500	27.2
Royal Caribbean	26	54,360	22.7
P&O	19	32,171	13.6
Star Cruises	18	27,068	9.8
Louis	17	10,770	2.8
Festival	7	7,358	2.3
Redisson Seven Sea Cruises	6	1,754	1.8
Disney Cruise Line	2	3,520	1.7
Cruiseinvest	5	3,510	1.6
NYK Cruises	3	2,504	1.3
Airtours plc	4	4,336	1.1
Others	103	43,000	14.1

Although cruises are not a new phenomena, they have been significantly developed to replace the loss of the previous sea passenger transport market. Many would argue that cruise traffic is not transport, as it is not a derived demand. The passengers do not pay to be moved to a specific place – in fact, they are usually returned to their starting place. They pay to have an entertaining, interesting and pleasant experience. To that extent, it is therefore a luxury commodity with a demand that can be directly stimulated by advertising and promotion.

The technical operation of the cruise ship remains largely the same as previously, but the commercial operation is a completely 'new ball game', having perhaps more to do with the hotel and holiday trade than what was traditionally considered shipping.

In the mid-1990s some 80 per cent of cruise passengers came from North America (6 million in 1999) and 16 per cent from Europe (2 million in 1999), though – as can be seen from the 1999 figures – demand in Europe is growing and comes from socio-economic groups with large disposable incomes. In the past, cruises tended to last for weeks rather than days, so a large proportion of the passengers were elderly and retired. However, since the advent of shorter (under one week) cruises, the average age of those taking cruises has come down considerably.

This photo shows how the modern cruise liner's superstructure can depart from the traditional liner – not a funnel in sight! (Courtesy of Malta Maritime Authority)

As the major market is in the USA (around 30 per cent of cruises start there), it is not surprising to find that the major cruising terminal is in Miami in Florida, with the Caribbean being among the most popular destinations. In 1998, Alaska was the third most popular cruise area.

Unlike the rest of shipping, the 1980s was a relatively profitable period for cruising, with this decade showing a general increasing demand of about 10 per cent per annum. As with the rest of shipping, the threat of over-capacity by increasing supply is always there and this sector of the industry has endured severe competition and ticket discounting. However, the price of the ticket (freight) is perhaps not such an important issue as it might at first seem as the total revenue on a typical cruise might be made up of:

10% from ticket sales

50% from sales on board

40% from casino profits

Different companies will cater for different 'ends' of the market. As we noted in Table 2.1, the USSR operated between 20 to 30 ships offering cheap good-value cruises.

Originally cruise ships tended to be relatively small – catering for less than 500 passengers – as they needed to be able to manoeuvre in and out of the smaller historical and romantic ports on the 'traditional' cruise itinerary. The market for these ships still exists, but the last few years has seen the development of megaships which can combine the economies of scale with a greater self-sufficiency in holiday needs – ie the ships become not just a vehicle, but a floating movable holiday resort. In *Lloyd's Annual Cruise Review of 1991*, it states that the cost per passenger berth on a 2,000-berth vessel can be 25 per cent lower than on smaller (1,000-berth) vessels.

If you look at Fig 2.2, you will see that this increase in the size of cruise ships is clear, and the following facts bear this out:

- In 1998, around 34 per cent of the cruise ship GT was provided by vessels over 70,000 GT.
- In November 1999, the *Voyager of the Seas* came into service owned by the Royal Caribbean Line. At that time she was the world's largest cruise vessel, having a GT of 142,000 and 3,114 berths.
- In 2002, the largest ship in service was *Carnival Conquest* at 952 feet LOA, with accommodation for 3,700 passengers and a crew of 1,200.
- In January 2002, work commenced on *Queen Mary 2*. At 150,000 GT, she became the largest ocean liner, having an LOA of 1,152 feet, 17 decks and facilities for 2,620 passengers.

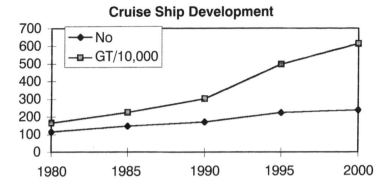

Fig 2.2   Graph showing that the sizes of cruise ships are steadily increasing.

Passenger ships: a technical description

The improved design of ships has meant that nowadays they can carry more passengers in greater comfort. In the 1950s and 1960s the average passenger ship carried one passenger for every 50 tons gross (see Fig 2.3), but the figure now is nearer to one passenger for every 30 tons gross. Also, the ratio of passengers to crew is nearer to 4:1 instead of the previous 2:1.

As we have already mentioned, passenger ships are very expensive – an average cost per berth in the early 1990s was in the range of $160,000 (USD). But it is also true that passenger ships enjoy a longer life span than most other ships. For instance, the *Achille Lauro*, which sank after a serious fire in 1994, was originally laid down as the *Willem* in Flushing in 1939 but not completed until 1946. But although passenger ships may have a long life expectancy, considerable money has to be spent on major refits and refurbishments to cater for the changing tastes, fashions and mores of each new generation. For instance, the 'class' separation of passengers has now largely gone, but there is a far greater choice for passengers as regards cabins, restaurants, entertainment, etc.

Passenger liners usually appear larger than a tanker or cargo vessel of equivalent tonnage due to the amount of superstructure. Of course, for passenger ships the dwt tonnage is virtually meaningless, as the weight of the cargo (passengers and their belongings) on a large cruise ship will only be, say, between 300 to 400 tons while the weight of fresh water that needs to be carried for them could be between 2,000 and 3,000 tons.

Most passenger ships will be fitted with stabilisers to reduce the amount of movement in bad weather and many have a bow-thruster to assist in manoeuvring when docking or turning in a small harbour. Apart from the various sizes of cabins, the number of berths and the amenities, all today's liners need restaurants (usually placed in the very centre of the ship where

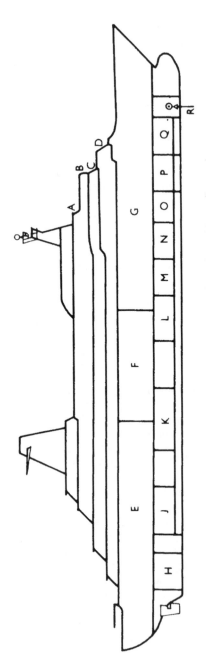

20,000 GROSS TON PASSENGER SHIP Ideal size for cruising or line service

A Observation deck
B Sun deck
C Bridge
D Lounge deck
These decks contain
most of the amenities
and luxury suites
E Cabins
F Shops & dining rooms
G Cabins

H Fuel
J Fresh water
K Engine room
L Sewage
M Fuel
N Fuel
O Fuel
P Fresh water
Q Fresh water
R 'Bowthruster' (a small transverse engine
   to assist docking)

Length: 550ft
Breadth: 79ft
Draft: 25ft
Speed: 21 knots (18,000 bhp)
Passengers: 767
Crew: 317

Fig 2.3 A typical 20,000 ton passenger ship.

there is least movement), a cinema, dance halls, swimming pools, bars, shops, hairdressers, gyms, lounges and libraries.

Passenger liners are, however, more than just ships with a band, a bar and 2,000 bottles of pickles, for the whole philosophy of construction and safety is in a different class to that of a cargo vessel. In passenger ships, the stress is on *prevention* rather than cure. In fact, to be designated a 'passenger' ship, it must be issued with a 'Passenger Safety Certificate', satisfying the latest SOLAS regulations. It is of course impossible to make anything 100 per cent safe, but in the modern passenger ship considerable money is spent trying to achieve this end.

The ship is divided into small watertight compartments that make it virtually unsinkable. Cargo ships cannot be constructed like this as small holds would ruin the stow and the space available for cargo. A further scourge of the passenger ship, though, is fire. The Americans favour the 'make everything non-inflammable' approach, but this is very expensive. Others favour detection and sprinkler devices with an economic level of non-inflammability. The IMO as a body is very concerned with the safety of passenger ships and both national and international legislation on this question is both strict and comprehensive.

Passenger ships used to be among the fastest ships on the oceans, but for cruising very high speeds are no longer so important. On the North Atlantic run, liners would compete at speeds in excess of 30 knots, but in holiday brochures advertising cruises speed is seldom mentioned. Rather than high maximum speeds, cruise ship operators are more concerned with the ability to operate smoothly between, say, 10 to 25 knots.

Cruising – like other forms of shipping – poses environmental threats. This is less obvious perhaps than in oil tankers, but it can take many forms:

- Some 2,000 tourists suddenly released on an unprepared sparsely populated area can cause many problems.
- A typical 2,000-passenger ship can generate about 3.5 tons of glass and tins, over 1 ton of food waste, and 1.5 tons of dry waste per day. If this were to be disposed of 'over the side', as used to be the case, there would be obvious pollution problems. A few years ago, cross-Channel ferry passengers caused quite a serious pollution problem by jettisoning their plastic drinking cups over the side.
- Sewage disposal has also been a problem that passenger ship operators have had to cope with over the last few years.
- Discharge of diesel exhaust gases in port.
- Toxic anti-fouling paints.

Before the Second World War, the combined cargo/passenger ship was very much in vogue, ie a ship that carried, say, 200 passengers and several thousand tons of cargo. But because of the increasing daily operating costs of the passenger section, and the increased danger of strikes and slow turnrounds in port for the cargo, this combination has not been an economic one since the 1960s. However, by increasing mechanisation and palletisation, a swift cargo turn-round can be achieved to synchronise with the passenger turn-round – and therefore the successful operation of the cargo/passenger combination. Perhaps one could argue that this vessel has been replaced by the Ro/Ro ferry.

Ferries

Ferries form a large and very varied segment of the passenger ship market, and one where over the last two or three decades many refinements have taken place. Competition from airlines – and alternative connections such as the Channel Tunnel – have done much to make ferry operators more customer-conscious.

For longer distances, the Ro/Ro ferries have increased in size (many now cater for over 2,000 passengers and have all the same basic design and operational features as cruise vessels). On the shorter more sheltered routes, there are still some hovercraft and hydrofoils but these seem to be less favoured than the high-speed catamarans – and in fact a new breed of larger catamarans are now appearing on the longer routes. The year 1995 saw the introduction of large high-speed ferries by Stena Line, and the largest HSS 1500 can carry 1,500 passengers and 375 cars (or 50 trucks and 100 cars).

The smaller ferries tend to be operated like aircraft at the upper end of the market, and like buses at the lower end. Like buses and trains, they are often used by commuters and may have daily peak loads, while others, like the cross-Channel ferries, will have holiday peak load periods.

The large Ro/Ro ferries have, as mentioned earlier, the particular problem of large openings and big car decks with few bulkheads (note the *Herald of Free Enterprise* disaster in 1987 and the *Estonia* in 1994). Also, ferries have the problem of frequently changing crews and of knowing precisely who or what has rolled or walked on board! In an aircraft, with everyone strapped in for take-off, it is a relatively simple matter of ensuring a standard safety procedure. In a large Ro/Ro ferry with everyone roaming around, often looking for seats, safety information is not so easy to disseminate. However, the industry is well aware of these problems and is taking steps to redress them.

General cargo ships

The general cargo liner ship has not changed fundamentally in the last 40 or 50 years. As shown in Fig 2.5, it is a multi-deck vessel of about 6,000–15,000 tons and is capable of loading dry cargo in either packaged or bulk form. A quick look at the ships from the Second World War shows that although the midship superstructure has been moved aft, fundamentally and functionally there is little real difference.

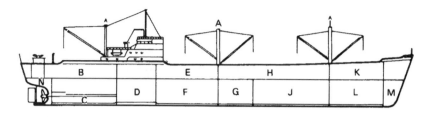

SD 14: 15,000 ton

A	5 tons	F	No 4 Hold	L	No 1 hold
B	No 5 hold	G	No 3 deep tank	M	Fore peak
C	Shaft tunnel	H	No 2 and 3 'tween deck	N	After peak
D	Engine room	J	No 2 hold		LWL 29'0"
E	No 4 'tween deck	K	No 1 'tween deck		Crew 25

Following the major losses of ships during the Second World War, various ship types were mass produced to reduce costs and increase production. The purpose of this statement is not simply to indulge in nostalgic reminiscence, but to underline two basic contemporary facts. The first is that the principles and advantages of mass production can apply equally to shipbuilding. However, although this is true, in contrast to other modes of transport, there is very little series building of ships at the present time.

The second fact is that the long life of the Liberty ship (there were over 2,800 built during the war and there were still 680 in service in 1967) showed that there was, and still is, a use for a cheap, universally known and understood workhorse class of tramp ship capable of carrying anything anywhere. As the last of the Liberties made their way to the scrapyard, there were launched a number of 'Liberty replacement' types, of which there are two particularly worthy of note:

Popular Liberty replacement – the SD 14 One of the most popular Liberty replacement ships was the British-designed and built SD 14 (Fig 2.4). Unfortunately, the famous Sunderland shipyard that produced these ships closed in the 1980s – though some were built under licence elsewhere.

Details of SD 14		Details of a Liberty ship	
Length	141 metres	Length	134 metres
GT	9,100	GT	7,254
NT	6,100	NT	4,420
dwt	14,000 tonnes	dwt	10,870 tons
Speed	14.9 knots	Speed	10.2 knots

Fig 2.4 The SD 14.

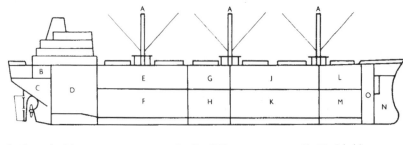

A	5-ton derricks	E	No 4 TD	K	No 2 hold
B	FW	F	No 4 hold	L	No 1 TD
C	AP	G	No 3 TD	M	No 1 hold
D	Pielstick diesel, 3,750 kw	H	No 3 hold	O	Deep tank
	18 tons per day, spd. 13 knots	J	No 2 TD	N	FP

Crew: 31
Length: 142m
Breadth: 19.8m
Depth: 12.3m

Draft: 9m
Deadweight: 15,000 tonnes
Gross tonnage: 10,903 tons
Net tonnage: 6,310 tons

Grain capacity: 19,950cu m
Bale capacity: 18,500cu m

Fig 2.5   The Freedom vessel.

The Freedom vessel   This was a Japanese-built Liberty replacement type. As can be seen from Figs 2.4 and 2.5, these are both unsophisticated ships with one 'tween or shelter deck. They are both very similar in size, though somewhat larger and faster than the original Liberty ship they replaced.

Since the advent of container vessels, general cargo vessels are often referred to as *breakbulk vessels* as the cargo is loaded into and broken out of their holds piece by piece. Because of the greater productivity of the container vessel, which is considered later, the number of cargo liners required will greatly decrease in the future.

Modern designs for breakbulk vessels have changed little from the above Liberty replacement types, though some of the tonnage used in the liner trades has taken the name of *multi-purpose carrier*. These may have one or more 'tween decks, large *open* hatchways and probably a heavy lift derrick.

The heavy lift derrick shown in the centre of Fig 2.6 is known as a *Stulken* derrick, one of the most popular of the patent shipboard devices for handling heavy lifts.

Table 2.3 (page 37), of ship types, shows that in 2002 breakbulk vessels had around 9 per cent of the carrying capacity; however, over the last 20 years new total capacity has fallen. In 2002, there were 16,448 such vessels according to *Lloyd's Register Annual Statistical Tables*, which makes it still the most common ship type – though it is clearly a declining species.

A Heavy lift ships

A 'heavy lift' ship refers to a vessel that carries an indivisible load greater than 50 tons. Hansa Line claims to be the first to enter this field in 1928 with a ship fitted with tackle capable of lifting 120 tons. Until recently this has remained the prerogative of the liner. However, since the container vessel has taken over as the common liner vessel, we have seen the emergence of specialist heavy lift ships. One such can lift 700 tons and Ro/Ro vessels can lift 1,000 tons. There are also some sophisticated vessels known as submersibles and semi-submersibles. These can flood their ballast tanks and submerge their decks to allow the heavy load to be floated above the deck. When in position, the ballast can be pumped out and the ship will rise under the cargo.

The Happy Buccaneer was built in 1984 with a GT of 16,341 and a dwt of 13,740. As well as being a heavy lift vessel, she can also be used as a Ro/Ro cargo ship. Note: Like many heavy vessels, she has Dutch registration. (Courtesy of Fairplay)

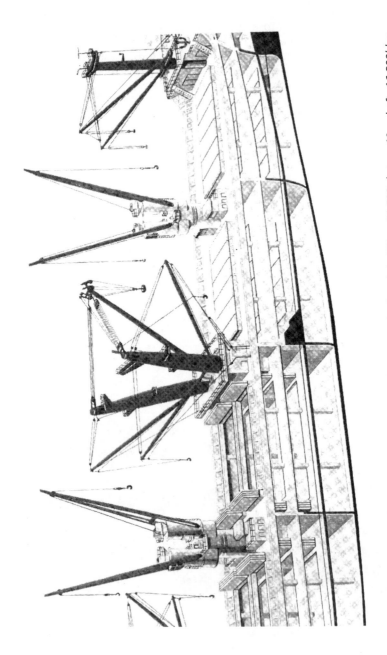

Fig 2.6 Nedlloyd multi-purpose carrier introduced in 1978; the length is 173m, 21,500 dwt on 10m draft; 16,800bhp; speed 17 knots; TEU capacity 676; maximum lift of Stülken heavy lift derrick is 225 tons.

Table 2.3 Carrier ships (2002)				
Type	No	dwt (millions)	Age	Percentage of total
Oil tanker	6,935	280	16	35
Bulker	5,021	274	15	34
Combo	180	12.6	19	2
Container	2,918	73	11	9
General cargo	16,448	74	24	9
Chemical tanker	2,681	32	15	4
LPG tanker	1,014	10.8	17	1
LNG tanker	138	8.7	15	1
Others		35		4

Container ships

The whole philosophy behind containerisation is the packing of cargo into uniformly sized boxes (containers) and then designing all carrying vehicles (road, rail and ship) for the swift, safe and efficient transport of these boxes, ideally from 'door to door'.

For the operation to be really successful it is essential that all parties are able to agree on what the uniform size of container should be. In most countries the limiting width and length are governed by the road vehicles (2.5 metres is the maximum width allowed in the UK). There is then the ISO (International Standards Organisation) to heed, which lays down standards for containers as regards their size, strength and lifting facilities. Originally, most maritime carriers adopted the 8 foot × 8 foot × 20 foot, and 8 foot × 8 foot × 40 foot size, but although the length and width have remained largely the same over the years – as change here would have caused problems with the cell guides – the height has become more flexible – 8.5 foot high and 9.5 foot high containers have become common.

Because of the larger road loads allowed in the USA and some other countries, some container operators have adopted even larger containers. Conversely, in mountainous countries such as Norway the road and rail tunnels cannot cope with 8 foot × 8 foot sizes and smaller containers have to be used (see Chapter 12).

As special terminals have to be built for container ships it is possible to create large deep water berths. Container ships therefore tend to be larger than the conventional cargo liner that has to fit into docks built over a century ago. They are usually faster, too, with speeds in excess of 22 knots.

The P&O container ship MV Nedlloyd Cook *at container terminal 3, Northport, Port Kelang. This ship is deployed on the Europe–Far East service of the Grand Alliance. Northport also services the OOCL* MV Shenzhen, *which, in June 2003, claimed to be the largest contianer ship with a capacity of 8,063 TEUs (LOA 323 metres).*

So that containers can easily be lowered into the cell guides, the ship must be upright and level at all stages of loading. Sophisticated and high speed ballast arrangements are therefore necessary.

Ships that work between dedicated container terminals which have all the necessary gantry cranes will be 'gearless'. This can, however, be embarrassing in an emergency such as grounding as it is difficult for them to jettison cargoes.

Containers can be – and usually are – carried on deck, and twistlocks are inserted into the lifting holes on the containers' corners to hold them together. But quick and efficient lashing systems must also be arranged.

About 50 per cent of containers are owned by some half a dozen leasing companies who hire their containers out in very much the same manner as ships are chartered. This can partly help solve owners' problems where an imbalance of trade occurs.

Although the dimensions of the container are uniform, this does not restrict the variety that is possible in the design of the container itself. There are some designed for end-loading, some for side-loading, others for top-loading, and some have only canvas sides or tops. There are also reefer containers and those designed to carry special bulk commodities such as beer, jam, chemicals, etc.

There are also hatchcoverless container ships. These were first designed in Australia in 1986 and the first ship to be built to this design was the *Bell Pioneer* which went into service in October 1990. This is a 301 TEU capacity ship for short sea trading. This design has reduced port turn-round times, increased voyages per year, and has significantly lowered labour and port costs. Ned Lloyd is operating similar but larger ships on the Europe to Far East service (for further details, see *Maritime Policy and Man*, vol 22, no 2, April–June 1995).

Advantages of using containers

The main advantages are listed below:

1 Speed and economy in handling, particularly at the interfaces (ie ports). Ten or twelve men can discharge and load a container ship in three or four days instead of a hundred men taking three to four weeks. This increased ship productivity and the reduced cargo-handling costs are probably the main reasons why shipowners converted to containerisation. By the end of the 1960s, liners spent more than 50 per cent of their time in port – and spent more than 50 per cent of their revenue on cargo-handling!
2 Safety both with regard to breakages and pilferage – the latter being a significant problem in transporting cargoes such as whisky and electrical goods such as CD players, etc.
3 Packaging can be reduced.
4 A real door-to-door transport service can be offered.

Disadvantages of using containers

These are as follows:

1 Money: It involves a massive capital outlay for the ship, which is more expensive than a conventional vessel.
2 Each ship needs three sets of containers, ie one set at each terminal, and one on the ship, and even an ordinary container is an expensive item of equipment. They have to be repaired and maintained and have a life of perhaps only about seven years. Special containers such as 'reefer' containers are even more expensive. One USCG study has indicated that:

45% of container damage is done at the terminal

30% of container damage is done during transit

25% of container damage is due to improper stowage

However, a more important factor is usually the specific trade. Containers handled at well-equipped container terminals on and off cellular container ships will have a longer life than containers swung onto a breakbulk vessel using a ship's derrick.

3 Special terminals have to be constructed using expensive high-speed cranes capable of lifting 40 tons or more. Expensive machines also have to be purchased to move the containers around the terminal.

4 Although the container does reduce the level of petty pilfering, it has opened up new possibilities for the organised criminal gangs who have not been slow to accept the challenge.

5 The problem of 'an imbalance of trade' in containerisable cargo. This leads to the unprofitable movement of empty containers. (Some 30 per cent of containers moved worldwide are empty, and on certain routes, such as the Persian Gulf trade, it can be as high as 83 per cent.)

6 There have also been a number of introductory problems involving Customs, documentation and legal difficulties, but these are now gradually being solved.

Definitions and abbreviations relating to containers

CSC = Container Safety Convention

FCL = full container load

FEU = 40 foot equivalent unit

ICD = inland clearance depot

LCL = less than a container load

TEU = 20 foot equivalent unit – eg one 40 foot container
       equals two TEUs

Other relevant points relating to containers:

- For a shipper with a full container load (FCL), the door-to-door service presents no problems, but with less than a container load (LCL), the shipper has to use an inland clearance depot (ICD).
- The Container Safety Convention (CSC) was set up by the IMO in 1977. Its function is to ensure that the containers are maintained in a safe condition. It introduced the 'safety plate' in 1984. This ensures that containers have regular safety inspections.

A brief history of containers

The idea of carrying things in containers is as old as mankind. However, what *is* new about the current practice of containerisation is the sophisticated but standardised container handling equipment, which enables one man to load a container with speed and precision. What is now generally meant when talking about containers possibly only goes back to about 1956 when containers were introduced on some American coastal routes. (Containers were first introduced in Australia and the USA, which is not surprising as these were the two countries with the highest cargo-handling labour costs.)

Relevant facts in the history of containers:

- *1950s* – first-generation container ships, around 10,000 dwt (pre-ISO-size containers).
- *1964* – *Kuoringa* – first purpose-built container ship.
- *1966* – the first transatlantic container-service began in mainly converted ships.
- *1967* – because of the large capital involved, shipping companies banded together and we saw the birth of several large container consortia, eg ACL (Associated Container Lines), Dart, ACT, OCL, etc.
- *1969* – maiden voyage of *Encounter Bay* – first OCL ship.
- *1970* – 167 container ships were in operation.
- *1971* – the *Frankfurt Express* was of Panamax size and able to carry over 2,000 TEUs.
- *1977* – 507 container ships were in operation.
- *1982* – 718 container ships were in operation.
- *1984* – 'Round the World' services were introduced by USL and Evergreen. These ships had a capacity of over 3,000 TEUs.
- *2000* – 2,590 container ships were in operation with a dwt capacity of 69.1 million tons and an average age of 10 years.

Fig 2.7 shows the increasing size of container ships over time, but it does not indicate a steady continuous growth; instead, there are sudden rises followed by long plateaux. (Table 2.4 gives further details.) By 1998, there were some 36 container ships with drafts greater than 14 metres. If container ship size continues to rise, then radical changes will be required in the terminals needed to service such ships.

Specific points relating to containers

- One serious constraint on building a 6,000+ box vessel was the lack of an engine that could generate the necessary 90,000 bhp capable of driving such a vessel at 24.5 knots on a single screw. However, the development of the Sulzer 12RTA96C and the MAN B&W 12K98MC-C reduced this problem.
- As ship's beam increases, cranes must also increase in size. This involves an increase in weight and there comes a point when the terminal cannot take the extra load without considerable civil engineering expense.

- As ship draft increases, the depth of water in ports becomes a problem. Virtually all major ports have 10 metres, but few can offer over 15 metres.
- For large ships to maintain the same schedules as their smaller brethren, cargo-handling speeds will have to be increased. From this it follows that the terminal area will need to be increased and the inland distribution facilities improved.
- Increasing the size of ships may well also increase the peaking factor, which can be a serious cost problem for a centre hub port.

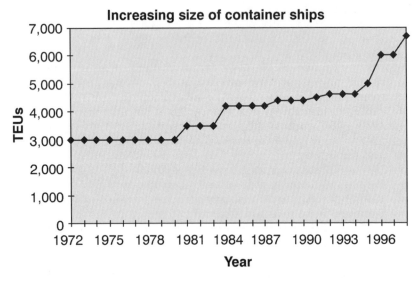

Fig 2.7   Increasing size of container ships – 1972 onwards.

Table 2.4 The increasing size of container ships						
Date	Generation	No of TEUs	Speed	Length (metres)	Draft (metres)	No in 1999
1960–70	1st Generation	< 1,000	16	200	9	831
1970–80	2nd Generation	1,000–2,999	23	275	10	1,136
1987	3rd Generation	3,000–4,000	23	290	11.5	222
Start of post-Panamax v/ls – max size for the Panama Canal = 289.5 m LOA. 32.3 m beam 12.04 m d						
1988	4th Generation	4,000–6,000	23	320	14.3	172
1996	5th Generation	6,000–8,000	23	310–42.8b*	14.5	22
2001	6th Generation	8,000+	23	338–46b*	13 m draft	P&O, Maesk

* Breadth in metres.

One of the interesting questions therefore at the moment is whether container ships will continue to grow, or remain at around 8,000 TEU?

There are proposed designs for Suez-max container ships for 9,000–12,500 TEUs and Malacca-max container ships for 18,000 TEUs.

Larger container ships lead to lower unit costs

One of the effects of the increasing size of container ships is the reduction in unit costs. This reduction in unit costs for container carriage has added to over-capacity on some routes, and the efforts made to reduce the carriage of empty containers means more and more bulk cargoes are being moved in containers. Containerisation has made significant inroads into the grain, sugar, fertiliser, scrap, steel and forest products trades over the last two decades and this gain looks likely to increase in the future.

Barge-carrying ships

A variation of the container ship is the barge-carrying ship where instead of carrying containers the ship carries loaded barges (floating containers). Although the vessels themselves are more expensive to construct than container ships, they do not need a purpose-built terminal – though in some cases this has been provided. In fact, in theory they do not need a port at all. They can simply come to an anchorage, discharge their barges (which are towed away by a waiting tug), and load the barges assembled ready. For countries like the USA with a large inland waterway network, this might seem to be an attractive proposition, but expensive ships need expensive high-freight cargoes. The original idea was to use this type of ship as a military support vessel for marines, which could have been the reason why in their heyday they were favoured by the USA and former USSR.

They seemed to have reached their peak of popularity around 1983 when Lloyd's Register listed 35 Lighter carriers, but since then there seem to have been few new buildings – though in 1994 *Lloyd's List* did report a contract for converting a heavy lift vessel to a LASH (lighter aboard ship)-type carrier.

Although small in number, they deserve a mention as they are an interesting idea and their main types are among some of the most spectacular ship types to observe while they are loading cargo.

Main types of barge-carrying vessels

- LASH (lighter aboard ship) (see Fig 2.8). In this, the most popular of all the types, the barges are loaded and discharged through the 'prongs' at the stern by the ship's own 510-ton gantry crane. The ship can carry just over 80 barges, each capable of holding 400 tons of cargo. The first LASH ship, the *Arcadia Forest*, came into service in 1970 operating between the US Gulf and London and Rotterdam. In 1975, FLASH was introduced. This

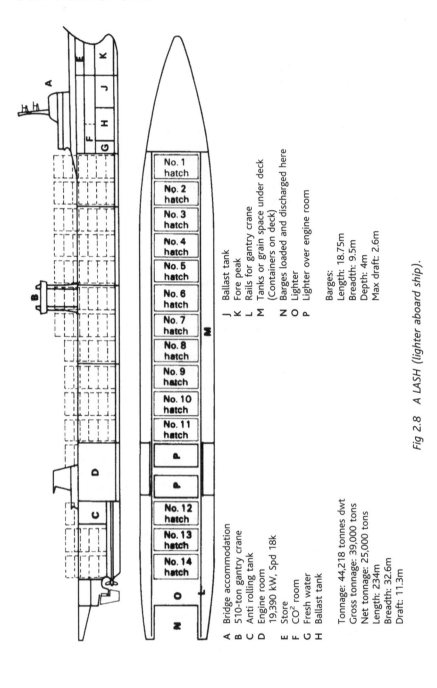

No. 1 hatch	
No. 2 hatch	
No. 3 hatch	
No. 4 hatch	
No. 5 hatch	
No. 6 hatch	
No. 7 hatch	M
No. 8 hatch	
No. 9 hatch	
No. 10 hatch	
No. 11 hatch	
P	
P	
No. 12 hatch	
No. 13 hatch	
No. 14 hatch	
O	
N	

A Bridge accommodation
B 510-ton gantry crane
C Anti rolling tank
D Engine room
   19,390 kW, Spd 18k
E Store
F CO² room
G Fresh water
H Ballast tank

J Ballast tank
K Fore peak
L Rails for gantry crane
M Tanks or grain space under deck
   (Containers on deck)
N Barges loaded and discharged here
O Lighter
P Lighter over engine room

Tonnage: 44,218 tonnes dwt
Gross tonnage: 39,000 tons
Net tonnage: 25,000 tons
Length: 234m
Breadth: 32.6m
Draft: 11.3m

Barges:
Length: 18.75m
Breadth: 9.5m
Depth: 4m
Max draft: 2.6m

Fig 2.8 A LASH (lighter aboard ship).

was a large towed unit which acted as a feeder unit for LASH. Then in 1978 an 11,000 dwt float-on barge carrier came into service known as SPLASH. However, by 2002 there were only two LASH vessels in service.

- Seabees. The first one of this type, the *Dr Lykes*, came into service in 1972. This vessel carried thirty-eight 1,000-ton barges which it lifted two at a time by huge powerful elevators at the stern. In 1985, though, the three vessels were retired to the US Reserve fleet.
- The BACO liner (barge and container). This is a 21,000 dwt ship that can carry 12 barges by floating them in through bow doors which are then closed and the water pumped out. As the name suggests, it can also carry containers, about 500 TEUs. The first of these ships started operating in 1979 and one was still in service from the north-west European ports to West Africa in 2002.

Pallets

This is another method of mechanised cargo-handling developed at the same time as containerisation for basically the same purpose – ie to reduce the handling costs and the time spent by the ship in port.

The idea with this method is to pack and attach the cargo onto pallets (trays that can be lifted by fork-lift trucks) and then load and stow the cargo using these trucks. Ideally, the cargo is palletised at the factory as it comes off the production line and is not taken off the pallet until it reaches the consumer or retailer.

It has the advantage over containerisation that it is much cheaper as regards initial capital investment – ie conventional ships can be used, and it can be introduced piecemeal.

Ro/Ro ships

The first record of a roll-on/roll-off vessel (see Fig 2.9) was probably Noah's Ark! The modern practice, though, was developed by a British shipowner from tank-landing craft used during the Second World War.

The words 'Ro/Ro ships' can cover a variety of vessels such as car ferries, specialist vehicle carriers (of which over 50 per cent are owned by the Japanese) and general cargo ships that are described as having Ro/Ro capability. It is this latter type that we are going to consider here. In 1994, *Lloyd's Register Annual Statistical Tables* gave a figure of 1,494 Ro/Ro cargo vessels with a capacity of 10.2 million tonnes dwt, and an average age of 14 years. Comparing these figures with those given for container ships, you would have seen that there were about the same number of ships for each type, but Ro/Ros had less than a third of the dwt capacity.

Ro/Ro ships are expensive – a 15,000 dwt size would be about twice the price of a conventional ship of this size. The 'wasted space' on Ro/Ro ships can be considerable, but their productivity is very high and their extreme

MV Emerald Highway, a 11,889 dwt Ro/Ro motor vehicle carrier with capacity for 3,000 cars. (Courtesy of Malta Maritime Authority)

flexibility – virtually anything can be rolled on (containers, heavy loads, large objects, etc) – makes them attractive to operate. These ships have also been referred to as STO/ROs in cases where the cargo is rolled on board by fork-lift trucks, which stow and handle the cargo as in a warehouse. Ro/Ros have also proved very useful in areas where congestion has occurred.

It was originally thought that Ro/Ros were only suitable for short distances, but many such ships have been operating for years between Europe and Australia and across the Pacific.

There are also ships which are part cellular containership and part Ro/Ro.

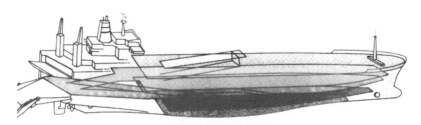

Fig 2.9   Deck layout of a Ro/Ro ship.

Bulk carriers

The dry bulk carrier

A bulk carrier is a large single-deck ship which carries unpackaged cargo. The cargo is simply poured, tipped or pumped into the holds or tanks of the ship.

Although there have been colliers for centuries carrying bulk coal, the modern concept of bulk cargo being loaded and discharged quickly into single-deck dry cargo ships from modern terminals equipped for handling bulk cargoes dates only from about 1957. Like container ships, they were born of economic necessity. Tramp freight rates were very depressed in 1957, so a cheaper means of carrying bulk cargoes had to be found. In 1969–70 they proved to be one of the most lucrative ships to operate and have been one of the largest growing types of ship outside the tanker fleets. Liberia and Panama are the main countries of registry. In 1962 there were only 21 bulk carriers over 40,000 dwt registered and the world total overall was only 611.

Great Motion – *a handy-sized bulk carrier. She was built in 1998 and has a dwt of 27,338. The four cranes have a SWL of 30 tons. Her steel hatchcovers can be seen folded open, presumably to facilitate cleaning and airing before berthing to load.*

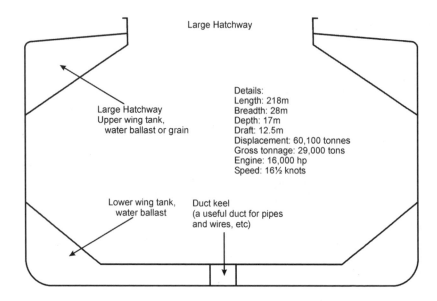

Large Hatchway

Large Hatchway
Upper wing tank,
    water ballast or grain

Details:
Length: 218m
Breadth: 28m
Depth: 17m
Draft: 12.5m
Displacement: 60,100 tonnes
Gross tonnage: 29,000 tons
Engine: 16,000 hp
Speed: 16½ knots

Lower wing tank,
    water ballast

Duct keel
(a useful duct for pipes
and wires, etc)

Fig 2.10   A transverse section of a 52,000 dwt bulk carrier.

During the last few years, iron ore, coal and grain have accounted for some 65 per cent of seaborne dry bulk cargo movements. Other important bulk cargoes include bauxite, sugar, wood, wood pulp, wood chips, fertilisers and cars. (Full cargoes such as cars and packaged lumber are sometimes referred to as neo-bulks.)

An OBO (oil, bulk and ore) ship has a similar cross-section, but would need the additional pump-room pipelines, cofferdams, heating coils and oil-tight joints.

Fig 2.10 shows a typical cross-section of a bulk carrier. Features are large hatchways to facilitate grab discharge and very strong bottoms to the holds to prevent grab damage. Also, the bottom of the hold is usually carried upwards at the bilges to facilitate discharge.

The upper wing tanks are shaped in the way shown so that when bulk cargo is being poured in, the amount of 'trimming' is reduced as the cargo is being loaded. When loading bulk cargoes, the danger has always been that the upper corners of the hold would be left empty with the consequent danger of the cargo shifting in bad weather.

Large bulk carriers usually trade between special terminals and therefore seldom have any derricks or lifting-gear. Smaller bulk carriers have to be prepared to discharge anywhere, so will usually have their own gear.

Popular sizes for bulk carriers:

- *20,000–45,000 tons dwt* – these are sometimes referred to as 'handysize' as they can trade to most ports in the world though 20,000 tons is about the largest size that can use the St Lawrence Seaway.
- *Panamax class*, which is the largest size that can use the Panama Canal. This is about 60,000 dwt, as the limiting lock width is just over 32 metres. This latter is important as much of the ore trade is through the Panama Canal.
- *Capesize bulkers*, which are 100,000 dwt+ and are used mainly for ore and coal on specific routes between well-equipped terminals.

In 2002, the IMO considered the double skin construction for bulkers with a length greater than 150 metres, but the idea was ultimately rejected. Also, SOLAS regulation XII/12 requires the fitting of water ingress detection systems on all bulk carriers, regardless of their date of construction, not later than the date of the first annual, intermediate or renewal survey of the ship to be carried out after 1 July 2004.

Forest product carriers

The year 1970 saw the closure of the Surrey Docks in London. For generations this had been a traditional timber port where virtually each plank was individually unloaded. Now, though, most of this trade has moved to specialised lumber berths at Tilbury where the timber, being made up into large symmetrical units, is handled very much like containers. Fig 2.11 shows the very large hatchways, whereby the timber can be placed directly into position and no further handling is necessary.

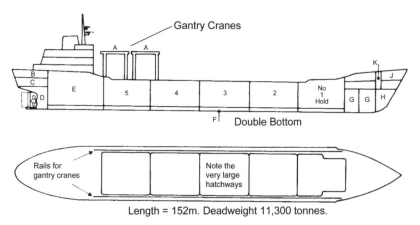

Length = 152m. Deadweight 11,300 tonnes.

Fig 2.11   A forest product cargo carrier.

Developments in tug-barge systems

Another variation in barge utilisation lies in their increase in size. Barges carrying in excess of 15,000 tons dwt are a well-established practice in North America – not only on the extensive waterways there, but also in the open sea, especially off the west coast of Mexico to Alaska. In Europe, however, barges of this type and size are still relatively rare.

Most of these combinations are towed in open sea conditions, but pushing is very much more economical and numerous ways of slotting the tug into the after end of the barge have been developed.

Since the early 1950s, attempts have been made to introduce the utilisation of integrated tug-barge systems (ITBs) whereby the tug is slotted into the barge so that the combination becomes, for the purposes of that voyage, a conventional ship. The economics and operational advantages of such a system are the same to sea transport as articulated heavy goods vehicles are to road transport. They have the advantages over separated tug-barge systems in improved fuel consumption, speed and manoeuvrability. However, the tug and barge in an ITB system have to be exactly matched – which calls for a high degree of standardisation if it is to enjoy full operational flexibility.

Technically there have been doubts as regards the seaworthiness of tug-barge systems, and over the last two or three decades various designs have appeared and operated in different parts of the world, but the idea has never 'taken off' on a large scale.

The oil tanker

There are about 7,000 oil tankers in the world with a total dwt tonnage of over 280 million tons and an average age of 17 years (Lloyd's Register statistics 2002). This is about 35 per cent of the world's total trading dwt shipping tonnage, and as the cargoes can be pumped on and off at far greater speeds than can be achieved for dry cargo, a tanker spends less time in port. In the course of one year, it can carry more cargo than a dry cargo ship of equivalent tonnage. More than half the cargo that is carried by sea is oil carried in tankers (this is comparing only the weight of cargo carried, not the value).

The world's consumption of oil increased at about 9 per cent a year until the price rise in October 1973. Since then, the demand has levelled off to about 5 per cent per annum. Crude oil makes up 78 per cent of the oil transported by sea, and 82 per cent of the oil ton miles. The average distance crude oil is carried by sea is 5,400 miles.

The first steam ship specially designed to carry bulk oil, the *Glückauf*, appeared in 1886 and had a dwt tonnage of 2,300. By the First World War these vessels had grown to 8,000 tons, which had crept up to just 12,000–16,000 tons by the end of the Second World War. In the early 1950s the supertanker of about 30,000 tons was introduced, and there was then a steady increase in size up to the mid-1960s when there was a tremendous leap from 100,000 tons to 200,000 tons (in 1967) and then to 350,000 tons (in 1969).

In 1972, the tanker *Globtik Tokyo* – of almost 500,000 tons dwt – was launched. After this, there were a few tentative plans for even larger tankers, but they have not materialised and even those over 250,000 tons do not seem to have been popular in the tanker market.

There are now basically two types of tanker: large and small. The large tanker, of which the 250,000 ton has become a standard type, is used only for the carriage of crude oil. These are known as VLCCs – very large crude carriers. Tankers above 300,000 dwt are usually referred to as ULCCs – ultra large crude carriers.

There is also the Suezmax tanker – which is about 145,000 dwt (around 1 million barrels). This is the largest tanker that can pass through the Suez Canal loaded.

The smaller tankers, of which 30,000 dwt is considered a standard size, are referred to as product carriers and are used for carrying the refined product from the refineries to the consumer.

The main difference between the VLCC and the smaller product carrier is in the number of tanks (see Fig 2.12). The VLCC has fewer whereas the product carrier carrying a variety of petroleum products needs more, usually about nine tanks from for'd to aft with each tank being divided into three. However, to reduce the risk of pollution after a grounding or a collision, the IMO now restricts the maximum size of any single tank.

In most tankers the pump-room is placed just forward of the engine room as with high discharging speeds considerable power is needed. The after tanks are usually smaller and can be used as slop tanks to take the 'slops' when washing out the tanks during a ballast voyage. These slops can then be discharged into the loading port's oily water reception facilities.

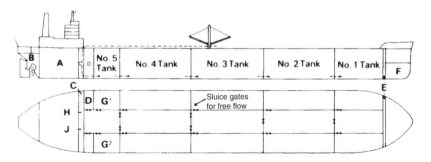

Fig 2.12   A 250,000 ton dwt very large crude carrier (VLCC).

It is also interesting to note that although the 200,000 ton tanker can carry 10 times the cargo of a 20,000 ton tanker, its dimensions – ie length, breadth and draft – are only about twice as great.

Apart from the obvious differences from a cargo ship – ie these vessels have tanks instead of holds – the tanks are separated from the rest of the ship by cofferdams. There is usually only one small crane or derrick to lift the flexible hoses aboard to connect them with the shore pipelines.

Because there are only small openings necessary on the deck, they are much less vulnerable to the seas breaking over the deck, therefore they are allowed to load deeper. This may mean that to enable the crew to move from for'd to aft in bad weather a catwalk or flying bridge may have to be constructed – this is particularly so in small tankers.

Traditionally, it has been rare for a tanker to have a double bottom. However, since the *Exxon Valdez* disaster in 1989 and the colossal clean-up costs involved, there has been a growing anxiety on oil pollution matters

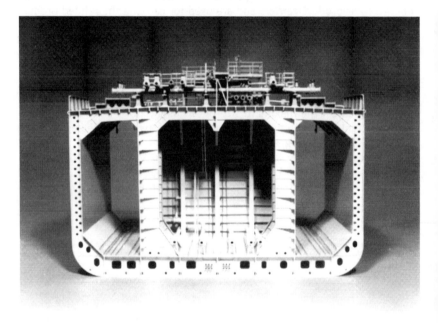

The photo shows a section through a modern double-skinned tanker. By being double-skinned, the inside of the tanks will be free from many of the structural elements which make cleaning and draining of the thick oils difficult in single-hulled tankers. The double skin can also be used as segregated ballast tanks. However, they are more expensive to construct and many argue that the double hull could harbour explosive petroleum gases which could in fact increase the danger! (Courtesy of Fairplay)

which has focused attention on possible improvements in hull design. As a result of this, the IMO has considered two major types of design:

- Double hulls. In December 2002, some 70 per cent of large tankers were still single-hulled but, following the loss of the *Prestige*, many countries are banning single-hull tankers from their ports and coastal waters.
- Design based on hydrostatic balancing – the idea being that in the event of collision or grounding, water would flow into the ship rather than oil out.

However, as a result of the very strong public opinion in the USA following the *Exxon Valdez* disaster, the US authorities unilaterally introduced OPA 90 (Oil Pollution Act 1990). This Act rules that all tankers trading with the USA must be double-hulled and the effect of this has been that virtually all new tankers constructed since this Act came into force have been double-hulled.

OPA 90 also requires *all* vessels trading to the USA to have *COFRs* (Certificates of Financial Responsibility). This is to ensure that any ship causing pollution within the USA will have the financial capability to pay for the clean-up costs.

The cargo is loaded by being pumped aboard by shore pumps or by having the shore tanks higher than the ship and letting it flow aboard under gravity. It is discharged by ship's pumps and bigger tankers can have bigger pumps and pipelines so that the discharging time should be fairly constant regardless of the size of tanker. As a rule of thumb, the pumping speed should be about 10 per cent of the dwt so that a 100,000-ton tanker should be able to pump the cargo at about 10,000 tons per hour. Some oils would be very difficult to pump if they got too cold, so steam heating coils in the tanks may be necessary.

A particular problem with tankers is cleaning the tanks. This is necessary not only to avoid contamination, but to remove all traces of oil which, if left, would vaporise and produce an explosive vapour-air mixture. Tankers are potentially most dangerous just after they have discharged their cargo. To help overcome this danger in the ballast condition, new tankers over 20,000 dwt are fitted with inert gas systems (IGS). This means that as the cargo is pumped out it is replaced by an inert, oxygen-free, gas. Many systems use the engine exhaust gases which have been cleaned and have had the excessively corrosive elements removed.

To facilitate tank cleaning and to ensure that the maximum amount of crude oil is discharged – as on a VLCC amounts of oil in excess of 100 tonnes could be left on board – the IMO now requires crude oil washing (COW) facilities to be fitted to all new crude-oil tankers over 20,000 dwt. By using this technique, the tanks are washed down with hot crude oil as the vessel is discharging. Crude-oil washing will slightly slow down the discharge, so it is not usual to wash all the tanks this way at each discharge unless the vessel is going in for repairs.

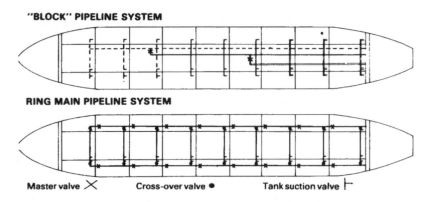

"BLOCK" PIPELINE SYSTEM

RING MAIN PIPELINE SYSTEM

Master valve ✕   Cross-over valve ●   Tank suction valve ⊢

Fig 2.13   Pipeline systems for conventional tankers with nine tanks, each divided into three: the starboard wing tank, the port wing tank and the centre tank.

Also, as it is difficult to get any tank absolutely clean, the IMO has ruled that all new tankers over 30,000 dwt should have segregated ballast tanks (SBTs). This should ensure that all seawater taken on as ballast can be pumped out again without any risk of pollution. With double-hulled tankers, the space between the hulls can be used for ballast. (See also the end of Chapter 11.)

Tankers have a relatively small crew, so to enable them to wash tanks quickly and efficiently, a variety of mechanical aids are provided. (See also the end of Chapter 11.)

Pipeline systems   Some of the VLCCs do not have pipeline systems, but simply large sluice gates in the bulkheads. Only one type of oil can be carried, but there are great savings in cost, weight and maintenance. This is known as the 'freeflow' system.

Product carriers that carry more than one grade of oil have to have a pipeline system. The more grades the tanker has to carry, the more complex the system has to be. Fig 2.13 shows the two most common systems. The purpose of the master and cross-over valves is to isolate sections of the line, and the purpose of the tank suction valve is to allow the oil in and out of the tank. The valves can be manually operated or from a central control room.

Combination carriers (Combos)

One of the economic problems of tankers and bulk ships is that they must inevitably spend half their working lives in ballast and therefore not earning freight (money). To overcome this problem, the combination vessel – which can carry both dry and liquid bulk – has been developed, and there are many permutations of this. In actual fact, they seldom do perform the 'full both

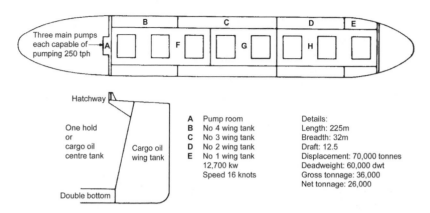

Fig 2.14   Combined oil/ore carrier (O/O).

way' voyages, due to the high cost and difficulties involved with the cleaning when switching from liquid to dry. However, they can switch from dry to liquid trades depending on which of the markets is offering the higher freights. From a commercial point of view, the importance of 'Combos' lies in the fact that they link the dry cargo and tanker markets.

In 2001, Combos made up 4 per cent of the dry bulk carrier fleet, and slightly less of the tanker fleet. In 1993, there were some 264 combination vessels forming some 5 per cent of the dry bulk carrier fleet tonnage, or 4 per cent of the tanker market. In 1983, there were 418 Combos, while there were 348 in 1986 – so there is clearly a declining trend in this type.

The O/O (Ore or Oil) tanker   An example of this is shown in Fig 2.14. It is more or less a tanker on which a hatch is provided on top of the central tank. For example, it can load ore in Brazil for Japan, thence in ballast to Indonesia where it could load oil for the USA – thus considerably reducing the time spent in ballast. Ore and oil are never carried simultaneously.

The OBO (Ore, Bulk or Oil)   Fig 2.10 (page 48) shows the transverse section of the large bulk carrier, and OBOs are basically dry bulk carriers modified to carry bulk oil. These ships are some 15–20 per cent more expensive to build than a tanker or bulk carrier of equivalent size and, as already mentioned, are fundamentally bulk carriers structurally reinforced to handle oil and high-density cargoes. It is a question of judgement and further research to see if this extra flexibility makes it an economic proposition.

Liquefied gas carriers

In the year 2000, there were about 1,126 such tankers, and they can be divided into two basic types to suit the two main cargoes concerned: natural

LNG tankers have tanks constructed of materials such as aluminium and nickel, which withstand very low temperatures.

gas (methane), and various petroleum gases such as butane. They are carried in liquefied form as this reduces the volume by about 600 times.

LNG (liquefied natural gas) is carried either by reducing the temperature to −160°C when it has to be carried in fast, well-insulated and expensive ships, or by converting it (an expensive process) into methyl alcohol and carrying it in conventional tankers. The economic advantages for each method depends fundamentally on the distance that the gas has to be carried. The latter method is better for longer distances and it is also inherently safer.

LPG (liquefied petroleum gas) can be liquefied at higher temperatures than above and is also, in some cases, liquefied by pressure or a combination of both. LPG carriers tend to be smaller than LNG carriers.

The International Gas Carrier Code (IGC Code) governs the construction of all such tankers built after 1 July 1986, but some of the main points that should be noted are:

- All LNG carriers must have double skins.
- Tanks must be constructed of material that will not become brittle at the very low temperatures required (aluminium, nickel, etc).
- Tanks must be insulated both to protect the mild steel outer hull from the very low temperatures that would make the mild steel go brittle, and

to reduce the cargo loss due to boil off. These tankers are possibly the only steam turbine ships still being built as the 'boil off' can be used in the boilers to power the ship.
- There are two main types of tank construction – independent or free-standing tanks, and 'membrane' tanks. The tanks that carry the liquefied gas within the outer hull must be adequately supported.
- Very strict safety precautions both as regards construction and operation apply.

Chemical parcel tankers

In 2001, there were in total about 2,681 of these specialised parcel tankers, and their design is very much governed by the IMO Code for the Construction and Equipment of Ships carrying Dangerous Chemicals in Bulk, which came into effect in April 1972 – ie the IBC Code (International Bulk Chemical Code). This code lays down three basic types:

- A type I ship is designed to transport products that require maximum preventative measures to preclude escape of such cargo. This type has a thick double skin.

MV Cape Benat, *a chemical tanker built in 1997/8. She has a dwt of 32,754 and operates under the Liberian flag.*

- A type II ship is designed to transport products that require significant preventative measures to preclude the escape of such cargo. This type has a thinner double skin.
- A type III ship is designed to carry products of sufficient hazard to require a moderate degree of containment to increase survival in a damaged condition. This type is similar to a sophisticated conventional product carrier.

All these types will have complex pipeline systems, often with several separate pump-rooms. The tanks will have special coatings, and the tank cleaning and preparation is of a much higher order than that required for conventional tankers.

This is a highly specialised branch of transport calling for specific training – not only for the crew, but also for the brokers and operating personnel.

Specialist ships

This term is not a precise technical expression, but is rather a catch-all phrase to cover ships designed and built for a dedicated purpose, ie where the ship has been built to suit the cargo, as opposed to the general cargo ship, where the cargo has to fit the ship. It could be argued that the container ship is not a specialist vessel as the container is a way of making the cargo fit the ship, whereas the tanker could be considered a specialist ship.

However, the term *specialist ship* is usually kept for relatively small categories of vessel where they do not enjoy, or perhaps deserve, widespread recognition as a type. Further, specialist ships can be separated into those such as heavy lift ships, which if they did not exist the cargo couldn't move at all, and those such as cement carriers, which enable the cargo to be transported faster, cheaper and safer.

Some of the more interesting specialist ships

The reefer This is a ship designed for carrying temperature-controlled cargoes (see Chapter 6). This category is probably too large a group to be put under the specialist heading, there being 1,553 vessels in 1993 (8.5 million dwt). Much reefer cargo is now carried in containers, but the need for dedicated ships remains. They are usually fast, have small hatches, and are well insulated. An interesting point about this type, seldom appreciated, is that one of the first ships fitted with refrigerated cargo capacity was the British ship *Dunedin*, which carried a cargo of frozen meat to the UK in 1882. The growth in the frozen meat trade obviously caused a major reduction in the livestock trade.

PCC (Pure Car Carriers) and PCTC (Pure Car and Truck Carriers) This type made a tentative start in the 1950s and properly developed in the 1960s, with the first purpose-built vessel appearing in 1965. Basically, they are floating multi-storey car parks! Problems include providing good ventilation systems, and their design – with high superstructure – gives them a high 'windage' and causes manoeuvring difficulties. The port of Rotterdam had to build an elaborate system of wind deflectors to allow such vessels access to their terminals during cross winds.

Cement carriers A few such dedicated ships were around in the early part of the twentieth century, but they were not developed to a great extent until after the Second World War. Today there is a large and varied fleet of such ships as regards size and capability. The main problems such a design has to overcome are dust, rain and speed of handling.

Fruit juice tankers These first appeared in 1985, and a typical fruit juice tanker would have a size of around 10,000 dwt and would be fitted with stainless steel tanks. The juice is carried at $-7°C$, and as it is of high density there has to be excess volume for buoyancy.

Molten sulphur tankers This type first appeared in 1960, and by 1991 there were some 30 ships between 1,000 and 30,000 dwt dedicated to this trade. Cargo is carried at $138°C$.

Phosphoric acid tankers This commodity is used in the production of fertilisers and the international trade in phosphoric acid developed in the late 1960s. By 1990, it stood at 38 billion ton miles with some 40 specialised terminals worldwide. In this same year, there were 12 phosphoric acid tankers, ranging between 10,000 to 59,800 dwt.

For specialist ship types to emerge, there needs to be:

- High demand, but a relatively low freight rate.
- Prospects of a relatively stable period of trade in order to make the long-term 'risk' involved in a non-flexible capital investment justifiable.
- Either an entrepreneur in the business prepared to seize the opportunity, or the commodity must form part of a large vertically integrated organisation that wishes to optimise the transportation link in the enterprise, such as you find in the banana trade.
- For a more detailed and complete description of specialist ships, see *The Shipping Revolution* (Conway Press, 1993).

Types of engines

The number and varieties of marine propulsion units developed for ships over the last two centuries are many and some of the basic types can still be found on older and smaller ships in many parts of the world; sometimes references to various aspects of these will be made in current documents – such as those used when chartering a vessel. However, for most new tonnage that has been built over the last few years, the diesel engine has become completely dominant.

The diesel engine

The diesel engine comes in two basic forms: the slow-speed diesel and the medium-speed diesel.

The *slow-speed diesel* is the original type of marine diesel engine. (The diesel engine was invented by Rudolf Diesel in 1893, and first went to sea in 1910.) As its name suggests, it is a slow-revving engine turning at just over 100 rpm at full speed. It can therefore be directly coupled to the propeller. They are very large heavy engines, but economical to operate – and the fact that they have been the most popular engine since the Second World War speaks for itself. At the present time, this type of engine would be the ship designer's obvious choice unless he had a pressing reason for choosing a medium-speed diesel engine or diesel electric. However, if building an LNG carrier, the choice would still probably be for a steam turbine as the 'boil off' from the gas can be used to heat the boilers. The maximum power of the

The photo shows a 12K98MC-C slow speed diesel engine on a test bed. It has an output of 68,520 kW/108,640 bhp at 104 rpm. The engine has a height of 12m, width 4m and length of 24m and has a weight of around 2,000 tons. (Courtesy MAN B&W Diesel A/S Copenhagen)

largest slow-speed diesel engine is around 100,000 bhp, which is adequate for all but the largest and fastest ships.

The advent of roll-on/roll-off ships – necessitating clear deck space without the intrusion of a large engine – brought about the introduction of the *medium-speed diesel* in the early 1960s. Its popularity has grown rapidly and currently these engines form a large percentage of the propulsion units for smaller tonnage and Ro/Ro types. The medium-speed diesel is smaller than the slow-speed diesel, being only about one-third of its weight and size. It obtains its power from higher rpm, which at full speed lies between 300 and 500 rpm depending on the make and model. As the optimum propeller speed for maximum propeller efficiency is between 80 and 100 rpm, the medium-speed diesel is too fast for direct drive and reduction gearing is necessary. Once the necessity of a gearbox is accepted, they have their advantages. Power for other purposes can be taken from the gearbox, and the ship – instead of having one large engine – can have two or three smaller engines driving into the gearbox. With this arrangement, the vessel is not immobilised in the event of a breakdown and can in fact repair and maintain her main engines while underway. Furthermore, by being physically smaller, not only is more space available for cargo, but the size of the components also become smaller, which makes such jobs as an emergency piston change while the ship is rolling in a seaway an easier proposition. One of the medium-speed diesel's main disadvantages is that it is offensively noisy for the engineers, who have to work in close proximity to it.

The diesel-electric engine

In this engine, one or more medium-speed diesel engines are connected to an electric synchronous generator and the propeller is turned by a synchronous motor. The speed reduction between the diesels and the propeller and the problem of reversing are achieved electrically. There is also great flexibility in the arrangement of the machinery space. No long shafts are necessary to transmit the power and the engines can be positioned anywhere and placed on cushioned mountings to reduce noise and vibration. This makes them the obvious choice for ships that rate passenger comfort higher than cost.

Steam reciprocating engine

This is a steam piston engine and was the earliest type of mechanical propulsion available. The first steam ship was the *Charlotte Dundas*, which was launched in 1801 and worked on the Clyde. The first power-assisted Atlantic crossing was that of the American ship, the *Savannah*, in 1819 – but it was some time before such engines were in common use on long runs due to the amount of fuel (bunkers) they consumed and the expense and difficulties in obtaining fresh supplies. A worldwide network of coaling stations had first to be set up.

This is a simple, robust and reliable form of engine, but it is limited in the power output available and it is relatively inefficient from the fuel consumption point of view. Some may still be found in older and smaller ships, and the Liberty ship was fitted with this type of engine.

The engine itself turns relatively slowly and can therefore be connected directly with the propeller. No intermediate gearbox is necessary.

The steam turbine

This was again a British invention, produced by Sir Charles Parsons in 1884. In this engine, high-pressure steam is forced through nozzles onto the turbine wheels where the steam pushing on the angled turbine blades causes it to revolve at high speed. Because of its very high speed, it has to be connected to the propeller via a gearbox.

It is also a single-direction engine – ie it cannot be reversed – so either an astern turbine has to be fitted (which is a big expense for possibly only a few minutes' use each trip) or a controllable pitch propeller can be fitted, by which the thrust from the propeller can be reversed. Where astern turbines are fitted, it is usual to economise by fitting a smaller unit. Many turbine ships therefore only have limited astern power.

In the past, the steam turbine was the most powerful and comfortable engine available, but its fuel consumption was significantly higher than a diesel of equivalent power, so after the fuel price rise in 1973 its decline was inevitable. It was the usual engine for VLCCs, as the steam power was available for both propulsion and pumps, but even these are now usually powered by slow-speed diesels.

The gas turbine

This engine first went to sea in 1947, and has now become the standard engine in the Royal Navy. A heavy-duty industrial engine appeared in the late 1950s in two merchant ships (a tanker and converted Liberty ship), but the trials seemed to evoke little enthusiasm.

In 1970, two large, fast container ships entered service with standard Pratt and Whitney aircraft gas turbines and a new wave of interest seemed likely – but in 1980 the two ships were re-engined with slow-speed diesels.

The fuel consumption of these engines is relatively high and the type of fuel expensive, but the engines are very small, reliable and can easily be changed – a new engine can be fitted in 24 hours while the cargo is being discharged. They also lend themselves to easy automation. This is yet another example as to how, in commercial shipping, cost is invariably the dominant factor.

Nuclear propulsion

The 1960s saw a wave of interest in experimental nuclear-powered merchant ships, ie the American cargo ship the *Savannah* was launched in 1962, but has long since been discontinued. The German bulk carrier the *Otto Hann* was launched as a nuclear-powered vessel in 1968, but she was re-engined with diesel in 1983. It is interesting to note that this change in power for the *Otto Hann* increased her dwt from 14,428 to 20,000. The Japanese also built a nuclear-powered bulk carrier, but again this was quickly discontinued. Only the Russian ice breaker *Lenin* seems to have been a success and repeated in other vessels.

Auxiliaries

In addition to their main engines, ships also need power for heat, light, ventilation, refrigeration, navigational apparatus, fire pumps, cargo gear, anchor windlass, etc. Vessels therefore need a collection of generators and other equipment. At sea, most of this power is taken from the main engines themselves, and therefore the auxiliaries have to be started up before the main engines are stopped – otherwise the ship can be thrown into a state of chaos. This means that there are problems if a ship wishes to stop her main engines without adequate prior warning.

Changes in methods of propulsion

Table 2.5 illustrates how the different types of engine have developed for British ships since 1925. The 1993 *Lloyd's Register of Annual Statistical Tables*

Table 2.5	The changes in methods of propulsion for British ships, 1925–82							
Year	Steam reciprocating		Turbine		Fuel		Diesel	
	% No	% GRT	% No	% GRT	% Coal	% Oil	% No	% GRT
1925	93	82	3	14	75	25	4	4
1930	90	75	4	14	72	28	6	11
1935	86	67	5	17	65	35	9	16
1939	80	57	5	17	60	40	15	26
1950	67	45	7	21	34	66	26	34
1955	56	31	9	26	12	88	35	43
1960	37	16	11	35	5	95	52	49
1965	19	5	12	40			69	55
1970	8	1	12	46	*	100	80	53
1978	3	0.3	6	47		100	89	52
1982	2	0.2	5	41		100	92	58

* A few large coal-burning ships have appeared on certain coal trade routes.

shows that of the total world tonnage for all ships, only 6 per cent of the number of ships are steam-powered, which accounts for about 30 per cent of the GT. However, as mentioned earlier, virtually all new tonnage is fitted with diesel.

Propellers

If you imagine the propeller as a screw – screwing into, say, wood – the *pitch* is the axial distance it would travel in one revolution. If the pitch were controllable and it was set at zero, there would be no forward movement. As the pitch is increased, then the vessel's speed will increase. This is the principle of the *controllable pitch propeller (CPP)* – by reducing or reversing pitch, the vessel can be manoeuvred virtually independently of the engine.

Controllable pitch propellers were first used at sea in the late 1930s for small ships, and they are now commonplace on large ships. With a CPP, control of engine power and direction (ahead or astern) is easily obtainable from the bridge. The pitch can also be adjusted to suit the weather conditions, thus giving greater overall engine efficiency. There remains, however, the question of high initial expense and the very considerable cost that might be incurred in the event of an unfortunately timed malfunction.

Over the last few years, engine and propeller manufacturers have developed engine pods that are fitted either in addition to, or instead of, the conventional propeller arrangement. The new *Queen Mary 2* has four such pods – two fixed pods and two azimuthing pods – that can be used for steering and manoeuvring. Such pods can be large and sophisticated, and the ones on the *Queen Mary 2* weigh around 250 tons each.

Power requirements and fuel consumption

Power is usually measured by *ihp* (*indicated horsepower*) with reciprocating engines, *shp (shaft horsepower)* with turbines, and *bhp (brake horsepower)* with diesel engines. However, with the advent of metrification, the standard measure is the kilowatt – kW.

One horsepower = 0.7459 kilowatts

One kilowatt = 1.3407 horsepower

Note: PS (Pferdestärke) is also used sometimes to indicate the power of marine engines, ie:

1 PS = 0.986 hp = 0.736 kW

Table 2.6 Typical power requirements for common ship types			
Ship type	Size	Speed	Kilowatts
Passenger	20,000 GT	21 knots	13,500
Container	56,000 dwt	24.5 knots	41,000
VLCC	280,000 dwt	15 knots	18,600
Panamax bulk carrier	63,000 dwt	13.5 knots	7,000
General cargo	15,000 dwt	13 knots	3,750

Fuel consumption

Table 2.6 gives a rough idea of the power requirements for various categories of vessel.

Specific fuel consumption (SFC) is the fuel used, in grams, for every bhp for every hour. Modern engines have an optimum SFC of, say, 125 gm/bhp/per hour. Therefore, the fuel consumption for a vessel with a 30,000 bhp engine, having a SFC of 125 gm/bhp/hr would be:

$$(30,000 \times 125 \times 24)/1,000,000 = 90 \text{ tons of fuel per day}$$

Different types of fuel

Crude oil is distilled at refineries, giving rise to *distillate fuels* – which include marine diesel oil and gas oil. Much of the residue left after distillation can also be used as fuel, and this residual fuel is known as *fuel oil*. As crude oils vary, so do the residual fuels; generally, though, they are thick viscous oils which may have sulphur, sodium and vanadium dissolved in them. However, these can be injurious to most types of engines. Also, because this is a residual fuel, it may contain other contaminants such as mud and rust.

Being a residual fuel, though, has one great virtue: it is cheaper than distillate fuels and by the use of heating, additives and cleaning, many of the problems can be overcome – and in fact most modern marine engines are able to use them. A compromise can be achieved by blending the two types to make what are known as *intermediate fuel oils (ifo)*.

Following the oil price rise in 1973, more distillate fuel was extracted from the crude oil. This is achieved by a process known as *cracking*. As the residue becomes a smaller proportion of the whole, the undesirable elements form a greater proportion of the residue, thus reducing the quality of many residual fuels (FO). By the early 1980s, quality control of FO had become a problem.

Table 2.7 A comparison of different fuel types

Type	Name	Viscosity cSt	Use
Distillate	Gas oil	1.7–4	Shipboard auxiliaries and small coasters
	Marine diesel	4–5.3	
Blends of distillate and residual fuels	Light fuel oil (ifo)	Blends vary from 30 to 180	Used in diesel ships
Residual fuels	Marine fuel oil, also known as Bunker C	180	
		380	Steam turbines*

* The cheaper, more viscous oils can be used in the diesel engine by heating the fuel before use, but the problem of the damage done to the engine by virtue of the ingredients remains unless due care is observed.

It is being suggested by the oil companies that, with improved cracking procedures, residual fuels may eventually disappear as virtually all the crude oil will be distilled.

A very common way of classifying oils is by viscosity, and until the end of the 1970s viscosity was measured using the *Redwood Scale*. This is a scale that measures the time it takes for a set amount of oil to drip through a standard size aperture at a temperature of 100°F. Therefore, the higher the figure, the greater the viscosity of the oil.

However, in 1977 the major oil companies supplying bunkers switched from using the Redwood No 1 scale to the SI system, where the viscosity is measured in centistokes (cSt) at 50°C for heavy oils and in centistokes at 40°C for the lighter oils (say those below 30 cSt).

Table 2.7 gives further details concerning fuel comparisons. The cost of oil varies not only with the grade, but also the distance it has to be carried – so fuel purchased from sources that are near to the oil wells are usually much cheaper than those further away. However, there may often be a surplus of residual fuel at large refinery areas such as Rotterdam, which can affect the market price. Also, most large users will enjoy a favourable contract price that they will negotiate individually with the suppliers.

3 TYPES AND TRENDS

We saw in the previous chapter that there are many types of ships and that these evolve and change their size and speed to adapt to circumstances. As in evolution, from time to time a species of ship becomes completely extinct, but sometimes there will be a mutation whereby a new type of vessel will emerge. In this chapter, we will consider the underlying factors that generate such changes.

The causes of such changes fall into four broad categories:

1 Changes in demand. In the case of passengers, the demand has switched from sea to air transport (see also Chapter 7).
2 Radical changes in technology, such as when iron and steel steam ships brought to an end the commercial wooden sailing ship. Although no such radical change has been seen in recent years, modern technology does give a greater freedom of design to the naval architect, and the computer enables the shipowner to calculate all the advantages that could be gained from each variation.
3 Relative changes in the cost structure of marine transport. For instance, the steep increase of cargo-handling costs expressed as a percentage of the total transport cost was a major stimulus for the introduction of containerisation (see also Chapter 8).
4 The removal or addition of some external constraint – eg the closure of the Suez Canal, the construction of a new deep-water terminal with high-speed cargo-handling facilities, a tax concession, or a financial incentive.

If considerable capital is needed to launch a new design of ship, then those putting up the money for this must of course be confident that this new type will be used for a number of years to come. To illustrate points 2, 3 and 4, the appearance of the container ship provides an impressive example as to how low freight rates and ever-rising costs in the late 1950s and early 1960s made shipowners look critically at the system then in vogue. A little research made it clear that:

- Dry cargo ships were spending 50–60 per cent of their time in port, and thus capital equipment was being poorly utilised.

Table 3.1	Total port cost (in pounds sterling) per ton (the figures are for 1969 for a developed country)		
	Breakbulk ship	Container ship quay-to-quay	Container ship door-to-door
Cost of ship's time in port	1.4	0.7	0.7
Capital equipment cost	1	0.7	0.5
Labour and staff cost	2.3	1.7	0.3
TOTAL	4.7	3.1	1.5
Estimated increase per annum over the next few years	6%	5%	

- The cost of lifting the cargo on and off the ship had risen from about 5 per cent to about 30 per cent of the total transport cost since the end of the Second World War.

A comparative analysis of port costs (Table 3.1) shows how containerisation can improve on the above statistics.

Although the container ship and containers were considerably more expensive to build than the breakbulk ship, Table 3.1 shows clearly that the port cost per ton of cargo carried was cheaper because of the extra voyages and quicker turn-round. For instance, a container ship turn-round time to Australia was 63 days, while for a conventional breakbulk ship it was about 146 days.

However, port authorities had to be convinced – and shippers assured – of the virtues and practicalities of the new scheme, and one of the trends in all forms of transport is the necessity of consultation with all interested parties.

A further point that made a change easier to contemplate was that in the early 1960s, some 20 years after the war, much of the tonnage built to replace war losses was now itself in need of replacement. Also, technologically it was now possible to build a container ship, which could not have been done 20 years previously – the very large hatch openings required would have been structurally impossible.

The final hurdle to be overcome was money, and this was achieved by the large liner companies coming together into a variety of consortia so that the necessary capital could be raised to start the venture. Obviously, by its very nature, containerisation is an all or nothing venture. You cannot just buy a couple of boxes to try out the idea! For containerisation to work successfully, it is necessary to set up the whole system – ie inland transport, port facilities, containers, container ships, computer tracking systems, etc.

The economics of ship size

What constraints are there on size?

1 Technical limitations Several ships of over 500,000 tons dwt have been built, and plans for a 1 million ton dwt tanker have also been considered as being quite practical from the technical point of view. However, if growth in size is too fast, there is always the possibility of some dangerous side-effect being overlooked — as, for example, when there were explosions aboard three 200,000 ton dwt tankers while tank-washing in December 1969.

2 Limitation of routes, canals and ports For 200,000 ton tankers there are only a limited number of ports outside of Europe and Japan where they can safely berth fully loaded, and many of these are only at the cost of expensive dredging. Even in the open waters of the English Channel and North Sea, the areas where there is an adequate safe depth of water are very restricted (see Fig 3.1).

For the 375,000 ton dwt tankers and above, the number of ports where they can discharge when fully loaded become even fewer. Certain important navigational channels, such as the Malacca Strait, should also be avoided by ships with such deep drafts.

The Suez Canal, which lies on the main oil route to Europe, can cope only with 150,000 ton dwt tankers loaded, though larger ones can go through in ballast. There are, however, plans to considerably enlarge the Canal.

3 Terminal facilities Large ships demand large storage and good distribution facilities, which alone prohibits the use of such ships for many

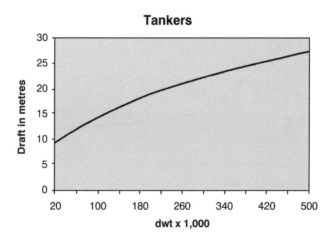

Tankers

Fig 3.1   Limitation of routes, canals and ports.

commodities. It is also important that ships can be discharged quickly –
ideally within five days, but certainly in not more than three weeks.
Therefore:

Maximum cargo-handling speed	Maximum size of ship
Tons per day	Tons dwt
1,000	20,000–25,000
2,000	40,000
5,000	80,000
20,000	150,000

For tankers this presents no great problem, and for some bulk cargoes (such
as ore) these speeds can be achieved at certain terminals. Port authorities
are, however, naturally loath to have expensive equipment and labour lying
idle for long periods with only occasional frantic employment. So there must
be a continuous demand for large amounts.

There must also be a long-term demand as large ships are not flexible and
cannot be used for other commodities on other routes. Before speculating,
therefore, the prospective owner will want to be assured of a long-term
charter.

Incentives to build large ships

- Reduced crew costs, as within very wide limits the same size crew is
  required regardless of the ship size (see Fig 3.2).

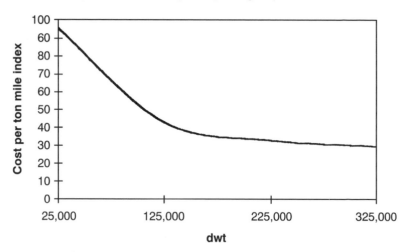

Fig 3.2   Relationship between ship size and costs.

- Reduced fuel costs, as consumption does not increase *pro rata* with size. The consumption of a 200,000 ton tanker is possibly only three to four times that of a 20,000 ton tanker.
- The building cost per ton is reduced. As mentioned before, a 200,000 ton dwt ship has only twice the dimensions of a 20,000 ton dwt ship and uses only three to four times the weight of steel. (*Note*: Although only twice the size, the plates are thicker.)

Disadvantages of large ships   Although the cost per ton is less, the overall cost is much higher. So if the money has been borrowed, high interest rates may have to be paid.

Apart from the constraints mentioned earlier, there are the possible dangers of putting all one's eggs into one basket, eg:

- Escalating insurance premiums.
- The possibility of massive pollution, followed by huge financial claims, and the loss of a good reputation and name.
- Any delay of 400,000 tons of *anything* could seriously embarrass the person or refinery awaiting it.
- Long tows may be necessary in the event of a breakdown to find a dry-dock capable of docking such a ship.

If we glance at this, it might seem that the disadvantages outweigh the advantages, but the facts speak for themselves. Large tankers have become the accepted mode of carrying crude oil; and the large ore-carrier is also now very common for the carriage of iron ore to large consumers who have their own special terminals. Container ships are also growing – and in fact most new ships on most routes are larger than their predecessors. An example of an exception to this trend is in the trade to the eastern Mediterranean where the Arab-Israeli conflict split the market into two separate divisions. A greater number of smaller ships in these trade areas was therefore required.

Finally, it must be stressed that the facts demonstrated in Fig 3.2 only apply if the ship is full – a large ship half full has a higher cost per ton than a ship half the size but full. In the vast majority of cases, though, it is the level of demand for that amount of a particular commodity that determines the trend in size of ships.

The optimum size of ship

The optimum size for the ship will therefore be the maximum size that the shipowner can fill and operate safely on the route and can 'turn round' with reasonable speed in port.

We must not assume, though, that as the costs per ton carried are cheaper for the shipowner with a large ship that he will necessarily make a bigger profit. The charterers are well aware of these cost reductions, and when chartering a larger ship will attempt to negotiate lower freight levels.

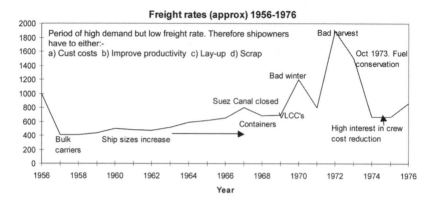

Fig 3.3   Effect of market conditions on ship types and operations.

Fig 3.3 is a simplified graph of the freight rates from the end of the Korean War, and indicates the effect that market conditions had on ship types and operation. From the end of the Korean War to the end of the 1960s, demand was growing – but so was supply, therefore freight rates were low. The shipowner could therefore only make a profit if he could cut his costs, and in this period the concentration was in two major areas:

1 As mentioned before, cargo-handling costs at this time had grown to a very large proportion of total costs, and in many trades had become the largest cost. In London, for instance, the cost of handling a ton of cargo had increased about 6.5 times between 1950 and 1970, and this was a period of relatively low inflation. Bulk carriers were therefore introduced at the end of the 1950s as this reduced the cost of, for example, handling a ton of sugar from around £10 a ton to 10p a ton. Containerisation took longer to introduce (about 10 years later) as it is a basic economic rule that the bigger the investment, the more cautious the investor. Also, although the cargo-handling cost savings were impressive, they were not quite so dramatic as with bulk handling.

2 Larger ships were introduced to cut the general transport costs. The increase in size was gradual at first and largely confined to tankers. During the 1960s, tankers grew from the 'supertanker' of around 25,000 dwt to 100,000 dwt, which was the largest size that could transit the Suez Canal. When the Canal was closed at the end of the 1960s, tanker size increased almost immediately to the VLCC of 200,000 dwt.

The early 1970s were boom years for shipping, which encouraged not only the usual round of new ship ordering but also enticed many newcomers – such as many developing countries – to enter the business. However, the boom was short-lived and, following the oil price rise in October 1973, the industry entered into a period of very low freight rates complicated by rising inflation. Propulsion and fuel consumption now became the target for cost cutting. *Slow steaming* was introduced, and ships with steam turbines were being re-engined with diesels. By 1980, bunker fuel had become so expensive that research was done with regard to the feasibility of returning to coal burning. At the same time, designs were introduced to bring back auxiliary sails for ships (computer controlled), and one or two ships were actually fitted with such sails. By the mid-1980s, bunker prices came down and crews became the high-cost item (see Chapter 4).

A more detailed cost analysis will be given in Chapter 8, but while considering ship types you might want to speculate as to what developments the next few decades may bring!

The economics of speed

Speed is an important factor with regard to passengers, perishable goods and valuable goods (especially where capital is tied up) in order to maintain schedules and to increase the ship's productivity. The graph in Fig 3.4 shows the relationship between horsepower and speed for 20,000 ton dwt vessels.

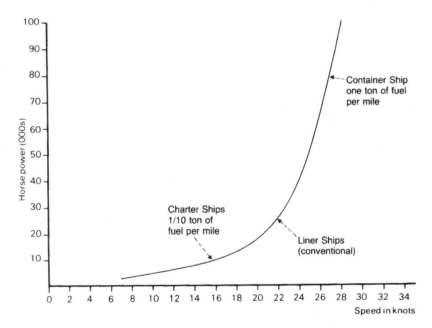

Fig 3.4   The relationship between horsepower and speed for 20,000 ton dwt vessels.

As this graph indicates, there is a very heavy financial penalty as regards increasing power. All transport does, of course, experience a rise in power requirement – and hence cost – with increases in speed, but water displacement vehicles do so out of all proportion compared with other forms of transport. This is mainly because, for ships, movement involves making waves. As a result of this, the maximum operating speeds of ships have altered little over the last 100 years – and in fact many passenger ships are running at slower speeds than they would have done, say, 30 years ago. It is also unlikely that any radical increase in operating speeds will be experienced in sea transport in the future, except with non-wavemaking ships such as hovercraft, hydrofoils and submarines.

However, although fuel costs increase with speed, the fixed costs – such as the capital costs, crew costs, etc – can be considered to be reduced as speed increases, as this lessens the time taken and increases the ship's productivity.

In 1994 the *Financial Times* referred to tests of a Japanese techno super liner with a speed of 50 knots (200,000 hp). Obviously this shows that there is interest in high-speed liners, but the fuel consumption is said to be 10 times that of liners with more conventional speeds.

Optimum performance in relation to earning capacity

The expression 'optimum' is frequently used very loosely concerning speed, and you often find that the speed under consideration is only being 'optimised' with reference to *some* of its dependent variables – not all of them. A truly optimum speed for a ship can only really be achieved by considering:

1 What speeds the ship can actually achieve, taking into account various mechanical constraints, the state of the hull (fouling), the draft and the effect of the weather.
2 What speeds we would *like* the ship to achieve, taking into account the costs, the profits and the pressures of schedules.

Also, the above considerations may need to be modified by an overall constraint that considers the safety of the ship, crew, cargo and environment.

However, in this section I would like to concentrate on those commercial/ economic factors considered under point **2**, and show how they can be applied to advantage by shipowners and charterers.

The basic principles 'Profit per ton carried' and 'profit per day' are two of the most useful transport indicators for measuring the level of operating surplus. If for the purpose of economic analysis the speed of the ship is adjusted to maximise these indicators, the solutions obtained will differ unless revenue equals costs.

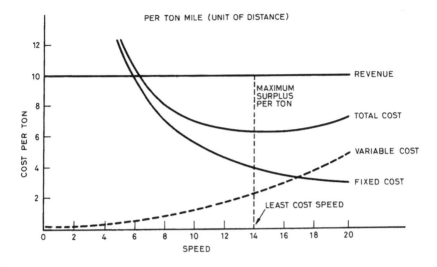

Fig 3.5   Cost curves.

If we look at Fig 3.5 we can see that the total cost curve is derived by adding the fixed cost curve onto the variable (fuel) cost curve. The important point to note, however, is that the revenue (freight) per ton is a fixed value per ton and appears as a horizontal straight line so that the maximum surplus per ton carried occurs where the total cost curve is minimum – which, for the case shown in Fig 3.5, is about 14 knots.

This optimum speed obtained is determined solely via the costs in carrying the cargo and remains constant for a fixed set of costs. It is not sensitive to delays, port time or freight rates, and therefore is more useful for long-run planning – particularly as the optimum speed based on profit per day will tend to fluctuate about this value as the freight rates vary.

The optimum speed determined by maximising the profit per ton carried is probably best referred to as the *least cost speed*, though it is also sometimes referred to as the *economic speed*.

If the profits and costs are considered on a daily basis (as is more common in commercial shipping), then it can be seen that the faster the ship goes the more voyages it can do, and the more profit it can earn (see Fig 3.6). The fixed costs are not affected by speed, so the problem can be seen to be that of setting off the variable (fuel) costs that increase with speed against the revenue (freight). In the case shown in Fig 3.6, this can be seen to be about 17.7 knots.

The profit per day indicator will maximise at the speed when the operating surplus per day is maximum. For most operating considerations, this is obviously a more desirable criterion – but it is very sensitive to fluctuations in freight rates, delays and port time, all of which are very difficult to

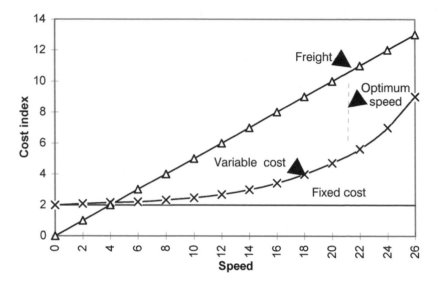

Fig 3.6   Revenue and cost per day.

predetermine and can therefore only be used for short-run planning. This optimum speed is referred to as the *most profitable speed*.

As already mentioned, the least cost speed equals the most profitable speed when the revenue earned equals the costs incurred. The freight rate that satisfies this condition, I will refer to as the *equilibrium freight rate* (EFR), which is so defined because although the freight rate will fluctuate daily, rates will tend to this level as the supply and demand for ships tends to an equilibrium position.

Figs 3.5 and 3.6 refer more to tramp ships than other types, and it has been assumed that at the end of the voyage in question, another will follow. For liners and passenger ships, the 'schedule' may be the critical factor – and here two ships going fast may save on the capital cost of having to buy a third.

The effect of varying fuel costs and port time

Fig 3.7 illustrates the effect on the speed-cost relationship, when (as in curve B) the fuel costs are increased. This obviously increases the total cost and cost per ton mile, but perhaps less obviously it makes the range of low-cost speeds smaller and the minimum-cost speed more critical. This can be seen when comparing the range of speeds in common operational use in, say, the 1930s, when fuel costs were low, compared to those of, say, the late 1980s.

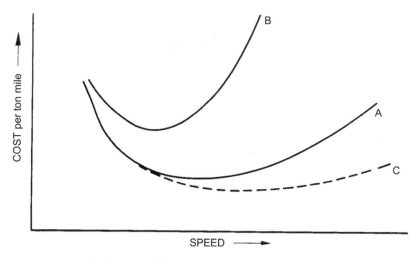

A = Standard ship
B = Standard ship where the fuel costs are increased
C = Standard ship where the port time has been reduced

Fig 3.7   The effect on the speed-cost relationship of varying fuel costs and port time.

In other words, fuel costs in 1930 were low so the curve was shallow, and in fact the range of operational speeds at that time was far wider than it is today. When (as in curve C) the port time has been reduced, the minimum-cost speed is increased – ie moves to the right. This is why container ships go faster than the traditional general cargo ship that they replace. It is perhaps interesting to note that when Cunard were considering building the two largest and fastest passenger ships ever – the *Queen Mary* and the *Queen Elizabeth* – they were described by the chairman of Cunard to the shareholders as '... in fact the smallest and slowest that would do the job'.

The importance of knowing the consumption of your ship

Knowing the bunker consumption of your ship at different speeds for different drafts and weather conditions is vital for efficient ship operation because:

- there are contractual obligations, as in time charters;
- it helps to establish the costs of operating under different possible scenarios;
- it is used to determine the *optimum speed* by trading off increase/decrease in speed/cost against profit.

How to establish consumption for different speeds The traditional way of doing this is to use what is known as the *Cube law*:

New consumption = (new speed)^3/(old speed)^3 × old consumption

My own researches have indicated that a better estimate can be achieved by using the 'J Curve':

$J = AV^3 - BV^2 + CV$

Average values for A = .000459, B = .0048, C = .04868

Where consumption at new speed = J × consumption at 14 knots

To achieve a reliable degree of accuracy, the values of A, B and C would of course need to be determined for each particular vessel.

For a motor bulk carrier, an estimate for a typical daily fuel consumption at 14 knots is given by the following formula:

Daily fuel consumption at 14 knots

= (19.5 + .00034 × ship's dwt) tons per day

Table 3.2, comparing the 'J' curve and Cube values, shows quite clearly that if the Cube law is used for estimating the consumption at, say, 10 knots, then the assumption could considerably underestimate the results, ie:

Consumption at 14 knots is 50 tons per day

Consumption at 10 knots using Cube law = 50 × 0.36 = 18 tons
    per day

Consumption at 10 knots using 'J' curve = 50 × 0.47 = 23.5 tons
    per day

If this cubic assumption is then used as the basis for the *optimum speed calculation*, then this operational decision could be significantly in error. Conversely, at higher speeds, if the Cube law is used it will probably exaggerate upwards what the actual figure would be.

The effect of draft Most ships will go about 10 per cent faster in ballast than at their loaded summer dwt – and for the same fuel consumption. For a large motor ship, an approximation of the reduction in consumption can be estimated:

Reduction in consumption = .004 (summer draft – new draft) ×
    TPI (tons per inch immersion)

Table 3.2   Comparison of 'J' and Cube multipliers

Speed (knots)	'J'	'Cube law'	Percentage difference
10	.47	.36	22
11	.57	.49	14
12	.69	.63	8
13	.83	.8	3.5
14	1.00	1.00	0
15	1.2	1.25	3
16	1.43	1.5	4.5

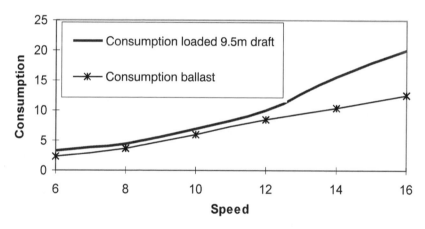

Fig 3.8   Consumption for a Freedom Mark 2 in calm seas.

Fig 3.8 gives an indication of the differences in fuel consumption for a Freedom Mark 2 between her loaded and ballast conditions in calm seas.

The effect of trim   The effect of trim is usually significant, but also difficult to assess. This effect is closely related to speed, draft and weather.

Trim may increase or decrease consumption, and data does indicate that large ships, at loaded draft and with bulbous bows, will at speed show a decrease in consumption if trimmed by the head.

To benefit from optimum trim, the best operating procedure is to fit the ship with an accurate fuel flow meter and then instruct the ship to adjust trim for minimum consumption for given speed, draft and weather.

The effect of hull roughness   Perhaps the most elusive effect is that of hull roughness, which is brought about by marine growth. Points to note are:

1 Roughness depends on the type of anti-fouling used. If self-polishing paints are used, then performance should actually improve over the first six months or so. If conventional paints are used, then there will be only a slight deterioration for the first few months. However, as the anti-fouling loses its efficacy, the build-up will become more prominent. But there is the added complication that anti-fouling paints are now being recognised as a water pollution problem in ports.

2 The degree of roughness will depend on where the vessel trades. In cold weather the build-up will be slight; in warm waters, particularly where there is an active concentration of marine life, it can be considerable. Other factors:

- This problem is worse where the vessel is slow steaming, and there are places – ie in the Persian Gulf – where a few days at anchor can have a catastrophic effect (eg speed reductions of 6 knots have been recorded).
- Visits to ports where the water is heavily polluted, though, may have a temporary beneficial effect.
- On average, a speed decrease of 1 per cent a month from dry-dock can be expected.
- Age and corrosion will also increase hull roughness, and hence reduce speed and increase consumption.

Basically, the above principles have been understood for some time, but quantifying them has become necessary because of the rise in bunker prices since 1973. It is now possible to do this because:

- modern navigational devices and fuel-flow meters have made accurate data possible;

Table 3.3   Percentage speed loss due to bad weather*

Beaufort Scale	Wind angle on the bow			
	0–30	30–60	60–150	150–180
2	1	1	−1	−1
3	3	2	0	−1
4	5	4	1	−1
5	9	7	3	0
6	14	11	6	2
7	20	14	8	3
8	27	16	9	5

*Note: This table indicates the percentage speed loss for an 8,000 dwt general cargo ship with containers on deck. Her 'fair weather' speed is 15 knots.

- computers have made analysing the data a simple and quick possibility.

The effect of weather and currents

Currents. Ocean currents and tidal streams do not affect the ship's speed through the water at all, but they can affect the ship's speed over the ground considerably.

In general, the broad flow of currents and tidal streams have been well known since Lieutenant Maury of the US Navy produced the first comprehensive atlas of currents at the beginning of the nineteenth century. Since then, current atlases have improved so that the majority of well-defined currents are now clearly tabulated. However, local meteorological factors can cause variations in the pattern and it is perhaps only recently that satellites with their 'all-seeing infra-red eye' have made it possible to quantify the day-to-day variations in ocean currents.

Wind and waves. The effect of wind and waves on the ship's speed is a much more 'hit and miss' affair to quantify. It will vary from ship to ship, depending on its superstructure, propulsion system, underwater form and ship length-to-wavelength ratio.

The direction of the weather relative to the ship will also make a difference to the speed reduction. As can be seen from Table 3.3, with a light following wind the speed can be seen to be very marginally increased.

4 THE CREW

The crew structure in Table 4.1 illustrates the typical crew that you would have expected to find on a 15,000 dwt general cargo ship at about the time of the oil crisis in 1973. However, this crisis brought to an end a very profitable period in shipping and the contraction of many traditional companies in the UK fleet.

As in any industry in a period of depression, high-cost areas – such as crew costs – present the management with obvious regions for possible rationalisation. But before analysing the changes made to crewing ships, largely brought about by the search for economies, it is useful to understand how this norm developed in the first place and what was expected from the different members on board.

In the days of sail there was just the deck department and the cook. Then came engines, and men with specialised knowledge were of course carried to operate them. The same situation occurred with the advent of radio, though as on the average ship the radio never required more than one or two men, it never established itself as a separate group. Finally, as society developed and shipping companies became more concerned for the welfare of the crew, and became responsible for such amenities as a balanced diet, bedding and cups and saucers, a separate catering staff evolved.

Typical duties of those on board

- The master, the official legal title for the captain, is responsible for the safe and efficient running of the ship as a whole. In some ways, it can be argued that his responsibilities have increased as ships have got bigger and more valuable, while on the other hand, with the increased development of worldwide instant communication, many of the vital decisions – which were originally his alone – are now shared with fellow managers in the shipping company.
- The chief officer, or mate, is the senior executive officer responsible for the efficient running of the ship. He usually keeps the 4–8 watch. (The watchkeeping officer is in charge of the ship. He ensures that the ship follows the track laid down on the chart, he avoids collisions with other ships, keeps a general eye on the safety of his own ship, and maintains a lookout for vessels and aircraft in distress.) The chief officer is also

Table 4.1	Traditional crew structure			
	Master (Captain)			
	Engine	*Deck*	*Radio*	*Cabin*
Officers	Chief engineer	Chief officer		Purser/Chief steward
	2nd engineer	2nd officer	Radio officer	
	3rd engineer	3rd officer		
	4th engineer			
	Electrician			
	0–4 Cadets	0–4 Cadets		
POs	Donkeyman	Bosun		Cook
	Storekeeper	Carpenter		
Ratings	Fireman/Greaser (3)	Sailors (6)		2nd cook
				Stewards (3)
				Cabin boys/galley boy

Note: *Figures in brackets are only a suggestion as to the numbers of this group that might be expected.*

responsible for discipline, the upkeep of the general fabric of the ship, and the cargo stowage.

- The 2nd officer usually keeps the 12–4 watch and has an overall responsibility for the navigation of the ship and the upkeep of the navigational equipment.
- The 3rd officer keeps the 8–12 watch and is often responsible for the ship's safety equipment.
- The cadets, both deck and engine, will spend part of their training period familiarising themselves with all the activities that go on aboard ship, part of their time ashore in a technical college learning the technical theory, and the final part understudying the officers.
- The bosun is the foreman of the crew and puts into effect the chief officer's directions on the day-to-day running and maintenance of the ship.
- The carpenter or general handyman is often carried for general deck repairs and maintenance.
- The deck ratings, composed of ABs and ordinary seamen, are divided up into watches where they help maintain a lookout, steer the ship when in confined waters and in fog when the automatic helmsman is not in use, and assist the bosun in the day-to-day running of the ship.

Duties of those in the engine room

- The chief engineer officer is responsible for the engines, in the same way that the captain is responsible for the ship. He wears the same insignia as the captain, the only visible difference being that his gold braid is on a background of purple.
- The 2nd engineer is the executive officer of the engine room. As many engines have been automated for some time (unmanned machinery space) now, it is not necessary for the engineers to keep watches. If they do, they would follow a similar pattern to that of the deck officers. The 3rd and remaining engineers would be allocated specific responsibilities depending on the type and requirements of the engine.
- The donkeyman is the bosun of the engine room and a storekeeper is often carried. On a tanker, a pumpman is necessary to operate and maintain the powerful pumps used in discharging the cargo.
- The function of the radio officer and the chief steward or catering officer and his department need no explanation.

Reductions in crew size

Crew sizes have steadily reduced in the years since the Second World War (see Table 4.2). Well-known UK cargo liners of perhaps 15,000 dwt in the 1950s had crews of up to 90 persons, where its replacement tonnage today would have a crew of, say, between 14 and 18, and there are plans for such ships of the future to operate with a crew of 10 or less.

A proud advertisement by the Australian Shipowners' Association in *Fairplay* (November 1994) asserted that the average crew size in Australian ships was 18 – well below the world average of 23.8. However, in 1988 Japan was operating 7 trial ships with crews of 11, known as Pioneer ships.

Just after the Second World War the desire to reduce crew sizes was prompted by a significant shortage of trained and qualified personnel, and many reductions were made possible as a result of technical improvements. Coal-fired ships, for instance, needed a small army of stokers, while automation – particularly in the engine room – reduced crew numbers

Table 4.2 Reductions in crew sizes 1955–2000	
Year	Typical crew for a general cargo ship
1955	42
1979	28
1994	22
2000	14

Table 4.3 How the number of UK seafarers has declined

Year	No of seafarers	No of ships	GT (millions)
1920	245,000	8,113	18.0
1930	236,000	7,856	20.3
1948	131,078	7,856	18.0
1952	135,950	5,912	18.6
1962	116,923	5,009	21.7
1971	98,000	3,785	27.3
1978	77,477	3,359	30.9
1993	31,957	1,747	6.0
2001	27,826	1,462	6.0

considerably. We could also list the effect of factors such as better paints, ergonomic design of equipment, etc.

By the late 1980s, though, the original reason – shortage of crew – had largely disappeared as a reason for crew size reduction, but other factors came into play. As already mentioned, following the oil price rise in 1973, shipowners were operating in conditions of under break-even freight rates and were therefore pressed to look for savings in their crew budget. One solution was to 'flag out' (this will be considered in a separate section), another was to do what was happening virtually everywhere – ie 'rationalise' the workforce. Consequently, dual-purpose officers were introduced, ie those who were qualified as both engineers and navigators. Today, with improved worldwide communications and the introduction of the GMDSS (1992), we see radio officers being replaced by fax and telex machines. For the ratings, general-purpose crews were based on the same philosophy as dual-purpose officers. These flourished for a few years, but now shipowners seem to prefer contracts whereby the seamen agree to be 'flexible' in their duties. The same kind of developments can be seen in ports among dockers – and in fact throughout most of the working world.

In Table 4.3 we can see that between 1920 and 1948 the number of ships and capacity (GT) remained very much the same, while the number of seafarers was greatly reduced. Much of this was probably a result of the change from coal-powered steam ships to diesel ships – and also losses because of the war. Between 1948 and 1962 the number of ships was reduced, but the size increased – which would seem to explain why the reduction in seafarers was less than *pro rata* for the number of ships.

In 1975 the UK merchant fleet reached its peak as regards tonnage (33.1 million GT), so by 1978 it was declining both in number and carrying capacity, showing a substantial reduction in the number of seafarers. By

Year	Officers	Cadets	Ratings	TOTAL
1952	44,300	3,150	88,500	135,950
1975	39,284	3,935	39,152	82,371
1998	15,248	1,477	10,750	27,475
2000	16,464	1,031	10,331	27,826

Table 4.4   UK seafarers, by rank, 1952–2000

1993, the number of ships had halved but the carrying capacity was only around 20 per cent of 1978 – showing that the large ships had been flagged out, leaving the specialist ships and ferries, so the rate of decline of seafarers was perhaps less than expected considering the UK tonnage. By 2001, the UK Registry was mainly a fleet of large ferries and the number of seafarers seems to have stabilised, though the introduction of a new tax system for ships under the British flag does seem to show an increase in UK tonnage. Table 4.4 gives further crew figures, by rank, for the period 1952–2000.

International crews

Crewing can no longer be viewed as a national issue. With the growth of open registers, second registers and special national and union agreements, ship managers can now, to a large extent, hire crews on the international market – just like ships. The regions shown in Table 4.5 provide the shown numbers of the world's total supply of seafarers.

In 1990, there were 403,000 merchant marine officers in the world and 838,000 ratings, giving a total of 1,241,000 seafarers worldwide. In 2000, there were 404,000 officers (40 per cent over the age of 50). In 2002, it was calculated that some 28 per cent of the world's seafarers came from the

Table 4.5   Regions of the world supply of seafarers (Source: ISF/Bimco)

Region	Numbers (× 1,000) of seafarers supplied Officers	Ratings	Cost in 2000 for full crew (wages) for Handy BC
OECD	147	191	
Eastern Europe	62	107	Russia: 450,000 USD
Africa and Latin America	35	89	375,000 USD
Far East	128	332	450,000 USD
India and Middle East	32	104	India: 500,000 USD

Table 4.6 Age distribution of seafarers worldwide in 2000			
Age range	Percentage	Percentage officers (OECD)	Percentage officers Far East
Under 20	2		
21–30	26	15	30
31–40	34	18	33
41–50	26	28	30
Over 50	12	50	8

Philippines, and it is estimated that in the year 2010 there will be a demand for 443,000 officers and 603,000 ratings.

The age distribution of seafarers worldwide and wastage

Table 4.6 gives further details on the numbers and ages of seafarers worldwide. Apart from retirement due to age, an ISF/Bimco report on the worldwide demand and supply position of seafarers in 1990 indicates that although approximately 11.7 per cent of officers change employers, only about 22 per cent of these left the industry altogether. With ratings, 77.6 per cent changed employers, but the report estimated that only 16.8 per cent of these left the industry.

Regulating crew size

Internationally, the IMO Resolution 481(X11) lays down the factors that should be considered when determining the size of crew required for the safe and efficient operation of a ship. These have been incorporated into Merchant Shipping Notice number 1501 for the guidance of British Flag Operators. This came into force in July 1992 and states that all UK ships of 500 tons or over, other than fishing craft or pleasure craft, which go beyond the limits of smooth water, must have a *safe manning document*, obtainable from the Department of Transport.

The principle of safe manning can be summarised from the IMO resolution:

- The capability of the vessel to maintain a safe bridgewatch, engine room watch and radio watch.
- The capability to manage all safety functions.
- The capability to maintain the vessel and its machinery in a safe working condition.
- The capability to moor and unmoor the vessel effectively and safely.
- Provision for medical care on board ship.

One of the major problems voiced by the unions, and others concerned with safe manning in an era of international crewing, is that of multilingual crews – ie crews made up of different nationalities and speaking different languages. During periods of routine operation there may be no problems at all with regard to this, but in an emergency, as many emergencies have shown, there can be considerable and dangerous consequences. One solution is to train the crew in a basic English as 'seaspeak'. In most cases this is mandatory for certain senior officers – but is it a realistic expectation for all?

Crew training

With the increase in the amount of sophisticated equipment in use and the growing number of specialist ships and trades, training of seafarers is obviously more important today than ever before. The safety and capability functions also require the appropriate member of crew to be suitably qualified. Of course, in an international situation the problem arises over agreed acceptable standards, and different administrations have in the past had different ideas on what constitutes minimum acceptable levels. To ensure acceptable standards and levels of training and qualifications for this international workforce, the IMO set up the STCW (Standard Training and Certification of Watchkeepers), and the IMO-revised STCW convention came into effect in 1997. For the first time ever, it was proposed that the IMO be given powers to enforce the convention.

The revised STCW convention also covers a wide range of other issues, including:

- Seafarers' hours of work and rest periods.
- Improved basic training for seafarers.
- Mandatory radar and ARPA (automated radar plotting aid) simulator training.
- Safe and efficient bridge procedures.
- Safety awareness and emergency training.
- Standards for personnel responsible for repair and maintenance of on-board electrical installations.

However, although everyone accepts the need for training, there is not always agreement as to who should pay for it. Should it be the employer, employee or the state? In the UK in the past there was an accepted formula for spreading the cost between all three. One of the criticisms made against flags of convenience, though, is that they poach trained personnel from other sources.

Where a vessel trades affects crew selection

In the administrative manning requirements, an important factor is 'Where will the vessel trade?', as this will affect the numbers, qualifications and experience necessary for the crew. The IMO advocates two main areas: coastal trading and unlimited trading. The UK used to have two areas – ie home trade and foreign-going – but in 1981 it decided to change this to three trading areas, as this fitted more closely the actual activities of the UK fleet. These three trading areas are:

- Limited European waters, which covers the near Continental areas from Brest to southern Norway and the Baltic in summer.
- All of the above, plus south to include the Mediterranean, and north to include most of the Norwegian coast and the Baltic.
- An unlimited trading area.

How crew are recruited

Someone wanting to find employment as a seafarer can either approach a shipping company directly or get on the 'books' of one of the many crewing agencies. Most ports will have such an agency and in the UK they must be registered with the Department of Employment.

Many shipowners nowadays do not, however, employ seamen directly but leave the manning and maintenance of their ship to a management company. In fact, you can meet masters these days who are appointed to a ship without ever meeting (or even knowing) who the actual owners are. At the end of 2001 it was estimated that there were some half a dozen ship management companies managing over 100 vessels – a dozen managing between 50 to 100 vessels, and some 200 smaller companies. The largest management company is Vships which has 600 ships, 25,000 seafarers and 1,000 shore staff in 20 offices around the world.

Pay and conditions

On British ships, and those of most developed countries, the conditions for the seafarer can be expected to be fairly good. So when attempting to estimate crew costs, it is important to know what these conditions may entail. For instance, British seafarers' salaries are low in comparison with many of their Continental counterparts, but their conditions of service – such as leave, repatriation conditions, etc – may be better and so add considerably to the crew costs.

Following the outrageous behaviour of the 'crimps' in the nineteenth century and the strength of the unions in the years following the Second World War, the conditions of service of the seafarer have been well regulated. The National Maritime Board was set up in 1917 as the main negotiating body between the shipowners and unions and it produced a Year Book that gave the latest agreed pay and conditions of seafarers. This Board no longer exists, and now – as with most other professions and trades – such matters are settled by individual negotiation.

Changing conditions do bring with them new problems – eg shorter voyages bring with them frequent changes of crew. If crews are changed frequently it is unlikely that the crew will take a great interest in the ship itself, which means not only does its maintenance suffer but also the shipboard communal life. Smaller crews with a highly efficient and productive work schedule means there is no slack in the system – although any illness or 'problem' can, and most probably will, create a fatiguing and stressful situation.

Industrial relations

By and large, industrial relations in this area have been quite good. The National Union of Seamen (NUS) was set up in 1887, resulting in shipowners banding together to form the Shipping Federation in 1890. By the early 1990s, though, the number of ratings had become relatively small so the National Union of Seamen combined with other transport unions to become the RMT (Rail, Maritime and Transport).

The major officers' union, the MNAOA (Merchant Navy and Airline Officers' Association) was not established until the difficult times of the 1930s (3 January 1936). Like the NUS, the MNAOA also suffered from falling membership and in 1985 reformed itself into NUMAST (National Union of Marine, Aviation and Shipping Transport Officers).

The strikes in the shipping industry can be listed in just a few lines:

- 1912: last national strike by the National Union of Seamen.
- 1920–6: series of local strikes culminating in the General Strike.
- 1947: strikes at major UK ports in response to the ending of special wartime conditions.
- 1955: strikes at two ports affecting liners only.
- 1960: nine-week strike over discipline.
- 1966: six-week strike.
- 1988: strike in Dover.

The International Workers Federation (ITF)

The ITF was founded by European seafarers' and dockers unions in 1896. Rotterdam dockworkers were on strike, and British maritime union leaders answered their call for support by organising an international trade union body that co-ordinated practical solidarity with this strike.

The ITF came into existence as a body designed to encourage practical support between transport workers – and this remains the central principle of the Federation. Soon after its foundation, the ITF grew from its seafarer and docker roots to embrace railway and road transport workers.

The Federation is a body made up of unions, not of individual workers. In 1993, it had more than 5 million members in 400 unions in over 100 countries. However, in one respect the ITF is unique. It intervenes directly in industrial relations for ships whose owners have chosen to operate under *flags of convenience* (more on this later) – seafarers serving on those ships who cannot join an affiliated national union are direct ITF members.

There can be no doubt that on the international scene there have been unscrupulous owners who have grossly exploited seafarers as regards their pay and conditions, and the ITF – by mobilising 'union action' around the world – has done much to draw attention to the worst excesses and it works hard to maintain reasonable pay and conditions for all crews under all flags.

Most reputable owners operating ships under a flag of convenience will operate with an ITF-acceptable agreement, who will issue a *blue certificate* for the ship. To obtain such an agreement, the ITF requires certain documents from the owners, such as a signed ITF special agreement, individual contracts of appointment, copy of ships' articles, a crew list, and the owners' contribution to the Seafarers' International Assistance, Welfare and Protection Fund for each seafarer. The ITF also has inspectors who will visit the ship to check that all is as it should be.

The International Labour Organisation (ILO)

The ILO was formed in 1919 to bring governments, employers and trade union representatives together for united action in the cause of social justice and higher living standards everywhere.

In 1946, the ILO became the first specialised agency associated with the United Nations, having special responsibility for social and labour questions, and the original membership of 42 nations has grown to over 150.

The special nature of conditions of work and life at sea has led the ILO to adopt an extensive range of over 50 conventions and recommendations applying specially to seafarers – eg the International Seafarers Code. The ILO minimum wage in 1992 was, for instance, $356 (USD) per month for an AB. We must note, though, that the ITF policy applies this minimum wage only to genuine national flag vessels. For flag of convenience vessels, the ITF sets a higher minimum wage, which in 1992 could be as much as $821 (USD) per month. In 2003, the ITF minimum wage for an AB was $1,300 (USD) per month.

5 NAVIGATION

Whose responsibility is this?

At an International Chamber of Shipping Conference held some years ago, the following resolution was passed:

The practical responsibility for safe navigation rests on masters and navigating officers. Nevertheless, the International Chamber of Shipping recognises that there are important management functions with particular reference to:

(A) effective supervision and appropriate guidance;
(B) the provision of appropriate navigational aids;
(C) the timely supply of all relevant information and publications;
(D) training;
(E) an up-to-date appreciation of all the navigational problems that arise at sea.

The High Court judgment on the Lady Gwendolen v Freshfield case underlines the importance of effective management supervision on the navigation of the ship. Furthermore, the trend towards taking legal action in the courts over the last few years indicates the growing management responsibility for all aspects concerning the safe operation of their vessels.
  In 1978, the IMO made the following recommendations:

1 No restraints should be placed on the master's professional judgement by the owner or charterer that are likely to endanger the ship.
2 The master should be protected from dismissal by the shipowner for exercising professional judgement with regard to safety.

The choice of route

Fundamentally, the choice lies between the shortest way, the quickest way and the simplest way.
  The shortest way is known as the great circle route and appears on the Mercator chart (the standard navigational chart) as a curved line. In the northern hemisphere – as, for example, on the North Atlantic run – the curve takes the vessel into higher latitudes than necessary, and possibly in winter into worse weather than the ship might expect to encounter if she kept further south. This is why the shortest way may not be the quickest.

The great circle route also involves frequent alterations of course and it requires a relatively sophisticated navigator if any significant advantage is to be gained over the simple direct rhumb line route. This is the one course which, if followed, will take the ship from A to B.

Least-time routeing, weather routeing or optimum routeing is a relatively modern technique and is only as good as the accuracy of long-range weather forecasts (ie on the North Atlantic, the ability to predict the weather for the next four or five days).

On the North Atlantic route, experiments have been going on since 1956 and the Netherlands Meteorological Office has been offering a North Atlantic routeing service since 1960. The British Meteorological Office has been offering such a service since 1968 on the North Atlantic and on the North Pacific since 1972. Also, there are now private companies offering routeing services, and these can be used by shipowners or charterers.

Savings of up to 14 hours can be claimed on a North Atlantic crossing, but far more important than this is the reduction in damage to the hull, engine and cargo. In fact, perhaps the major use of weather routeing services is in settling disputes after the voyage has been completed!

The simplest route really speaks for itself. One of the reasons why mandatory routeing in the English Channel was introduced was that the majority of ships using this waterway preferred coming along the English coast rather than the French coast, because it was navigationally simpler to do so. Hence the heavy congestion and high collision risk that developed in this region. Because of this, traffic routeing was introduced into the English Channel in June 1967, and since then the IMO has recommended the introduction of similar routeing disciplines at many other traffic focal points. These are now published in a booklet by the IMO – but subsequent collisions have illustrated that management has not always drawn the attention of their masters to the existence of these routes. However, since September 1972 many of these routes have been mandatory.

Other factors for choice of route

- Insurance policies and charter parties often put restrictions on the choice of route.
- The possibility of fog and ice, the ship's draft and manoeuvring ability, and the navigational devices she has on board must all be taken into consideration. (And, of course, passengers on a cruise expect to pass close enough to shore to enjoy the scenic delights on the ship's advertised itinerary.)
- There are also minefields still in existence and military exercise areas to be avoided.
- Concentrations of small fishing boats, some with dimly lit drift nets extending up to 5 miles, can create a problem – particularly when the migrating herring are moving across a busy shipping lane.

- In 1977, the IMO recommended that all vessels should have 3.5 metres under keel clearance (UKC). If this recommendation were to be followed rigorously, it would severely limit the choice of routes available to, say, ULCCs. However, where possible, the UKC should be determined for each ship and port. The major UKC allowances are made up as follows: wave allowance, squat, allowance for tidal prediction error, change in water density, and other safety factors. Squat is an effect in shallow water whereby the ship's draft can be increased. For a typical 15,000 dwt general cargo ship, this could be up to 1.5 metres—and for a large tanker it could be more.

Further, in shallow water the ship's speed will be reduced, and if the shallow water is on one side of the vessel the steering may become erratic − a problem that can occur when a ship moves out of the centre of a narrow channel.

The ship's navigational hardware

The compass

All ships must have a magnetic compass but, of course − due to a combination of the earth's magnetic field and the ship's magnetic field − this device may have sizeable errors. The gyro compass, developed during the First World War and became common on merchant ships during the Second World War, was made compulsory by the IMO 1974 SOLAS Regulations, which came into force on 1 September 1984. The gyro compass gives true direction, but being mechanically sophisticated it is liable to suffer from mechanical failure and is carried in addition to, and not instead of, the magnetic compass. The modern gyro compass is, however, very reliable.

Other ancillary compass devices are:

- The automatic helmsman which, as the name suggests, steers the ship automatically. This should not be used in fog, near the coast, or in areas of high traffic density. The ship should also be fitted with an alarm in case the automatic helmsman goes haywire. Serious casualties have occurred because of this.
- Repeater compasses to assist the navigation.
- A course recorder, which keeps a graphical record of all courses steered.

Radar

Radar was developed during the Second World War, and became available commercially immediately after 1945. Of all the modern technological marvels that have been developed since the war, radar is worthy of special

The bridge of the Isle of Innisfree, *built in the late 1990s. In the central 'bay window' is situated the command position where the controls and information are grouped around two seats: one for the captain and one for the officer of the watch. On the far side of the bridge can be seen the port wing docking control station, where the captain can control the berthing operations. This control station is duplicated also on the starboard side of the bridge.*

mention. It serves a twofold function: combining that of an easy-to-use position-fixing device with that of an all-weather lookout.

Unlike many modern black boxes, it does require a well-trained and able operator to comprehend its message fully. Many incidents that have occurred illustrate all too clearly the possibility of the untrained observer not realising the full significance of the radar picture he has been observing. The IMO STCW Convention stresses the need for watchkeeping officers to have undergone a practical radar simulator course as part of their training.

Fundamentally, there has been little change in radar since its introduction, although it has become easier to use, more discriminating and more reliable. It is compulsory (IMO) for virtually all ships on international voyages, and since February 1995, ships of 10,000 tons and over must be fitted with two independent radars.

In 1956, a radical change in presentation was first made available, known as 'true motion display'. This offers a presentation on the screen of the actual courses and speeds of the vessels within range, at the same time showing the actual course and speed of the vessel itself. On the conventional radar display the observer appears to be stationary and the courses and speeds of other ships displayed are all relative to the observer. It is the interpretation of this relative motion that is very often at fault and is the cause of misunderstanding. To help the mariner, there are now some very sophisticated radar sets with built-in computers known as ARPA (automated radar plotting aid). Their cost is four or five times that of a basic conventional radar, but since 1984 it has been compulsory for all new ships over 10,000 dwt to have them.

Automatic identification systems (AIS)

Since July 2002, the IMO, under SOLAS Ch V, requires AIS to be fitted for all ships greater than 300 GT.

Charts

This must be the most used and the most essential piece of navigational equipment. Every day, lights and buoys and underwater obstructions are changing their character and position, so the chart must be kept up-to-date and the management must ensure that their ships are supplied with the necessary information. British Isles charts used the Ordnance Survey of GB 1936 datum (Ireland, the 1965 datum) until March 2000 when it switched to European Terrestrial Reference System 1989 datum (ETRS).

Electronic charts are now available, so the question of keeping them up-to-date is today a simple matter of changing discs. Also, further electronic charts can be combined with other sophisticated electronic navigation systems – autopilot, etc – to form a fully integrated navigation system. With such a set-up, the waypoints can, for example, be programmed in and the ship will automatically proceed along the route decided. In 1998, the Maritime Safety Committee of the IMO allowed two basic modes of electronic chart displays:

1 Raster chart display system (RCDS). This is simply a scanned paper chart and therefore has no intelligence so cannot be interrogated.
2 The ECDIS system. This is when ENC data is used (an ENC is a vector chart). It is compiled from a database of individual items, so it can be interrogated to give a user selection of data.

The log

This is the traditional name given to the device that measures the ship's speed. (The 'log book' was originally the book for recording the number of knots that had run out when the log was cast.) There are now a large variety of patent devices, many of which are very good. All new ships of 500 tons and upwards making international voyages must have a log. The Walker's towed log goes back to 1878.

The integrated bridge system as seen by the officer of the watch in the command position in the centre of the bridge of Sky Wing *built in 2002, a double-hulled VLCC.*

Astro-navigation

This is a long-established and universally practised method. It requires considerable skill, but it is a skill that most professional navigators can be assumed to possess, though its role nowadays is that of a back-up system. It can be used anywhere in the world where it is not excessively cloudy, and the apparatus required is relatively cheap and reliable. The time required for a fix is longer than with most modern electronic methods but, when out of sight of land, speed of position-fixing is seldom critical. The navies of the world still take considerable interest in this method as, unlike most electronic methods, it is free from interference from a hostile agency.

Radio direction finder

This first became available in 1912 and was made compulsory on all ships over 1,600 GT. With this device, the bearing of known radio beacons can be taken and also the bearing of radio distress signals. It therefore had a safety as well as a navigational use. However, under SOLAS 2002, it is no longer required and most of the beacons have been taken out of service.

Decca navigator

This was developed by the British during the Second World War and was first used during the Normandy landings in 1944. It had a range of some 300 miles and the coverage included nearly all north-western Europe and many of the other navigationally difficult areas of the world. Its popularity and coverage grew until 1981, when there were 51 chains throughout the world. Since then, it has been declining as a result of competition from accurate, cheap and easy-to-use satellite systems. In Europe and in most other parts of the world, the system was shut off at the end of 1999.

Loran (derived from long range navigation)

There were two models: standard Loran or Loran A, and Loran C. Standard Loran (Loran A) was developed by the Americans in about 1942. It was a middle- and long-range navigational device and was operated mainly by the American Services. However, on 1 January 1980, the Americans switched off their last remaining stations.

Loran C has been available since 1959 and is a very accurate long-, medium- and short-range device which is available over much of the northern hemisphere. In its early days it was complex and expensive, but subsequently it became cheaper and easier to use. The US military, who are the main providers of the system, have estimated that this system will continue in operation at least until 2005.

Omega

This had been experimented with since the mid-1950s, but became commercially available as a worldwide system when the eighth permanent station in Australia became operational in 1982. This system provided a continuous position anywhere on the earth's surface to an accuracy of 1 mile or less. Omega closed down on 30 September 1997.

Navigational satellites

- In 1964 the US Department of Defense introduced the TRANSIT satellite system, which became available for commercial use in 1967. It was a discontinuous system, which means it was only possible to obtain a 'fix' at intervals that could vary from 30 minutes to a couple of hours. By the 1980s, the equipment had become cheap, available and easy to use, and by the early 1990s it was reckoned that there were some 95,000 users. However, because of the introduction of GPS (global positioning system), the US authorities discontinued it in 1996.
- Navstar GPS was born in 1973, but has offered worldwide coverage for commercial shipping only since 1991 – and only since 1995 has its

complete potential been available (ie a continuous, accurate, three-dimensional position fixing that can be used anywhere in the world). It is so accurate that the US military authorities have deliberately degraded the accuracy for commercial use to within 100 metres. However, it is possible to restore the accuracy to within a few metres by a method referred to as Differential GPS (DGPS). Many countries offer free DGPS (+− 19 metres) for vessels sailing up to 150 miles off their coast, eg north-west Europe, Spain, the USA. It is hoped that by the year 2006 GPS will no longer be deliberately degraded.

- GLONASS is the Russian equivalent of GPS and has only been available since 1995. Accuracy is claimed to be within 15–20 metres and the authorities have apparently made no policy decision deliberately to degrade the accuracy of the system.
- There are plans by Inmarsat to offer a combined GPS/GLONASS system.
- The EU is considering its own satellite system, Galileo.

Echo sounder

This is a sonic device that measures the depth of water under the ship. It can display the depth either as a graph or otherwise as required. It is fitted to nearly all ships, and the IMO recommends it for all ships over 500 GT.

VTS (vessel tracking systems)

In most major ports and traffic congestion areas, such as the English Channel, the movements of vessels are tracked and monitored and recorded. This latter point can be useful for inquiries following a disaster in the channels under surveillance. This 'control' centre also provides an excellent link for 'damage control' in the area.

Weather facsimile recorder (weatherfax)

This enables ships at sea to receive weather forecast charts from the main forecast centres of the world. It can be considered both as complementary to, and in addition to, external weather-routeing.

There are many other devices, both experimental and operational, and when we take into account the fact that for most navigational devices there are many models and many different makers, the problems of comprehensive and reliable instruction for their safe use and maintenance can be appreciated!

Communications at sea

Communication is absolutely vital to shipping. In fact, the development of the shipping industry as we know it today can be traced back to the invention of the telegraph in 1844 rather than to iron ships or steam ships. Before international communication existed, 'finding cargoes' was very much in the hands of enterprising masters.

Communication has two main functions:

1 Safety. This includes the sending out of distress signals, co-ordinating rescue action, and warning ships and those concerned of any dangers. Medical advice and diagnosis can also be given and help summoned.
2 The commercial operation of the ship.

Following the introduction of the telegraph was the telephone, in 1876. But from the ship's point of view, radio was the major breakthrough. Marconi showed its possibilities in 1895, and by 1903 an international conference had established some of the ground rules for its use at sea. By the time of the first SOLAS convention in 1914, following the *Titanic* disaster in 1912, ships carrying more than 50 passengers had to carry a radio with a range of at least 100 miles. (The *Titanic* did have radio, and must have been one of the first ships to use the new SOS signal.) Nowadays, all vessels over 1,600 GT must be able to maintain some kind of radio contact.

From the early days of radio, *wireless telegraphy* was used for long-range communication as it is not so much affected by the various forms of interference as the spoken word.

Medium Wave radio/telephone can be used for making link telephone calls via the coastal radio station.

VHF radio/telephone is a short-range radio telephone used for talking to other ships, pilots, tugs, etc. Many port and canal authorities insist on ships being equipped with this.

Inmarsat

The date of 1 February 1982 marked the opening of the London-based Inmarsat service – a worldwide satellite communication system for use by shipping and offshore industries. It is established under an IMO convention, and using the Inmarsat system a ship can enjoy virtually the same communication facilities enjoyed by any well-equipped office ashore, ie telephone, fax, computer links, etc.

In 1992, implementation of the GMDSS (Global Maritime Distress and Safety System) began. This system attempts to ensure that shore-based search and rescue authorities and vessels in the vicinity of a ship in distress are quickly alerted and rescue operations more effectively co-ordinated.

6 TYPES OF CARGO

Some important definitions

Dunnage

As already defined in Chapter 1, this is anything used to protect the cargo. There are two main types of dunnage:

1 *Permanent dunnage*. This may take the form of battens of wood fixed to the side of the ship to allow air to circulate and to keep the cargo off the cool side of the ship, where condensation might occur.

   The bottom of the hold may also be covered with wood to reduce the risk of damage to both ship and cargo from any impact as the cargo is loaded, to assist ventilation, and to prevent contamination from any liquids that drain down to the bottom of the hold or leak through from the bunkers in the double bottoms.

2 *Non-permanent dunnage*. For the most part, this consists of planks of soft wood but could be anything that is used to assist ventilation and drainage, and stop the cargo moving, chafing, etc. This dunnage has, of course, to be paid for, and for cargoes requiring large quantities it can form a sizeable expenditure.

Broken stowage

This means cargo space that is lost because of the shape of the cargo, packaging, dunnage, shape of compartment, pillars, etc. For example, one of the effects of palletisation is to increase broken stowage.

Stowage factor

The stowage factor of any commodity is the number of cubic feet (cubic metres) that a ton (tonne) of that commodity will occupy in stowage. This figure should include an allowance for broken stowage.

   The purpose of Table 6.1 (stowage factors) is to show the range from the heaviest types of cargo (pig iron) to one of the lightest (cork). Water has been included as it is the dividing commodity. Those heavier are considered *deadweight* (dwt) cargo, and those lighter are sometimes classified as *measurement* cargoes.

Table 6.1   Stowage factors

Commodity	ft³/ton	m³/tonne	Angle of repose
Pig iron	11.31	.36	
Iron ore	11–17	.31–.47	30–75
Bauxite	20–32	.56–.89	28–55
Scrap	20–40	.56–1.11	45
Sand	11–28	.5–.98	30–52
Salt	29–40	.81–1.12	30–45
Cement	23–29	.67–1.00	8–90
Sulphur	27–36	.74	35–40
Coal	40–55	.79–1.53	30–65
Water	36	1.0	0
Wheat bulk	47–49	1.31–1.37	25
Wheat bags	52–54	1.45–1.5	
Urea	47	1.17–1.56	28–45
Petroleum coke	48–55	1.25–1.67	33–42
Canned goods	55–60	1.53–1.61	
Wood chips	110–160	3.07–4.46	45
Esparto grass	190	4.0	
Cork	200	5.57	

Note: *1 cubic metre per tonne = 35.8 ft³ per ton.*
1 cubic metre per ton = 35.3 ft³ per tonne.

Therefore to find the space required by any consignment, the weight of the cargo is multiplied by the stowage factor or, conversely, the space divided by the stowage factor will give the weight that might be put in that space. However, there are other factors that have to be considered. For example, a 20-foot container has about 32 cubic metres, but the amount of pig iron you could load into it is not 32/0.31 (the stowage factor of pig iron) as this would give you an answer of over 100 tons, which you might physically be able to put into the container, but an ISO TEU is only constructed to take 20 tons. There are various other legal weight limits such as axle weights for road vehicles, etc that will limit the amount of pig iron you can actually put into the container. There is also the problem of broken stowage – for instance, if you were trying to load cargo in cartons into the container, you would find, unless you were very lucky, that you were left with gaps at the side and top of the container.

Pre-shipment planning

There are four general principles with regard to this, as follows (1 being the most important factor and 4 being the least):

1 Safety of ship and crew. Where there are dangers in this respect, as with explosives or cargoes such as grain which are liable to move, then there is a considerable body of national and international law to be complied with.
2 Safety of cargo. This is the shipowner's liability in respect of the Hague/ Hague Visby/Hamburg Rules.
3 Highest possible port speed.
4 The most efficient use of space.

It could be argued that the major change or revolution in shipping over the last few decades has been the change in the order of priority of the above points. Prior to the 1950s, the most efficient use of space would have been considered more important than the highest possible port speed.

The stowage plan

When loading a general cargo at a variety of ports, to distribute to a variety of ports, the problem of which hold (horizontal distribution) and which deck (vertical distribution) to use is quite intricate (see Fig 6.1). It is usually solved by the ship's chief officer, but this may be done by a cargo superintendent when loading at the home port.

With container ships running between specialised container berths, this is now being tackled by the terminal computer – but the ultimate responsibility for the ship's safety remains with the ship's chief officer and captain.

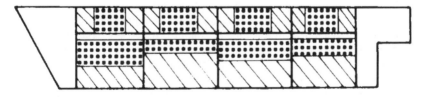

▓▓▓▓ 1st port of call
◤◤◤◤ 2nd port of call

Fig 6.1   A simple stowage plan.

Considerations for the horizontal distribution of cargo

1 Speed of working. If, for instance, the ship is loading for Melbourne and four other Australian ports, the more holds containing Melbourne cargo, then the more gangs of stevedores or more gantry cranes that can be employed for the fastest discharge at Melbourne. At many ports, only one gang of stevedores per hatch is allowed for safety reasons.

2 The ship's trim (ie whether the ship is level or down by the head or stern). When the ship sails from Melbourne for the other discharge ports, her trim must be reasonable. Many ships become difficult to handle if down by the head. For instance, pilots at the Panama Canal may refuse to take the ship through the Canal if trimmed by the head, unless a tug is in attendance.

3 If the horizontal weight is not evenly distributed at all stages of the voyage, including loading and discharging, the ship may be bent excessively. This can be a real problem in very large ships.

Considerations for the vertical distribution of cargo

1 The ship must be stable at all times (see Chapter 1).

2 Cargoes in the same compartment must be compatible, ie cargoes that give off moisture or a strong odour must not be put near cargoes that absorb moisture or odours. Heavy cargoes must obviously not be stowed over or next to light cargo, and it must be remembered that all liquid cargoes are liable to leak.

3 Accessibility. For example, when the ship reaches Melbourne, cargo for subsequent ports should not have to be moved before Melbourne cargo can be reached as this wastes time and money. This is, of course, the ideal and may not be attainable.

Stowage and discharge

It is during this period that loss of or damage to cargo is most likely to occur. Some of the more common causes of damage or loss are:

1 Breakage due to careless winch or crane work, usually from the impact of cargo being lowered too fast. Ideally, for handling containers, gantry cranes are needed, as in this type of crane the driver sits directly above the container. This is necessary if the crane driver is going to be able to position the spreader onto the container, and the container into the cell guides quickly and safely.

2 Hook damage. To avoid having their hands or fingers crushed, stevedores handle cargo with large sharp hooks. Carelessly used with delicate cargoes, hooks can do considerable damage.

3 Dragging cargo through the hold.

4 Improper use of special appliances. There are many specialised gadgets used for handling particular cargoes. If incorrectly used, damage can be caused.

5 Lack of walking boards over already stowed cargo.

6 Pilferage – security is difficult in the dim recesses of a ship's hold.

7 Inadequately dunnaged cargo, which has not been secured to prevent movement. This is particularly important for containers stowed on deck.

Note that factors 2 and 4 may be reduced with containerised cargo, but similar damage can occur when stowing the cargo into the container. In fact, most of the traditional principles of stowage apply to containerised cargo. In this context, containerisation can be considered as a method of pre-stowing the cargo to facilitate loading.

The separation of identical-looking units

When there are different consignments of identical-looking units on board – eg bags of grain, cartons of tinned food, bundles of timber, etc – they must

Cargo being handled in the general cargo ship BOSCO ASR, *owned by the Bonyad Shipping Co, at Bandar Abbas. Note the pieces of wood lying on the cargo – examples of dunnage (see Chapter 1).*

be kept separate. This is done in a variety of ways, such as by using special paint, chalk, sheets of paper or plastic, tarpaulins, lengths of rope, etc.

The care of cargo during the voyage

Damage to cargo during the voyage may arise from:

1 The cargo breaking loose and, in extreme cases, going through the side of the ship. A frequent inspection of lashings is necessary, particularly when rough weather is forecast.
2 Infestation by rats, weevils, etc. This hazard can be reduced by inspection before and during loading.
3 Heating. Many cargoes such as swarf (oil-covered scrap metal turnings), coal, cotton, etc are liable to heat up spontaneously on passage. With such cargoes, facilities must be available for monitoring the temperature and the officers must be given ample instruction as to how to cope with the situation should it arise.
4 Water damage, which can either be from salt water or fresh water. If it is from salt water, it is probably due to leaks through the hatchcovers – but it could be from a leaking ballast pipe passing through the hold. If it is from fresh water, it could be from the cargo itself, rain while loading, or leaking pipes, but most likely it will be from condensation. This condensation is often referred to as *sweat*, as the beads of condensed water on the ship's side, or on the cargo itself, give this visual impression. (This process can and does go on inside containers.) This condensation can only be avoided by correct ventilation, and indiscriminate ventilation may aggravate the situation. In liner ships on long voyages to the Far East, where considerable temperature variations can be expected, continual monitoring of air temperatures and humidity levels in the hold is necessary.

Many modern ships, in addition to having powerful electric extractor fans, can if necessary dry the circulating air.

In fine weather, the hatchcovers can be opened if required to increase the ventilation.

Examples of cargoes with special features

- *Cement* – in paper bags or bulk; this is very dusty, and must be kept dry.
- *Coal* – three main risks: (a) fire in the body of coal, which may only be detected by constant monitoring of the temperature in the hold. If the temperature exceeds 55°C, head for the nearest port. *Do not use water at sea.* Use inert gas if available. (b) Gas explosion due to lack of surface ventilation. (c) Shifting of cargo – especially with small coal.
- *Copra* – this is liable to heat and is highly inflammable; it has a rank penetrating smell and is subject to weevil infestation.

- *Crushed bones* – this has a strong odour, and should be stowed away from cargoes liable to become tainted.
- DRI (directly reduced iron – briquettes and pellets) – these are liable to spontaneous heating when wet and may involve hydrogen, a flammable gas. If the angle of repose is less than 35, then precautions are necessary to prevent shifting.
- *Esparto grass* – this is very inflammable and liable to spontaneous combustion if wet; it is often carried on deck, covered with tarpaulins.
- *Fertilisers* – these usually absorb water; they must be kept dry and away from all foodstuffs.
- *Fishmeal* – strong odour and high fire risk.
- *Flour* – is easily tainted; must be kept dry and away from goods with a strong smell.
- *Hides and skins* – these are shipped either dry or wet; must be stowed away from fine goods and other items that taint easily. Hides should be kept away from the steelwork and they are often weevil infested.
- *Iron and steel* – pig iron, steel billets, round bars, pipes, etc; all these are liable to shift and need to be well secured. Should be levelled off before overstowing with other cargoes.
- *Metals* – lead, copper, tin and zinc ingots; bottom stowage, often in refrigerated compartments below the refrigerated cargo.
- *Rice* – this contains a large quantity of water and is, therefore, liable to sweat; adequate ventilation is required. It is usual for shippers to provide wooden ventilators for use in the hold. On completion of stowage, cargo should be covered with mats or waterproof paper to prevent sweat falling back and causing damage to the top tier of cargo. Bags should be kept well away from all metalwork, and all pillars and ventilator shafts should be well matted.
- *Tinned goods* – these need top stowage to avoid being crushed; good ventilation is required to stop damage to cans by sweat.
- *Tea* – liable to damage by taint.
- *Tobacco* – liable to taint and will also taint other cargo; stow away from edible and fine goods.

(For bulk cargoes, see the IMO Code of Safe Practice for Bulk Cargoes.)

Refrigerated, chilled and temperature-regulated cargoes

- *Deep frozen cargoes* – carried at around −5°F.
- *Frozen beef* – carried at 15°F.
- *Frozen lamb and mutton* – carried at 15°–18°F; stowed on good clean dunnage. Carcasses should be frozen hard and any soft ones should be refused.

- *Chilled beef* – carried at about 29°F. Due to relatively soft nature of the meat, it is always hung on hooks. Remains in prime condition for about 30 days.
- *Butter* – carried at 15°F and liable to taint.
- *Fish* – carried at about 10°F; stowed only with other fish.
- *Cheese* – carried at 40°–45°F.
- *Eggs in shells* – carried at 33°–40°F; liable to taint, stowed in a compartment by themselves.
- *Apples* – carried at 31°–34°F. Concentration of CO_2 gas is liable to build up – this should not exceed 3 per cent or fruit will deteriorate.
- *Pears* – carried at 30°–32°F; not to be carried in the same compartment as apples.
- *Citrus fruit* – carried at 36°–41°F; requires adequate ventilation and leaves a strong smell.
- *Bananas* – carried at 52°–54°F; temperature is critical; usually carried in specially built vessels.

Stuffing containers

In general, the same principles of stowage and the same problems of carriage exist for cargo loaded into a container as for cargo loaded directly into a

Bags of cocoa being 'stripped out' of a container in Amsterdam. (Courtesy of Fairplay)

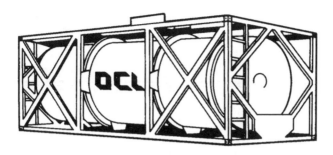

Fig 6.2   A tank container.

ship's hold. The advantages of loading into a container are that it can be done under cover in relative comfort and safety and if there are any delays these need not necessarily involve the ship that will carry them. Furthermore, as there are a variety of ships for certain types of cargo – ie refrigerated cargo and fruit – so there exist a variety of containers (see Figs 6.3 and 6.4).

All containers have securing points set into the floor, doorway and corner posts, but in addition the majority have arrangements for securing points in the side walls. The floor is made of wood.

Tank containers

Tank containers (see Fig 6.2) are available for the carriage of various bulk liquid cargoes. Such tanks are supported within standard ISO steel frames and are equipped with hatches to allow access for cleaning. Some are fitted with heating facilities and may also be suitable for the carriage of hazardous cargo.

Bulk cargo

Bulk cargo carried in ships specially designed to carry that particular type presents few problems that the naval architects and the technical department have not overcome in the basic design of the ship. Bulk cargo carried on a general-purpose cargo ship can, however, present certain dangers and the IMO has drawn up a Code of Safe Practice for Bulk Cargoes, of which the following summarises some of the basic points:

(A) Improper weight distribution resulting in structural damage.

1 Excessive concentration of weight on decks or on inner bottom.
   Department of Transport notice suggests that:

the maximum height of stow in the 'tween decks

$= $ (Ht of 'tween deck$/50$) $\times$ Stowage factor

20ft GENERAL CARGO CONTAINER	Minimum Interior Dimensions			Door Dimensions		Cubic Capacity (Minimum)	Tare Weight (Maximum *)	Payload (Maximum)
	L	W	H	W	H			
20ft × 8ft × 8ft 6in	232in	91.7in	93.7in	91.7in	89.4in	1,154.8ft³	4,850lb	39,947lb
6.1m × 2.4m × 2.6m	5,900mm	2,330mm	2,380mm	2,330mm	2,270mm	32.7m³	220kg	18,120kg

*The tare weight for a 20ft general purpose container can vary between 3,747lb (1,700kg) and 4,850lb (2,200kg) depending on materials used in construction.

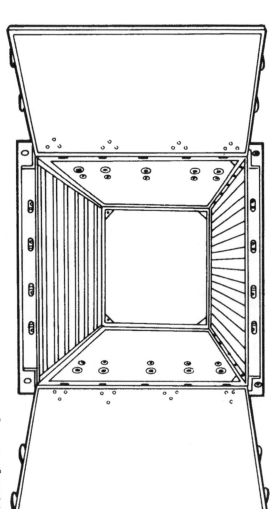

Fig 6.3   General purpose container.

20ft DRY BULK CONTAINERS	Minimum Interior Dimensions			Door Dimensions			Cubic Capacity	Tare Weight	Payload
	L	W	H	W	H				
20ft × 8ft × 8ft	232in	91½in	86in	89¼in	81¼in	1,060ft¼³	6,150lb	38,650lb*
6.1m × 2.4m × 2.4m	5,893mm	2,324mm	2,184mm	2,267mm	2,064mm	30.01m³	2,789kg	17,531

Fig 6.4   Dry bulk container.

111

Therefore the maximum height of ore with a stowage factor of 15 cubic feet to the ton, in a 'tween deck of 10 feet in height, is:

$$10/50 \times 15 = 3\,\text{feet}$$

2 Improper distribution of weight between the holds.

(B) Improper stability or reduction of stability during the voyage (see Chapter 1). This is mainly a problem of cargo shifting – see comments on angle of repose and bulk grain.

(C) Spontaneous heating. In common with some other cargoes, a few of the commodities covered by this Code are subject to spontaneous heating (see comments on coal).

In addition to these dangers, a ship operator must also consider the damage done as the bulk cargo is dropped or poured into the hold. For instance, some cargoes of scrap iron include such items as large car engines and these may simply be dropped some 50 or 60 feet into the hold.

Many cargoes may also bring with them an all-pervading cloud of penetrating dust, so machinery and living spaces must be protected.

Discharging by grabs can also cause damage in ships not strengthened to take the battering that these devices can give.

Bulk cargo definitions

- *Angle of repose* is the angle between the horizontal plane and the cone slope when bulk cargo is emptied onto this plane (see Fig 6.5). Obviously the smaller the angle of repose, the greater the tendency the cargo has to flow. It is recommended that when the angle of repose is less than 35°, the cargo needs trimming (levelling out).

- *Concentrate* is the material obtained when a natural ore has undergone some purification by the physical separation of undesired ingredients. The natural ore, when shipped, includes a considerable percentage of large lumps; concentrates, on the other hand, consist of either fine particles or small pellets.

- If moist, the concentrate tends to flow. The level of moisture at which the flow state develops is known as the *flow moisture point*.

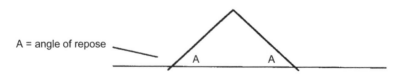

Fig 6.5   Angle between the horizontal plane and cone slope.

A large consignment of grain (52,750 tonnes of wheat) is being loaded aboard Pacific Peace *at Teesside bulk handling terminal. (Courtesy of Fairplay)*

- *Transportable moisture limit* is the maximum moisture content of a concentrate deemed safe for carriage by sea in a general-purpose cargo ship that is not specifically fitted for this type of cargo.

The carriage of bulk grain

British ships and ships trading to British ports are covered by the Merchant Shipping (Grain) Rules 1980. These British regulations reflect the IMO SOLAS Rules, so their application can be considered worldwide.

To carry grain, a ship must have a *document of authorisation*; this must be stamped by the administration of the country the ship is registered in. This document is a booklet that shows the different ways that grain can be stowed aboard that particular vessel, and the appropriate precautions that must be taken for each method.

The first safety problem with grain is that it is light, with a small angle of repose. It is also difficult to make a solid stow in any compartment as the vibration and motion of the ship will cause the cargo to settle – say, about 5 per cent. One method of keeping a solid stow is to build a 'feeder' in the 'tween deck hatchway; another method is to level out the grain and overstow with a thick layer of bagged grain. An alternative solution is to treat the grain as a liquid and subdivide the cargo by shifting boards.

A variation of overstowing with bagged cargo is *strapping*, and this is particularly useful for part cargoes. The grain is trimmed so it has a slight dome in the centre of the hold, and then covered over with tarpaulins followed by wooden gratings. This covering is then 'strapped' down onto the grain by wires across the hold which must be kept tight throughout the voyage.

In many loading ports, there are governmental or shippers' restrictions on hygiene and hold cleanliness.

Dangerous cargoes

The legislation concerning dangerous cargoes is fortunately mostly international in character and substance, as most countries have based their legislation on the IMO Dangerous Goods Code – the IMDG code.

The British law based on this Code appeared in 1965, updated by the Merchant Shipping (Dangerous Goods) Rules 1982 and the recent edition, which came into effect on 1 January 2001. This latest edition has endeavoured to harmonise the regulations concerning dangerous goods, for all modes of transport. The practical detailed advice on the 'Carriage of Dangerous Goods by Sea' is given in the Blue Book, an official publication that gives the relevant characteristics and properties of the goods, details of packaging, advice on stowage, and how such problems as fire-prevention and firefighting should be tackled.

Goods classified as dangerous are not allowed on passenger ships and they must always be declared by the shipper, and the packages need to be clearly marked with the agreed international symbols. They must be accompanied with a dangerous goods note (DGN). Ships arriving in port with dangerous cargoes on board are usually required to notify the port authorities in advance so that any necessary preparations can be made and precautions taken.

Containers carrying dangerous cargoes are usually carried on deck on the top layer at the side where they can be easily jettisoned if necessary. The Code does, however, contain details as regards constraints as to where dangerous cargoes can be stowed.

Deck cargo

This is also covered by legislation, ie the Merchant Shipping (Load Lines) Deck Cargo Regulations 1968. Basically, these regulations state:

1 Excess deck loading should be avoided.
2 Great care must be taken regarding stability as:

(A) this is top weight, which may – as in the case of timber – absorb moisture, and become even heavier as the voyage progresses;

A good example of deck cargo: the walkway built on the top of the cargo on the port side can clearly be seen. (Courtesy of Fairplay)

(B) beam winds will have an even greater effect;

(C) bottom weight will be lost during the voyage if the ship uses bunkers from the double bottom.

3 The deck cargo is not to interfere with the ship's equipment (particularly safety equipment) or the working of the ship. (*The Times* (22 April 1995) carried a report of a vessel being detained in Southampton, having sailed from Bangkok with deck cargo that prevented a proper lookout being kept from the bridge.) If the crew have to cross the deck cargo, safe walkways are to be provided.

4 The cargo must be securely lashed with facilities for safe and quick jettisoning of the deck cargo if required.

5 Special conditions must be fulfilled if the ship wishes to take advantage of any special lumber load lines.

Types of cargo carried on deck

- Cargo too large to be put anywhere else.
- Dangerous cargo – so that it can be jettisoned if necessary.
- If the ship is full but not down to her marks, deck cargo offers the possibility for earning more freight.
- Livestock.

(*Note*: Cargo carried on deck is not covered by the Carriage of Goods by Sea Act and is usually at 'Shippers Risk'. However, cargo carried in containers on deck is not – for the purposes of the above Act – considered to be deck cargo.)

Points on tanker cargoes

- These cargoes are highly inflammable and give off poisonous and explosive gases, so precautions have to be taken during loading, while carrying, and even on the ballast voyage when not gas free.
- Charterers will wish to inspect the tanks on loading to ensure that they are empty, dry, and in a fit state for the cargo they are loading.
- As the cargo is loaded, the distance from the top of the tank (known as the *ullage*), the specific gravity and the temperature are noted. By means of these three facts, the amount of cargo loaded is determined. A mistake in any one of them will cause a discrepancy, and many claims for subsequent short landing might be due to such a mistake.
- Oil cargo is often loaded at quite high temperatures to make it easier to handle. During the voyage it will cool and contract. As it contracts the inert gas in the ullage space must be kept at the right pressure – ie just above atmospheric pressure. The cargo must not be loaded too hot – say, above 135°F – as this could damage tank coatings and seals. If the cargo is of a high density, it may need heating during the voyage, otherwise it will be slow and difficult to discharge.

- On discharging the cargo, it is not unknown for, say, 1 per cent of the cargo to be left behind – by adhering to the tank sides and caught up in the structure. If drainage holes are blocked by a build-up of sludge and the pump and pipelines are in bad condition, this makes things worse. With crude oil washing, the percentage of oil remaining on board can be reduced.
- During the ballast voyage the tanks may be washed, the oily slops collected, and at loading terminals these slops should be discharged into special reception facilities and processed. Such reception facilities have been mandatory since 1983, but Mr Kulukundis, the chairman of Intertanko, stated in 1995 that 70 per cent of ports that receive tankers have inadequate or no reception facilities!

7 WHY CARGO IS MOVED

Before looking in detail at the subject of demand, there are three basic points that need to be made:

1 With certain exceptions, such as cruising and yachting, people and goods are not moved for the pleasure of movement, but because the customer wants safe arrival at a certain destination – in other words, the customer does not actually care who moves his goods or how they are moved. The main concern is getting them safely to the destination at the minimum cost – which is why economists refer to this demand as a *derived demand*. This has considerable implications as to how a transport service should be advertised and marketed – do we produce beautiful pictures of our ships, or information concerning our price schedules and safety record?

2 Demand for the commodity is not the same as demand for transport. Demand for transport should be measured in tonne/miles, ie it is a function of the weight and the distance. For instance, when the Suez Canal was closed in 1967 the demand for oil from the Persian Gulf to the UK hardly altered, but as the distance the oil had to be moved was virtually doubled, the demand for tankers greatly increased.

  Likewise, we need to study the statistics following the oil price rise in 1973 (see Table 7.1). In actual fact, during this period the demand for oil remained virtually constant, but the greater use of pipelines (substitution by other means of transport) reduced the amount of oil carried by tankers, and the exploitation of indigenous sources nearer the customer meant that the distance the oil was carried fell even further – hence this was a bad period for tanker operators.

3 The value of a commodity is not its price or its cost, but its 'desirability', which can invariably be increased by transport. For example, coal a mile underground has no value, but mined and moved to a person freezing in winter, it can have considerable value. As transport becomes cheaper, then the competition between sources increases, thus reducing prices. With large bulk carriers reducing costs, then coal from Australia can compete in the UK with British-mined coal. This indicates that reducing the cost of transport can increase the demand for transport. We need to note, though, that this will not necessarily increase the demand for coal. Specialised cheap transport for, say, exotic foods and fruit can, however, increase both the demand for the goods and for the transport.

Table 7.1	Tanker cargo	
Year	Million tonnes oil cargo	Tonne/miles × 1,000
1976	1,950	11,463
1985	1,198	5,440
1991	1,523	8,000
2000	2,024	10,420

The theory of trade

Trade between people must be the oldest civilised human activity – or at least the second oldest! Trade results from the fact that others have skills (or things) that we need and want, but haven't got. Therefore the basis of trade is that different groups of people in different areas purchase different goods from other areas. The reasons for this usually lie in their different natural resources and factors of production, which are classically designated *land, labour and capital*.

These factors are of course interrelated and can further be subdivided into those factors that give a particular group an *absolute advantage*, and those that give this group a *comparative advantage*.

What can give a group an absolute advantage?

Group A might have *resources* – such as crude oil, ore, uranium, gold, etc – that are not easily obtainable by Group B. Group A are therefore in a good position to trade with Group B, but although this might be considered an absolute advantage it is not a fixed or eternal advantage. For example, the source might be a very limited one, such as oil, or a similar source may be found in Area B itself, or an enterprising person in Group B may invent a synthetic substitute that is as good as, or cheaper than, the original. Until the oil price rise in 1973, little serious attempt had been made to drill for alternative sources of oil or to look for energy substitutes.

Climate and the quality of soil can be considered natural resources that enable some countries to produce goods in a way that is not possible in others. For instance, can Norway produce oranges and grapefruit on a commercial scale? Modern scientific methods can and do, though, change these absolute advantages to comparative ones. Work in Israel has shown that what was considered arid deserts can now, with an injection of capital, be made profitable agriculturally. And Saudi Arabia now exports a surplus of home-produced wheat!

Capital is also often considered to be an absolute advantage. Certainly, having capital is an advantage, and not having it may be such a disadvantage that all the other factors of production may not be able to be utilised. Changes in available capital resources may therefore suddenly bring on whole new areas of transport demand or just as quickly turn them off.

In 1976, there was a sudden upsurge in trade in many of the oil-producing countries as a result of their new wealth created by the oil price increase in 1973. This in time produced port congestion in some of these countries, with considerable knock-on effects in all aspects of shipping.

It must be remembered that trade is a two-way exchange. If no customer exists to buy your goods, your capital investment becomes worthless. Therefore it may well be in the interests of a rich group to lend capital directly, or by means of a joint venture, to a poorer group, so they can produce something with which to trade.

What can give a group a comparative advantage?

Aspects that might be considered to give a comparative advantage are *labour, skills, and an established production and market.*

Some countries have relatively *cheap labour*, which gives them a comparative advantage in labour-intensive industries – and in the 1980s we have witnessed the growth of shipbuilding in South Korea to the detriment of shipyards in Western Europe. However, it does not take long before workers in successful low-cost countries expect a share in their countries' increasing wealth. Workers' salaries doubled in South Korea between 1987 and 1991 while their currency appreciated against the US dollar by about 20 per cent in the same period.

Countries with high labour costs have developed greater automation and made greater use of *skilled labour* and *capital-intensive industries*. And countries with old-established industries should enjoy lower costs due to *economies of scale* – ie a trained workforce and an established market with secure outlets that gives them a comparative advantage in trade. But how long can this advantage be maintained? This was certainly once true for British shipping – but has it maintained this advantage? The strength of the historic comparative advantage situation depends very much on how easy it is to get in and out of a new venture, and shipping is a relatively easy industry to enter and leave.

Up to now, only the basic economic factors affecting trade have been considered, but there are also those that are of a *political* nature. If the concept of groups is extended to political boundaries and trade between countries is solely considered, then the balance of trade in and out of a country has to be considered. To increase its balance of payments, a country may artificially increase its comparative advantage for some particular commodities to increase sales as it needs the foreign currency.

Furthermore, when the UK joined the EU, old-established trade patterns with the Commonwealth were dropped in favour of EU internal trade. This meant, for instance, that the UK consumed the same amount of sugar, butter, meat, etc, but from different sources – so the impact on the established shipping demand was considerable. To overcome this problem, countries such as Japan exported their skills of production, and built and operated factories in the EU to produce their cars – and so we have seen the decline in the demand for PCCs.

A further fundamental policy that could affect world seaborne trade could be the nature of what is exported. At present, something like 70 per cent of world trade is in the carriage of raw materials – crude oil, coal, iron ore, etc – with much of the trade being from the developing countries to the developed ones. It is surely inevitable that in time the trend will be to process this raw material in the developing country and to sell it semi-processed. This will not only mean less in terms of quantity, but the product will need to be shipped in different types and sizes of ships.

What has been said so far is true of *all* forms of transport, so those in the shipping industry should think of themselves as being 'in transport' rather than 'in shipping'.

What is different about sea transport?

1 Sea transport is slow – ships carrying raw materials (tramps) move at around 13–15 knots, while ships carrying expensive cargo (liners) travel at 18–25 knots.
2 Sea transport is cheap because it can take advantage of the economies of scale (ie use large ships), which can reduce the cost per unit carried. Large ships are also the most energy-efficient means of moving anything.

Where land is separated by water, the choice is only sea or air, and air is more expensive. However, we have to take into account the growing use of tunnels/bridges where water separation is small, eg the obvious possible consequences to UK seaborne trade with the EU brought about by the Channel Tunnel.

How much cargo is actually moved?

As can be seen from Fig 7.1, dry cargo has been rising steadily since the Second World War – in fact, more than doubling in the 1960s. Tanker cargoes follow a similar pattern, except following the October 1973 oil price rise (see also Table 7.2).

Supply v demand – the crux of the problem

As Fig 7.2 shows, supply and demand in the shipping world are seldom in balance. In the early 1970s they were close, which was why these were profitable years for shipowners. In 1973 demand exceeded supply, so this was a very profitable year but in October 1973 came the oil price rise

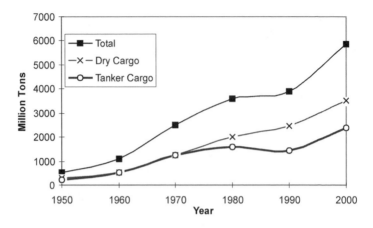

Fig 7.1   Growth in world seaborne trade.

Table 7.2 World seaborne trade in ton/miles	
Year	Billion ton/miles
1970	11
1980	17
1990	17
2000	23

following the Arab-Israeli war. Ever since then, there has been surplus tonnage, with the inevitable lowering of freight rates. The surplus does not have to be large. If there are 10 shiploads and 9 ships, the shipowner can be a *price maker*, but if there are 10 shiploads and 11 ships, the shipowner will be a *price taker* and can be beaten down to the break-even cost of the cheapest operator.

If the shipping market were a genuinely *free* market, we would expect supply and demand to remain in step, but the shipping market has specific problems:

- Ships take a long time to build. There will be a rush of ordering during periods of high freight rates and it may be several years before they are actually delivered. The new owners will be reluctant to sell as prices will probably also be low and the new owners will also not wish to 'lay up' as they will usually have to make monthly payments to a financier.

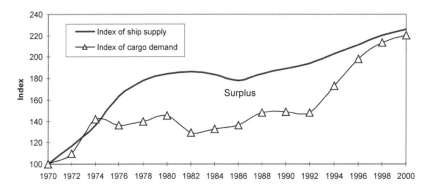

Fig 7.2   World shipping supply index v trade demand index.

- Many of the new shipowners enticed into shipowning following the very high rates of 1973 were state enterprises, many in developing countries, who thought they had found a solution to their hard currency problems. When the freight rates started to fall, many received the advice 'to hang on' as the market would recover in a few months. Governments were therefore encouraged to intervene with subsidies and financial help and therefore the surplus increased.
- Note that Fig 7.2 is a global one and the actual situation has been different in each market. For instance, the dry-cargo market has never actually seen a decrease in demand, but since 1973 the supply has outstripped it.

The general global trend in the future would seem by most forecasters to be one of continued growth (see Table 7.3). However, to be a success in demand forecasting and analysis it is not sufficient to take only the global view – the demand for specific commodities must also be considered, as must the trends in growth rates on routes and in regions.

Regional differences in seaborne trade

The last decade or so has seen the growth area shift from the north Atlantic to the Pacific rim. From 1970 to 1990 the regional container throughput in Asia and the Far East grew at almost double the rate of that of northern Europe and North America. Table 7.4 shows the top ten container ports and illustrates the point that eight of the ten are in the Pacific rim.

Japan is often considered to be one of the most important shipping-related economies, as of all countries it is probably the most dependent on shipping for its economic success. In fact, Japan accounts for some 25 per cent of the world's seaborne bulk trades.

Table 7.3 Quantities of products transported by sea

Year	Crude oil	Oil products	Iron ore	Coal	Grain	Other	TOTAL
1970	996	245	247	101	89	804	2,482
1980	1,170	262	314	188	198	1,255	3,387
1990	1,190	336	347	342	192	1,570	3,977
2000	1,612	412	455	520	225	2,150	5,374

Table 7.4 Top ten container ports in 2001

Rank	Port	No of TEUs
1	Hong Kong	18.0
2	Singapore	15.5
3	Pusan	8.1
4	Kaohsiung	7.5
5	Shanghai	6.3
6	Rotterdam	6.1
7	Los Angeles	5.2
8	Shenzhen	5.1
9	Hamburg	4.7
10	Long Beach	4.5

As is pointed out in the 1992 UNCTAD *Review of Maritime Transport*:

Developments in the world economy have a direct impact on the derived demand for global shipping services. Three key economic indicators are changes in real GDP, world merchandise trade, and industrial production. In 1992, real GDP increased by 0.8% over 1991. The GDP of OECD member countries grew by 1.4%, while that of developing countries experienced an increase of 6.1% over the previous year. Growth was particularly strong in Asia and the Middle East. However, formerly centrally planned economies experienced a 17.2% annual decline in output.

The graph in Fig 7.3, drawn from data of the IMF, *International Financial Statistics*, shows clearly – as you would expect – that there is a definite correlation between industrial production and seaborne trade. However, there does not seem to be any such demonstrated relationship between the performance of the financial markets and seaborne trade. Following the Wall Street stock market collapse in 1929, the ensuing depression greatly affected

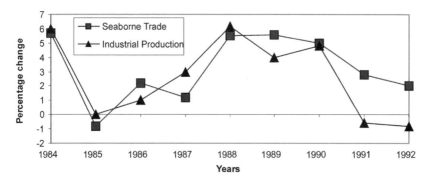

Fig 7.3   Annual change in OECD industrial production and seaborne trade 1984–92.

seaborne trade. In contrast, the massive fall in the stock markets worldwide in the late 1980s seemed to make little impression on worldwide seaborne trade.

Cost of transport and competitive advantage

Competitive advantage as a factor of demand in world trade can only be realised when considered in conjunction with transport cost. If transport costs are reduced, then new regions can exploit the competitive advantage they might enjoy as regards lower prices for their goods and services. For instance we only have to consider how cheap jet air travel opened up the holiday/tourist possibilities for many Mediterranean countries. I would estimate that the cost of carrying, say, a ton of coal, by a modern large bulk carrier, is perhaps 30 times cheaper in real terms than it was a century ago –

Table 7.5   Freight costs as a percentage of import values for 1980, 1990 and 2000 (*Source*: UNCTAD *Review of Maritime Transport*)

Country group	Freight costs as a percentage of import values		
	1980	1990	2000
World total	6.64	5.22	5.06
Developed countries	5.49	4.4	4.07
Developing countries	10.44	8.6	8.06

hence it can now be economically viable to carry coal from Australia to Newcastle!

Table 7.5 shows that the transport cost varies in different regions, with the greatest difference being between the developed and developing nations. The irony and implications of this are obvious in that the countries that most need to stimulate their economies face the greatest financial hurdles.

Forecasting demand

Forecasting – or at least anticipating – demand is obviously an essential element for any service operator. Where the demand is increasing or decreasing following a simple *trend*, the forecast presents little difficulty. However, problems occur when an unforeseen 'wildcard' presents itself – such as the oil price rise in 1973, which caused violent changes in demand in many fields. We could argue, for instance, that the port congestion in Nigeria a few years later was a direct result of the price rise.

Many factors can upset the pattern either on a long-term or short-term basis, such as strikes, wars, weather (particularly cold and drought), a radical change of political power in a region, a change of technology, or the invention of a cheap important substitute. But when such events have occurred over the last few decades, very few seem to have anticipated the change. However, commercial success can be observed in those people or companies who react quickly and positively to such changes and can see the potential advantages that might be offered.

8 COSTS AND FREIGHT RATES

Cost classification

The ways of classifying the costs involved in operating ships is remarkably standard and has altered little over the last 100 years. Where possible, the variables on which the costs depend are indicated so that the causes of the change can be better understood.

These costs are usually divided into three groups:

Group 1: Administration costs and depreciation

In tramp companies, these two costs are often only known to those in the accounting and secretarial side of the company – and are often completely unknown in the operating department, who ignore them anyway in their voyage estimating. In liner companies, nominal values are often given for them but, as will be discussed later, they are often difficult to define precisely from an operating point of view.

Group 2: The daily running cost (DRC)

DRC costs (crew costs, stores, repairs, insurance, P&I, etc) are usually totalled for a year and then divided by the number of ship operational days in a year – ie 365, minus expected days under repair. This figure is then referred to as the *daily running cost*. They form the basis of the operational time-related costs, which the shipowner has to meet no matter where, if or how the vessel is trading. Some maritime economists refer to this group of costs as the *operating costs* – however, I have tried to avoid using this term as so many authors use it to mean different things.

Group 3: Propulsion, cargo-handling and other port costs

These costs vary a great deal depending on route and distance. In the tramping situation, the ship is often fixed 'FIOT', which means that the cargo handling is paid for by the charterer. These three groups of costs fit in very well with the three ways that a ship can be chartered:

- Under a demise or bareboat charter, the shipowner pays only the group 1 costs.
- Under a time charter, the shipowner pays only the costs in groups 1 and 2.
- Under a voyage charter, the shipowner pays all the costs – unless FIOT.

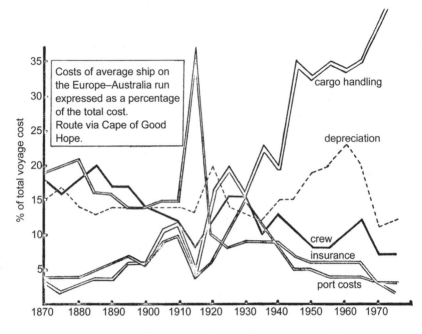

Fig 8.1   Costs of an average ship on the Europe–Australia run.

In the liner shipping situation, the shipowner, as the carrier, is responsible for *all* the costs.

Fig 8.1 shows how the shipowner's 'cost mix' has developed and changed over the last century or so. I have chosen 1870 as the starting date because, as explained before, this is the period when shipping as we know it today can be considered to have started. It is this 100-year period from 1870 that I am referring to when I talk of 'the period' in this chapter.

Perhaps the most interesting cost is that of cargo-handling, which started the period as one of the least costs, but after the Second World War 'went wild'. The large surge shown by insurance during the First World War was due to the fact that during most of this war the owners carried the risk, whereas in the Second World War the government accepted it.

There is in the data considerable evidence to support the obvious theory that change will tend to follow the dominant cost in the cost mix. For instance, if we were considering sailing ships in this period, the crew cost was the dominant cost – so there were attempts to reduce this cost by rerigging vessels as barques and schooners and cutting crews' wages and size. By the same token, on tramp ships, where the cargo-handling is usually paid for by the charterer, the dominant cost was crew and propulsion, which probably explains why tramps have traditionally paid their crews less and had a slower speed than liners.

For power-driven vessels in general, however, considering all costs from 1870 to 1920, the dominant cost was propulsion, so research and change was concentrated here; after 1940, though, cargo-handling becomes the dominant cost. The question is perhaps, in this case, why didn't bulk carriers and container ships therefore come about sooner? The answer is probably threefold.

First, it would not have been technically possible to build a container ship in the late 1940s as the large hatch openings required would have been impossible until the new high-tensile steels were developed in the postwar period.

Second, once the new fleets were built in the immediate postwar period of reconstruction, any immediate radical change became impossible. For instance, the massive capital commitment to containerisation made any dramatic change in this area almost unthinkable over the next decade.

Finally, as the late Professor Parkinson has pointed out, management will only consider radical changes during periods of falling prosperity. Therefore a law for technological change could perhaps be propounded – that large technological change will take place when a cost mix change takes place, and one cost becomes significantly dominant over the others. This change will, however, only take place if:

- It is technically possible.
- Revenues (freight rates) are low or falling.
- New capital investment does not make current recently acquired equipment obsolete.

Table 8.8 on page 140 also shows a comparison between percentage costs for different ship types.

Administration costs and depreciation

The data for administration costs is perhaps the most difficult of all the costs to analyse and compare rigorously for three reasons. The term 'administration' is a very broad one as the meaning of 'shipping company' can embrace a very wide range of activities. Indeed, one ship could provide a reason for existence for three shipping companies. The first could own it, the second could manage it, and the third could operate it. Fundamentally, however, in the administration of a ship there are two basic spheres of activity:

Activity A: 'Husbandry', or keeping the ship stored, crewed and technically functioning and generally ensuring that the vessel is seaworthy.

Activity B: Routeing, scheduling and finding cargoes for the ship.

Activity A can be relegated to a completely separate company known as a management company. In the early days of shipping, much of this would have been done by the master of the vessel.

Activity B for a tramp company can be solved in good times by simply phoning one's shipbroker. For a liner company, however, the inward and outward freight departments may require a large staff or this may be subcontracted to various loading brokers. In the early days of shipping, much of this activity would also have been done by the master of the ship.

Comparing the administrative cost per ship of a typical tramp company, an own account company, such as a large oil company – and a large liner company – at least from the early 1920s, and expressing the administrative costs for ship of the tramp company as unity, the comparative indexed costs are shown below:

- Tramp company $= 1$
- Own account company $= 3-4$
- Liner company $= 10-12$

The changes in the administration throughout the last century or so are greater and more radical than the changes in the ships themselves. The changes in communication from letter to telegraph to radio, to the latest communication satellites that provide worldwide radio, fax and computer contact, have revolutionised, several times, the whole operation of world trade and markets throughout this period. Furthermore, many of the administrative jobs done by the shipping companies are now done by separate specialist consultants and independent organisations.

Percy Harley, in his book *My Life in Shipping 1881–1938* (Bayliss, 1939), indicates that the present-day chartering activities of the Baltic dates back to the early 1890s, when the River Plate entered the market for steam tramps, and the modern (Centrocon) style of printed charter party became the custom.

Today's ship management companies indicate that it is uneconomic to run a company with fewer than ten ships, ie the fixed costs for ten ships are the same as those for one ship. Although difficult to measure, I would estimate that in real terms the fixed cost element (or the basic unit) to operate one ship became bigger in real financial terms as the period progressed. The basic personnel unit in 1870 would be about four, whereas in 1970 it would be about ten. I suspect it reached maximum numbers in the early 1950s, as the long period of depressed freight rates during the late 1950s and early 1960s brought with it a wave of rationalisation, work study, mechanisation and inevitable pruning. However, it is difficult to estimate the growth of the consultancy element that has undoubtedly taken place in the last 20 years in the whole area of what can loosely be termed 'administration'.

Throughout most of the last century the number of shipping companies decreased in number and tended to centralise, moving their head offices to London, and in *My Life in Shipping*, Percy Harley gives a self-explanatory table of this trend (Table 8.1). However, latterly some companies have moved out of high-rent 'City' offices to locations near London Airport.

Table 8.1 The decrease in shipping companies: 1836 and 1933		
	No of shipping companies in the port	
Port	1836	1933
Liverpool	93	44
Newcastle	90	52
Cardiff	61	75
West Hartlepool	48	9
Middlesbrough	18	6
Hull	22	12
North Shields	15	1
Glasgow	72	45
Dundee	19	5
Leith	18	8
Aberdeen	18	9

It is in the area of administration finances that the very complex subject of 'tax avoidance' enters with mergers with non-marine enterprises, the creation of foreign subsidiaries, subsidies, grants, discriminations, etc. The costs involved here are very real, but they have been ignored.

Because of these complications, the administrative cost has been equated with the fee charged by management companies as this is data that is more readily quantifiable and does reflect most accurately the cost involved in moving the 'space' and 'safe arrival'.

Administrative costs are not a function of the size of the ship, but are more dependent on the route, type and the mode of operation.

International Ship Management Association (ISMA)

The ISMA was created in April 1991, and by 1998 had as members 40 companies from 16 countries, which managed over 2,300 ships, comprising around 50 per cent of the world's managed ships.

The initial cost of purchasing a new ship

This is invariably one of the largest single costs, but it is also one of the most difficult to quantify with any precision. There are large variations in the price of similar ships built at the same time for different owners, and the fluctuations in the supply and demand for ships has caused new prices to move (up and down) by as much as 20 per cent in one year. Secondhand

Table 8.2 Percentage market share of the world shipbuilding order book

	1938	1950	1967	1978	1986	1992	2000	2002
Japan	11.6	9.9	47.5	24.6	42.7	36.1	26.1	23.7
S Korea				2.4	16.8	16.5	42.8	36.3
E Europe + China				20.3	9.3	10.9	5 Poland	11.8 China + Poland
W Europe	77.2	74.4	38.0	28.3	20.9	28.0	23.0	15.8 EU
USA	11.2	7.1		12.9	1.1	0.3	1.7	1.2
Others		8.6	14.5	11.5	7.1	6.8	1.4	11.2

prices can be even more unstable: when the oil freight fell in 1974, the secondhand price of one particular VLCC dropped from over £30 million to £12 million in just a few months.

Since the end of the Second World War there have been geographical variations in price, with the Japanese yards offering lower prices for certain types of snips (see Table 8.2 for further details). This has led to a variety of political pressures and economic complications, and the inducements of grants, easy payment terms, etc. It is interesting to note that in 1956 UK shipyards still had 35 per cent of the market, but this had dropped to 3.5 per cent by 1976.

For new buildings, most countries provide official shipbuilding credit schemes to support their shipyards. In order to regulate competition on this front, most shipbuilding countries will attempt to be seen to follow the financing regulations laid down by the OECD, but during the years when shipyards have been desperate for work, some shipowners, one suspects, have had some very good deals. Secondhand ships, on the other hand, nearly always have to be purchased with a bank loan paid back over a period of five years, *and* with higher rates of interest than most credit packages for new ships. The irony of this is that some shipowners (or potential shipowners) with cashflow problems may find it better to obtain financing for a new ship rather than a secondhand vessel, as some 'imaginative' credit schemes for new vessels allow the 'pay back' to be over a much longer period.

Table 8.3 shows representative prices for ships built in the Far East and the secondhand prices that such ships were fetching in 2001. However, as already mentioned, ship prices are like property prices in that they fluctuate depending on the state of the market.

Perhaps a better way of comparing prices for ships is to compare their prices per dwt ton rather than the actual price for the ship, though the method you adopt will depend on the point you wish to make.

Table 8.3 Representative prices (millions of $(USD)) for ships built in the Far East				
Ship type	New buildings		Secondhand tonnage 2001	
	1980	2001	Price	Age
15,000 dwt general cargo ship	14	18	10.1	5 years
2,500 TEU container ship	42	34	22	5 years
30,000 dwt bulk	17	18	16	5 years
Panamax bulk	24	20	14	5 years
250,000 dwt tanker	75	72	60	8 years
125,000 m³ LNG	200	162		
75,000 m³ LPG	77	58	55	3 years

In most cases the cost of the ship will be the shipowner's/operator's biggest cost, but there is no universally accepted method as to how this cost should be allocated by the operator when estimating what charge should be made to the user. One way would be to take the:

(New cost – secondhand value)/period of ownership

But if you decide on this method, do you use the shipyard price or the amount you have to pay to the bank every month which includes interest? Also, until you sell the ship, you will not know its secondhand value. Most Greek shipowners will hope the value of the ship will appreciate and that they will be able to sell it for more than they paid for it, so for them the problem does not arise.

Table 8.4 Costs for a typical 'tweendecker, 9,000 GT (European flag) per day in $(USD)				
Year	Crew	Bunker	DRC	Depreciation
1960	79	500	202	159
1965	123	450	273	162
1970	179	450	377	211
1975	490	1,950	836	605
1980	1,200	3,600	1,826	905
1985	1,611	2,500	2,375	1,300
1990	2,000	2,100	2,968	1,730

In fact, in chartering tramp trades, when the operator is preparing a voyage estimate, this cost is usually ignored and it is usually considered satisfactory to calculate the operational surplus or deficit for the proposed voyage.

In Table 8.4, the depreciation shown is simply a straight line depreciation of 6 per cent per annum on the building price of the ship, assuming a life of about 15 years.

The daily running cost (DRC)

For the purpose of this analysis, it is assumed that the DRC is made up of crew costs, stores and repairs, insurance, P&I – and perhaps also the management fee if the ship is 'managed' by a separate management company. As can be seen from Table 8.4, all the costs have increased in the period from 1960 to 1990. Nowadays, we tend to accept inflation as a fact of life, but 'serious' inflation only really hit the shipping world towards the end of the 1960s. As you will see, the rise in DRC between 1965 and 1970 was much less than the rise between 1975 and 1980. One of the effects of rapid inflation over this period was the reluctance of owners to accept long-term charters of, say, 15 years – which was in fact quite common in 1970. This in turn created an effect of instability in many companies, as they no longer had an assured cash flow projection for the future.

Crew costs

As can be seen from Table 8.4, crew cost under European flags increased faster than other costs, and the DRC group of costs is usually the largest cost. Journalists writing about shipping often refer to crew costs as the owner's largest cost. This would probably only be true for a tramp with a very old ship on *time charter*.

Table 8.6 is an example of many such tables that appear in the press, comparing crew costs for crews of different nationalities. Although the exact amounts are seldom precise, as it is not always clear as to what is being measured, the costs of crews from different countries do show considerable variations. For instance, an American crew may be ten times the price of a Chinese one – hence the attraction to the shipowner to 'flag out' (more on this later). But we must remember when comparing labour costs that it is not sufficient to compare salaries – leave and pension payments must also be considered, as must any repatriation costs, etc. It is also difficult to quantify the money saved by having a loyal, dedicated and efficient crew!

Stores and repairs (S&R)

Table 8.5 gives an estimate of the amount we might expect for this cost on two different vessels. On more sophisticated ships it would, of course, be

Table 8.5 Comparison of costs in $(USD) per day between a 400 TEU 7,000 dwt container vessel and a 55,000 dwt bulk-Panamax European flag in 1999 (each vessel is five years old)

	Container vessel (Liner)	Panamax (Tramp)
Capital cost		
Depreciation + interest	2,500	7,250
Operating cost		
Crew	1,218	1,903
Repairs + maintenance	451	520
Oils and lubricants	61	50
P&I + hull insurance	437	474
Stores	64	61
Overheads	142	142
TOTAL DRC	2,373	3,150

Table 8.6 Crew cost comparison 1993 in $(USD) month[*]

Nationality	Master	AB
Sri Lanka	4,000	468
Chile	3,700	790
Poland	3,200	1,020
Philippines	2,975	929
Russia	2,600	700

[*]Inclusive of wages, vacation, overtime and social costs.

larger – and, unlike the crew cost, would tend to grow as the ship size increases. It is often convenient to consider stores and repairs two costs together as there are so many areas of overlap. Even within one company, there is not always consistency as to which account an item will appear on. For instance, the cost of painting can appear as stores if done at sea, but as repairs if done in port. The only significance in drawing attention to any distinction in these cost areas is that in the last 40 years or so, repair costs have been escalating faster than store costs.

It is interesting to note that the very rapid rise of repair costs has given rise over the last few decades to a number of technical improvements and innovations, and these have combined to make it possible to extend the *annual* dry-docking period. In addition, the introduction of the continuous survey a few years ago means that the work load and maintenance costs can be spread out more or less evenly over the five-year cycle.

The factors that affect this cost are size of vessel type, engine type and age. Of these factors, the age is probably the most important one. This cost is also related to crew cost – in that as crews are reduced in number to save money, more money has to be spent on the maintenance that would previously have been done by the crew.

Insurance costs

Hull and machinery As can be seen from Fig 8.1 on page 128, which shows the changes in percentage costs over the last century, the insurance costs have reduced from one of the largest costs to one of the smaller ones. For the most part, this is due to the undoubted fact that shipping and sea transport have become much safer over the last 100 years, but is also a result of the high level of competition in this field over the last few decades. Many have argued that marine insurance has been too cheap over recent years, and the financial difficulties of some of the underwriters does perhaps bear this argument out. Marine insurance underwriting never seems to have been a scientific art.

Manley Hopkins, in *A Manual of Marine Insurance*, published in 1867, writes in his chapter on marine premiums that whereas life assurance premiums are fixed by a fairly precise formula, 'Marine insurance premiums are a mixture of experience, tradition and personal fancy. They fluctuate with the seasons and the states of the barometer; they are affected by locality, by storms and by political events, by prejudice, by the comparative strength of the two contracting parties. They are too uncertain to be tabulated.' This viewpoint is still very much reflected in the attitude of many brokers and underwriters today. And in addition to the points made above, liner owners with large modern fleets constructed and maintained to the highest standards will enjoy considerably lower premiums than a tramp owner with one old ship.

In 1867, the 'time risk' book of the Thames and Mersey showed that during that year their annual rate of premium in hull risks ranged between 4 to 12 guineas per cent. Owen, in *Ocean Trade and Shipping*, published in 1914, says in his section on the cost of ship insurance that the rate for an annual policy is £3–£4 per cent for ships of the highest class, but 5 to 7 guineas for tramp steamers. He offers £6 per cent as a good average figure. Of the premium he tells us that the brokers get 5 per cent and the owners are usually allowed 10 per cent for prompt payment. It is interesting to read that as steamers tended to keep close inshore, working from headland to headland round the coast, they ran greater risks from grounding and collision than the sailing ships which preferred to stand well off.

For the present variety of ship types and size, an average typical figure becomes more difficult − but an approximation for a general cargo ship's premium in sterling might be given by:

$$(1.5 \times dwt + .003 \times value \ of \ ship)$$

Finally, it should be noted that insurance is not mandatory, and that in hard times an owner may choose to operate without it or reduce the extent of his cover.

Shipowners' mutual protection societies − P&I clubs These are concerned with insuring the shipowner against those extra risks not covered by ordinary marine policies − in particular, nowadays they cover the shipowner against his liabilities, which have been the fastest growing area of risk since the Second World War. The first such club, Tindall Riley & Co, appeared in about 1866, and the relatively high rates in the first part of the period probably was caused by the relatively small membership.

In their early days, these mutual insurance clubs underwent frequent changes as regards the cover they offered and how they charged for it. Most of them offered 'mutual hull insurance' as well − in fact, most of them were an extension of the already existing Hull Clubs. This applied until about 1890 when the competition from the commercial market changed, due to legal constraints being removed, and made the Hull Clubs no longer a viable option. However, the Swedish Club in Gothenburg still offers these facilities. The actual size of the annual P&I club call will of course depend on the owner's claims record, the type of ship, where it is trading, and the type of deductibles the owner decides on.

Originally, the mutual aspect was obtained by simply grouping together owners who operated similar ships on similar trades. Now the mutuality is achieved by an underwriter who endeavours to ensure that each owner carries only his fair share of the risk.

Since the Second World War, P&I club costs have increased rapidly − reflecting the growth of social legislation increasing the liabilities of an employer to an employee. For ships on the American run, there will be a surcharge of 55 cents per GT (1995) over and above the normal calls due to the very high claims allowed by the American courts. In addition, although not directly P&I club costs, the introduction in 1995 of COFRs (Certificate of Financial Responsibility) by the US administration − to ensure that the shipowner can meet any oil pollution liability − brings in a substantial new cost. For example, a 100,000 dwt tanker can expect to pay in the region of $20,000 (USD) for such cover.

Propulsion, cargo-handling and other port costs

Bunker costs

Chapter 3 analyses the economics of speed in some detail, and Fig 8.2 shows how after the initial oil price rise in October 1973, the price continued to rise until the early 1980s. During this time every effort was made to reduce this cost – slow steaming, re-engining with more efficient engines, a consideration of return to sail, or coal burners etc. However, another effect of the increase in the price of this globally important energy was to cause inflation, so it can be argued that in *real* terms bunker costs by the late 1980s were cheaper than they had been before the initial price rise – ie when the inflation curve rises and crosses the bunker cost curve. It is interesting to note, though, that when the initial problem had disappeared, many in shipping management retained a subconscious knee jerk reaction to the effect that bunker prices were still a problem. This is perhaps a general problem of management training in that great emphasis is placed on making management aware of new problems and how to deal with them, but there is no equivalent de-programming when the threat or problem has passed. However, in 1999 crude oil increased in price from $10 to $24 (USD) per barrel, dragging the bunker price up from $52 to $140 (USD) per tonne at Fujairah.

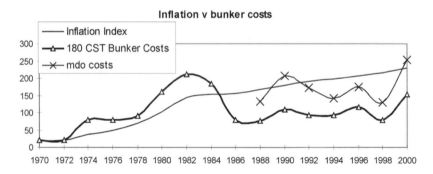

Fig 8.2   Bunker prices 1970–2000.

Port costs

From a practical point of view, these costs can be split into two – 1: all port non-cargo-handling disbursements, and 2: total terminal cargo-handling charges.

1 All port non-cargo-handling disbursements *Charges per NT in $(USD)* — the following suggested figures are arrived at by taking random samples of port charges from at least 50 ports worldwide in 1994.
Dry cargo vessels:

> Average = $2 (USD) per NT, of which ship-handling costs were 57 per cent of the total. STANDARD DEVIATION = 1.5

Tankers:

> Average = $1.5 (USD) per NT, of which ship-handling costs were 55.5 per cent of the total. STANDARD DEVIATION = 0.97

These costs are usually made up of three groups:

- *Agency costs* — these costs are usually based on a scale of charges agreed by some appropriate national organisation. The fee charged will depend on the nature and scale of work involved.
- *Harbour dues* — this is mostly the rental charged for the use of the terminal. A random sample from 120 ports worldwide showed for dry cargo ships an average of 0.186 per NT with a standard deviation of 0.47, while for tankers the average was 0.0618 per NT with a standard deviation of 0.19.
- *Ship-handling charges* — made up of pilotage, boatmen and tugs. From the same sample of ports, the average for dry cargo ships was 0.707 per NT with a standard deviation of 0.77, while for tankers the average was 0.5963 per NT with a standard deviation of 0.63.

There are other charges by some ports; in the UK, for instance, charges are levied for the maintenance of lights, navigational aids and dredging. (Further details are given in Table 8.7.)

Table 8.7 Examples of port and canal charges in $(USD) — from *Lloyd's Shipping Economics* 1992

	20,000 dwt	60,000 dwt	250,000 dwt
Rotterdam	34,000	76,000	248,000
Ras Tanura	3,000	7,000	26,000
Yokohama	16,000	31,000	85,000
Panama Canal loaded	49,100	68,000	too large
Suez Canal ballast	71,000	114,000	295,000
Suez Canal loaded	84,000	135,000	only part loaded

2 Total terminal cargo-handling charges

Per TEU – average = $136.8 (USD) for terminal handling charges, with a standard deviation of 56.5

per ton of grain	$2–7 (USD)
per ton of pig iron	$5–15 (USD)
per ton of coal	$2.5–10 (USD)
per ton of general	$3–20 (USD)
per car loaded – around	$19 (USD)
per ton of paper pulp – around	$10 (USD)

The figures in Table 8.8 were compiled from costs for specific vessels on specific voyages, and therefore the shown percentage values could change if a ship of different age and flag on a different voyage was used. What it *does* show is that the method of grouping costs does not fit so neatly on liner trades or ferry trades. For the VLCC and Panamax bulker, I have shown the three groups and their major components, while for the container ship and ferry I have shown the major costs.

The importance of Table 8.8 is that it shows how for different ship types, different costs assume a different importance. We need to note, for instance, that for the container ship, the cargo-handling is a major cost, but usually of no concern for the others – for the Panamax bulker one would expect the charterer to pay for the cargo-handling, ie FIOT. Crew becomes more important for the ferry – because not only will it be relatively large, but most

Table 8.8   Ship cost groups as a percentage of the total cost

Tanker (VLCC)		Panamax		Container		Ro/Ro ferry	
Capital cost	34.7	Capital cost	41	Capital cost	15.7	Capital cost	50
DRC	19.6	DRC	26	Leasing	10.3		
Insurance	4.4	Insurance	6	Insurance	1.5	Insurance	4
Crew	4.7	Crew	10	Crew	4.5	Crew	15
Management	1	Management	2.5	Admin	4.4	Admin	6
S&R	9.5	S&R	7.5	S&R	3.7	S&R	3.5
Voyage costs	45.7	Voyage costs	33	Cargo handling	22		
Port dues	10.9	Port dues	15.5	Port dues	3	Port dues	10
Bunker	21.2	Bunker	8	Bunker	7.5	Bunker	7.5
Canal charges	12.3			Feeder	7		
Tank heating and cleaning	1.3	Hold cleaning and preparation	9.5	Positioning	5.4		
				Agency	15	Advertising	4

ferries will have two or three crews per ship. The large agency cost for the container ship is for the loading brokers processing the large amounts of documentation required in liner shipping.

Freight rates... the key to the problem

There is really only *one* thing necessary to be a success in commercial shipping, and that is to be able to understand and anticipate the constant fluctuations in the freight rate. Ultimately, nearly all important decisions in sea transport operations depend on the ability to judge the future trend in the freight rates. A ship may appreciate in value three or four times in a few weeks on a rising market and depreciate perhaps even more quickly on a falling market. It has been said that more money can be made out of buying and selling ships at the right time than by operating them successfully.

The freight rates depicted in this chapter only show the overall global trends. There will be day-to-day fluctuations in different markets, and markets will also depend on what type of charter is being offered. A charterer faced with a sudden problem may well pay above the going rate for a 'spot' vessel – ie a ship of the right type that is just where he wants it in his moment of crisis.

There are also those who say that to talk of freight rates at all is grossly simplistic. The problems involved in drawing up a freight scale have been well summed up by Mr Angier in criticising a paper given to the Royal Statistical Society in 1936:

It was perhaps presumptuous of one who was on the classical side at school, and even there rarely got more than *gamma* + for his mathematical efforts, to criticise the productions of eminent statisticians. However, the fact that his family had been accumulating figures about freights for about a hundred years might serve as an excuse for his daring. The Angiers had never been able to convince themselves that there was any satisfactory way of ascertaining average rates of freight which could be applied universally. Most outward coal freights treated by the method used by Dr. Isserlis would yield results approximating the truth, but almost no homeward freights. It had seemed to them (and *pace* Dr. Isserlis, they were not singular among denizens of the Baltic in holding this view) that to arrive at the average rate for, say, January from the River Plate by lumping together all the fixtures reported in that month, whether for loading in January or at any other date, would result in a figure which meant really nothing. One could suggest other ways, e.g. that the rate for January should be based on the freights of all ships loaded in that month, whenever fixed, which would be less illusory, but still open to serious objection. For in almost all homeward trades nowadays, the charter party gave the charterers various options, both as to the loading and discharging, at various rates, so that even if all fixtures were reported fully and truly, one could not tell which option would be used and therefore what rate would be earned. In the River Plate fixtures were often done to one or more of a range of ports at different rates, and the variance between the highest and lowest might well be 2s. 6d [12.5p] – say, on today's minimum schedule rate, 10 per cent or more. This had always seemed to him completely to prevent the attainment of any sound basis for an average. In other trades similar conditions prevailed with even wider variations in the rates which might actually be earned, but he used the River Plate as an illustration, as it was the most important tramp market.

It should also be stressed that since 1938 the much greater variety of ship size and type has made the compiling of a 'meaningful' freight index much more difficult. However, having said all that, freight scales and indices *are* produced – and although they lack precision, they do provide a useful tool to help analyse and understand the fluctuating fortunes of shipowners.

Fig 8.3 shows the freight rates for just over 100 years from 1870 to 1975. From this graph, we can suggest that:

- Freight rates are low for longer periods than they are high. This low plateau should in theory be the 'equilibrium freight', or break-even freight, where the shipowner's revenue is only just slightly above that point where he would consider laying up.

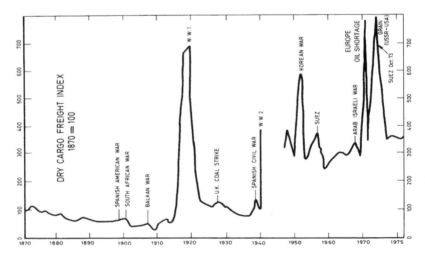

Fig 8.3   Freight rates from 1870 to 1975.

- The high freight rates are not caused by high demand as such, but where some unexpected 'disaster' creates a temporary need for more ships. If you were cynical, you might observe that strikes, famines and wars were good for shipowners (though note the exception of the Arab–Israeli war in October 1973).
- The high rates in the First World War were due to the high insurance premiums charged at this time.

Fig 8.4 shows the tramp freight rates from the end of the Korean War and through the long ensuing period of low freight rates in the 1960s until the 'boom' period of the early 1970s. Unfortunately, the oil price rise in October 1973 gave rise to rapid inflation and, as the quoted freight rates are in actual money rates, Fig 8.4 is misleading as it gives the impression that the shipowner was doing well. In Fig 8.5, the actual freight rate is shown from 1968 to 2002, while underneath the actual freight rates I have tried to indicate in *real money* terms what the rates were worth in values comparable to those of 1968.

As already indicated, it is unlikely that any upward trend or 'boom' in freight rates will last for long, for as soon as any general upward trend in freight rate is discerned, ships are brought out of lay-up and new ships are ordered, so that supply eventually catches up with demand – and then the rates quickly come down until an equilibrium pattern is established, where the freight rate equals the running costs of a reasonably efficient owner in a relatively low-cost country.

The future of this simple pattern of free market forces, however, would seem to be liable to serious problems due to growth in 'protectionism' – not only to shipping, but also to shipbuilding, where there is a danger of supply being artificially increased at times where there is no demand. This aspect will, however, be considered in greater detail in the next chapter.

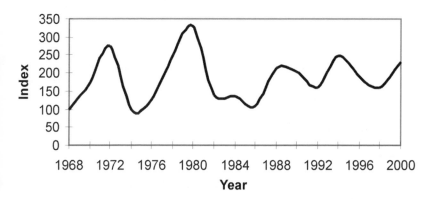

Fig 8.4   Tramp freight rates: 1968–2000.

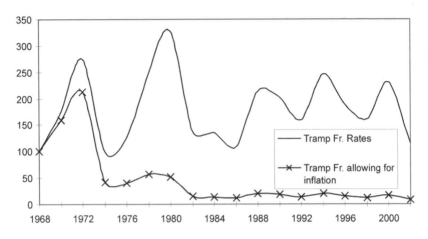

Fig 8.5   Effect of inflation on freight rates.

A demand pattern that can be discerned in most years is shown in Fig 8.6, which is an average of the annual curves between 1985 and 1990. In this average year, the rate rises in the first part of the year until May, then it falls until July. From July until the end of the year, it rises slowly.

The Baltic Freight Index (BFI)

The BFI was created as the basic marker for the Baltic International Freight Futures Exchange (Biffex), which began trading in May 1985 at the Baltic Exchange in St Mary Axe and remained there until the building was severely damaged by a bomb in 1992. Biffex calculated the BFI daily by taking an average of the rates for the major ship types on a dozen of the major dry-bulk routes, which are carefully weighted to reflect their overall market importance. By taking advantage of Biffex, owners can hedge against a future fall in freight rates and a charterer against a rise, while an entrepreneur can simply speculate as to the future performance of the freight market. On 1 November 1999, the *Baltic Panamax Index (BPI)* superseded the BFI as the instrument of settlement for Biffex.

Liner freight rates

The previous freight figures have referred directly to the charter market. A freight rate scale for liner shipping is even more complex as a result of the very great variety of rates charged by the conferences, and the Bundesministerium für Verkehr of Hamburg appears to be the only body that attempts such a task.

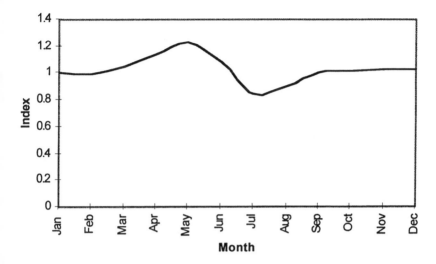

Fig 8.6 Typical freight fluctuations during an average year.

From Fig 8.7 it would seem reasonable to deduce that:

1 Fluctuations in liner freight rates are much less violent than those for tramp vessels.
2 On average, liner rates are higher than tramp rates, for the same basic reason that in air transport charter flights are cheaper than scheduled flights, ie they enjoy higher load factors and experience more open competition.
3 The liner freight rates seldom go down, but when tramp rates are low the liner rates rise less sharply. In periods of low tramp rates, tramp owners will become more interested in liner-type cargoes, and competition between the two markets will become much keener than when tramp rates are high.
4 Liner rates tend to keep more in step with inflation than tramp rates.

General points on liner rates

- Liner freight rates can be commodity-based, in which case a different rate is charged depending on what the commodity is. These may be very detailed where many thousands of commodities are itemised, or they may be split into a few broad classes (see CBR, below). The alternative is to charge so much per unit, and this is a growing practice with containers (see FAK rates, below).
- Freight rates based on the commodity may be either revenue-based – where the freight is calculated on the value of the goods, ie 1.5 per cent *ad valorem* – or cost-based, where the cost of loading, discharging,

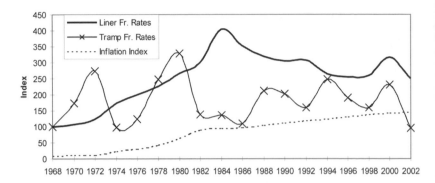

Fig 8.7   Comparing liner and tramp freight rates.

carrying, etc are assessed and the charge estimated accordingly. Surcharges are usually applied for large (more than 40 feet) and heavy (more than 5 tons) units of cargo.

- Revenue-based freights are usually for expensive items of cargo, but may also be used for very inexpensive items of cargo that would not be carried if cost-based freights were applied. The result of this is that valuable cargo subsidises inexpensive cargo. The effects of air transport creaming off the very expensive cargo can therefore be deduced.

- The tonnage used in assessing freight may be either tons weight or tons measurement. The latter is used if the commodity has a density of more than 40 cubic feet to the ton, or 1,000 kilos per cubic metre.

- The purpose of most government interference, as in the Australian trade, is to provide an objective assessment of the costs and thus protect the interests of the nation's exporters. Unfortunately, with the rapidly rising costs and the slowness of the procedures for increasing freight charges, the shipowner's expenses have tended to exceed his income, and profit margins have been low over the last few years.

- In a growing number of cases, governments may be directly involved both as shipper and shipowner.

- Various regulatory bodies, including those applying the UNCTAD Liner Code, require notice, often as much as six months, before conferences can increase their freight rates. However, to meet sudden cost changes, certain surcharges are allowed, ie:

  CAF – currency adjustment factor, to allow for changes in exchange rates, as most tariffs are quoted in dollars.
  BAF – bunker adjustment factor, to allow for changes in bunker prices.
  Port congestion surcharges, to allow for the extra cost of port delays, are also sometimes applied.

The effect of containers has been to simplify the system by:

1 CBR – commodity box rates; for example, on 1 July 1982, the Far Eastern Freight Conference replaced its 3,000 individual tariffs with CBR, ie 106 items grouped into 13 main categories.
2 FAK rates – freight all kinds. This is where a fixed rate is charged per unit moved, regardless of the commodity. It is used on some coastwise routes and by some non-conference liners. Although FAK has obvious attractions, particularly for the shipper of high-value goods, it could penalise the shipper of low-value goods to the extent that several low-value commodities might stop being shipped altogether.

A few definitions in relating to freight

- *Advance freight*. Most liner cargo freight is paid in advance on signing the bill of lading. Advance freight is not recoverable even if the goods are lost.
- *Destination freight, freight forward or freight collect*. This is freight payable on the delivery of goods. A shipowner has the right to hold the cargo (possessory lien) until all freight has been paid.
- *Dead freight*. If a charterer fails to provide a full cargo, the shipowner may claim for dead freight. This is computed on the basis of loss of freight, less the expenses that would have been incurred earning it.
- *Backfreight*. Where cargo is over-carried due to the cargo-owner's failure to take delivery at the intended destination, or if the shipowner is unable to deliver for reasons outside his control, he may have a claim for backfreight in affecting delivery at a second port or eventually the original port of discharge in a second attempt.

9 WORLD TONNAGE

The supply of shipping is made up of the carrying capacity of ships to move cargo. This comprises four main factors:

1 The number of ships Over the last century, the number of *ships that carry things* has declined, but the total tonnage of ships has greatly increased.

2 The size of ships Ships have consistently grown bigger over the last century or so. The growth was slow from 1880 to 1955, but from 1955 to 1975 the growth was spectacular as owners quickly realised the possibilities of new technologies and trade routes. The year 1975 was the time of construction of the last of the ships ordered before the oil crisis ended the boom of the early 1970s. Since then, the situation has stabilised – tankers, for instance, have not grown any bigger, but ferries have.

3 Port time The less time ships spend in port, the more cargo they can carry in a year. Hence reducing port time increases the supply of ships – which is why one container vessel can replace several conventional general cargo ships. As noted in Chapter 3, the increase in size is also related to port speed, as port speed is probably the factor that held back the growth in ship size up to the mid-1950s.

4 Speed Increasing speed obviously increases the supply of ships and vice versa. This is the only way supply can be adjusted in the short term – apart from laying ships up and reactivating them. As stressed in Chapter 3, reducing speed by 2 or 3 knots can show significant economies, so 'slow steaming' can be a valid strategy in the attempt to balance supply and demand.

A brief history of the supply of shipping

Apart from learning a lot of quaint nautical jargon, from a commercial point of view it is not necessary to go back much further than the middle of the nineteenth century, as it was about this time that there were three major developments. This period produced the shipping evolutionary equivalent of *Homo sapiens* – ie modern shipping. These three major developments were:

1 The development of worldwide communications. (This point, of course, has already been stressed in previous chapters.) Trading in an organised way requires communication. Without it, you could only give your

master a ship-load of, say, coal, and hope he could trade it for something interesting. If you've read *The Merchant of Venice*, you will realise the problems merchants have in not knowing when ships will return!

2 The development of iron ships. Some argue that the British shipbuilders were forced into this new technology by the lack of available wood, and if this is true then it was a happy result from what must at the time have been seen as an environmental catastrophe. The Admiralty, we are also told, resisted the change strenuously, refusing to believe that iron could even float! However, as we now know, iron – being much stronger than wood – enabled lighter, larger ships to be built, giving British shipping and shipbuilders the edge for several generations.

3 The development of a suitable reliable power source and a method of harnessing it – ie the propeller. Steam engines had been around for some time, but until this period they were not efficient or reliable enough for ocean passages.

The supply of steamships ran into one of its earliest problems with the opening of the Suez Canal in 1869. On the one hand, this gave the steam ship a major advantage over the still competing sailing vessels, but on the other it created over-supply – particularly with regard to the important India trade. This was probably the reason why the first Liner Conference was convened in 1875.

By the end of the nineteenth century, the Baltic Exchange, standard charter party forms and chartering procedure were all well established.

The sophistication of the 'unsinkable' *Titanic* in 1912 shows how advanced shipping had become by this time, but the First World War, with the following depression, kept the development and evolution at a modest pace until the mid-1950s when low freight rates and growing demand – coupled with the technological advance of the Second World War – launched the shipping industry into a renaissance. Those who do not wish to go back to the nineteenth century in their study of shipping can usefully start their exploration of modern shipping from the postwar period.

Dr Mech, in one of his papers, calls the period 1965–73 the 'Golden Age of Expansion', with more rapid evolution of ship types (eg container ships, chemical, gas carriers, Ro/Ro, car carriers etc) than any other. This period also saw the expansion of national fleets and those of flags of convenience (see page 150–52).

Then came the years following October 1973, which brought this Golden Age to an end and forced the industry into a period of cost-cutting and the search for greater efficiency. This period, which for many has been a period of trying to survive, has been made even more difficult, perhaps, because it has also been the period of growing awareness of the need to consider environmental sustainability and the growth of operators' liability.

The growth of national merchant fleets

In 1914, Great Britain owned and operated about 45 per cent of the world's merchant tonnage. In 1978, it was only in the region of 7.6 per cent, and by 1992, it was 1.35 per cent. If we were to consider these statistics alone, it might be thought that British shipowners have failed. However, a glance at Fig 9.1 and Table 9.1 shows that, apart from the war years, the British merchant fleet grew reasonably steadily until 1975, since when it has declined. This British dominance of the shipping scene in the period when shipping as we know it today developed is why London became the centre of the shipping world – not just for owners, but for all the services it requires – eg banks, brokers, traders, underwriters, P&I clubs, arbitrators, etc. Since January 2000, the UK fleet can opt for a *tonnage tax*. Under this system, the tax is on the tonnage – not on profit – but it requires one cadet to be supported for every 15 officers, or to pay a levy into a training fund.

The American curve is notable for its rapid growth during the wartime periods. It is also perhaps no coincidence that during the early 1950s the Liberian fleet grew as the US fleet declined. The growth of the Liberian fleet since 1955 is outstanding, as is the Greek fleet from 1970 (Table 9.1 and 9.2). If, however, it is remembered that much of the Liberian fleet is Greek and American owned, it is probably true that Greek and American nationals own the largest merchant fleets in the world. The growth of the Japanese and Norwegian fleets speak for themselves. It is perhaps worth noting that these were the only two fleets to show any appreciable growth during the depressed years of the 1930s.

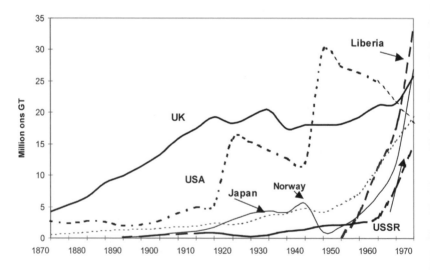

Fig 9.1   Growth of six major national fleets, 1870–1970.

Table 9.1 Major national fleets (1970–2002) in million tons (average age of ships registered under major flags in 2000 was 18 years)

1970		1980		2000				
Country	GT mill	Country	GT mill	Country	No	dwt mill	% share	GT mill
Liberia	33	Liberia	80	Panama	5,088	162.9	21.5	107.7
Japan	27	Japan	41	Liberia	1,511	77.5	10.2	50.0
UK	26	Greece	39	Bahamas	1,124	44.6	5.9	30.0
Norway	19	UK	27	Malta	1,462	44.5	5.9	26.9
USA	18	Panama	24	Greece	1,089	41.8	5.6	24.6
USSR	15	USSR	23	Cyprus	1,417	36.0	4.74	23.2
Greece	11	Norway	22	Singapore	992	34.2	4.51	21.6
			Rank	TOTAL		759		
			8	Norway	1,178	33.0	4.35	21.5
			9	China	2,098	22.5	2.96	15.1
			10	Japan	3,215	22.5	2.96	16.1
			13	USA	361	12.8	1.69	9.4
			14	UK	472	8.8	1.16	6.9

If instead of using tonnage as the main criteria for listing the largest fleets, and the number of ships is used instead, then the pecking order in the list changes and Japan can be seen to have the largest fleet (see Table 9.1).

In 2000, several nations could claim the lead position. Panama had the largest GT and number of ships. Japan has a great number of ships, but if the table were to show nationality of owner rather than country of registration, then Greece would be in the lead. However, with the growth of the internationalism of shipping, the value of analysing the supply of shipping on a national flag basis would seem to be of limited value. For instance, the ships could be owned by a multinational company with its head office in one country, but registered in another, managed in another, crewed from still another, the profits banked in a different country again, and carrying cargoes from yet a further set of countries (see Table 9.2).

Perhaps a more useful analysis is to consider the supply from the different types of vessels (see Table 9.3).

The 2000 columns give a complete list of cargo-carrying ships with regard to their number, their GT and their age (ie 50 per cent of the number of ships in the world, but 95 per cent in terms of GT). The blanks in the 1965 and the

Table 9.2 Registered and controlled fleet of major shipping nations – in dwt (millions) in 2002

Country	Registered fleet ships > 300 GT	Controlled fleet ships > 1,000 GT	Average age
Greece	49	148.9	22.1
Japan	16.6	104.5	11.2
Norway	32.4	59	23.7
China, People's Republic of	23	41.9	22.7
USA	10.6	40.6	25.8
Germany	7.2	40.2	12.9
Hong Kong	23.7	35.2	11.4
Korea, Republic of	9.3	25.7	19.5
Taiwan	7.1	23	16.2
Singapore	32.9	18.1	14.1
SUBTOTAL	211.9	537.1	17.1
UK	7.8	18.2	14.9

1980 columns merely indicates that *Lloyd's Register Annual Statistical Tables* did not give so much detail in these years. These years are, I think, worth including as they do show, for the main types, where the increases and decreases are. General cargo ships, for instance, remained fairly constant in the 1970s, but their numbers and GT are now both declining, while container ships have grown consistently throughout the period. O/Os and OBOs peaked around 1980, but as a type they seem to lack popularity now.

The average age figure is interesting. The world's supply of ships would seem to be getting older – probably due to the relatively low freight rates since 1973, leaving insufficient margins for reinvestment. It should also indicate that during the next decade there must either be a reduction in supply or a boom in shipbuilding.

We must note that not all the ships in the supply side of the equation shown in Table 9.3 will always be available for transport. At a conservative estimate, at any one time at least 4 per cent of the total will be undergoing repairs and maintenance and others will be laid up until their particular market improves.

The decision to lay up a ship

At what point will a shipowner consider laying up his ship? In other words, withdrawing it from active trading.

Table 9.3 Summary of the world's cargo-carrying ships by type

Ship type	1965 No	GT Millions	1980 No	GT Millions	2000 No	GT (millions)	Age	dwt (millions)	2002 dwt (millions)
Liquefied gas	5	0.059	631	7.4	1,126	19.7	14	18.5	19
Chemical			649	2.2	2,534	17.5	14	28.7	8.5
Oil	5,307	55	7,112	175	7,009	155.5	16	283.7	303.2
Other liquids			120	0.2	345	0.5	23	0.7	0.7
Bulk dry	1,316	17.6	4,282	83.4	4,886	142.7	14	255	277.1
O/O and OBOs	87	3.4	424	26.2	205	8.6	17	15	14.1
Self dist bulk dry					165	3.2	26	5.4	
Other bulk dry					1,086	6.7	17	8.9	
General cargo	22,000	50	22,676	81.3	16,755	54.9	22	78	72
Container			662	11.3	2,590	60.2	10	69.1	76.1
Refrigerated					1,414	7	18	7.4	7.2
Ro/Ro cargo					1,882	27.1	17	13.7	7.4
Passenger/Ro/Ro cars					2,574	13.1	21	3.8	5.6
Passenger					3,366	10	22	2.1	2.1
Other	500	2			268	2.1	24	2.2	9.6
TOTALS	29,215	128	36,565	387	46,205	528.8	19	792.2	799.8

Table 9.4 The costs of laying up a ship		
Freight rate	*Profit if trading*	*Profit if laid up*
$9,000	$1,000	−$3,000
$8,000	$0	−$3,000
$7,000	−$1,000	−$3,000
$6,000	−$2,000	−$3,000
$5,000	−$3,000	−$3,000
$4,000	−$4,000	−$3,000

Consider a shipowner with fixed costs of say $3,000 per day – ie he will have to spend $3,000 a day even if his ship is laid up. For a specific voyage, he has $5,000-a-day voyage costs but he does not have to spend this if he lays up.

If the freight rate is $9,000/per day, then profit = $9,000 – ($3,000 + $5,000) = $1,000 per day. If the freight rate is $8,000/per day, then profit = $8,000 – ($3,000 + $5,000) = 0.

However, if at this point he were to lay up, he would lose $3,000. We could therefore build up a table such as that shown in Table 9.4.

Although not an elegant proof, it is fairly obvious from Table 9.4 that when *the freight rate = the voyage costs*, which in this case were $5,000, the shipowner stands to lose more by trading than by laying up. On reaching this point, an operator will not necessarily lay up, as laying up and reactivating can be quite expensive processes, but a decision will have to be made as to whether to:

- continue trading at a loss;
- lay up;
- reduce his costs;
- scrap or sell the ship.

Which of these options he selects will depend on his *expectations* of the market's future. In other words:

- Will freight rates pick up soon?
- Will freight rates remain low for months?
- Will freight rates remain low for such a period that he cannot anticipate any future profitability for the ship? In which case, scrapping or selling becomes the solution.

We need to note that as ship's costs are different, not all ship operators will reach the lay-up point at the same time. We also need to take into account the fact that new ships tend to have higher fixed costs and lower voyage costs than old ships, so old ships will tend to lay up before new ships. (For example, in

January 2003 there were 252 ships of 14 million dwt laid up, having an average age of 32.1 years.) The official statistics on lay-ups are given in Lloyd's Register, though it is worth bearing in mind that the real figures will probably be higher as prudent operators will use these occasions of low-freight periods to fit in repairs and dry-dockings, etc. If the operator anticipates the bad period will be short-lived, he may slow steam or 'hang around' in port or try to position himself where he hopes a spot opportunity might occur.

In 2001, 623 ships of 14.3 million GT, and with an average age of 27 years, were scrapped or otherwise disposed of.

Tramp price fixing and tonnage stabilisation schemes

There have been various attempts among owners of tramp ships to regulate prices – ie the Baltic and White Sea Conference in 1905 set up minimum freight rates for sailing vessels. One of the more successful was in 1935 when British owners, along with owners from other major tramp-shipping nations, were able to establish a price-fixing scheme. Minimum freight rates were fixed on a limited number of routes.

In 1958, the International Chamber of Shipping drew together some 12 concerned leading maritime nations and decided to form an International Tonnage Stabilisation Scheme. The idea of this particular scheme, as with most tonnage stabilisation schemes, is that member owners pay into a common fund to create resources with which to compensate members who agree to lay up their ships. Since 1958, there have been many meetings and discussions and some action (in operation for six months at the end of 1964), but no great success.

During the low freight-rate periods following the fuel price rise in October 1973, efforts in both the tanker and dry-cargo markets have been made to find a solution to this problem.

Problems with such schemes

1 To be successful, the majority of owners must co-operate. This is difficult considering the entrepreneurial spirit among owners of tramp ships.
2 The large variety of types and sizes of ships today makes the mechanics of any such scheme very complicated compared with those of the pre-war scheme.
3 Owners operating modern ships with large depreciation costs, and low operating costs, stand to lose more by laying up than owners operating old tonnage with little or no depreciation costs and high operating costs.

Reasons for encouraging and sustaining national fleets

1 It is a traditional occupation that the nation does well and for a profit, eg Norway and Greece.
2 To earn foreign currency, eg developing countries.

3 To save foreign currency, eg countries with a very large overseas trade, such as Japan.

4 To avoid dependence on others, eg the USA.

5 For military and prestige reasons.

For many countries, such as the UK, it may be a mixture of all the above reasons.

The growth and development of the world's merchant fleets is the result of the interplay of many constraints, which can loosely be classified into:

- Technical constraints;
- Economic constraints;
- Political constraints.

These three constraints need to be understood if we want to comprehend the mechanics of supply.

Technical constraints

The growth of the British fleet at the beginning of the twentieth century was very much dependent on her being the first to develop large iron stream-driven ships. Also, the change in the design of ships in the last 10 years, and the advent of container ships, bulk carriers and very large tankers, could become a reality only after changes and improvements in shipbuilding technology. On the other hand, politicians may through their administration develop policies which, like OPA 90, can bring about a whole range of technical changes in hull design for safety reasons. In the case of OPA 90, this was a unilateral decision on the part of the US administration, but one that others may copy. Most such technical problems are, however, settled through the IMO. The importance of policy technical changes on supply is that they can, by changing the legal requirements, make many ships obsolete. The same can be said for propulsion units, and much of the ancillary equipment that is now essential for the safe and efficient operation of ships. (Most of these aspects have been covered in previous chapters.)

Economic constraints

Shipowners need to make money and can do this in two principal ways:

1 By buying ships cheaply when the freight rate is low, and selling for a profit when the rates are high. A ship's 'value' has been known to increase two or three times on a rising market, and therefore profits can be made by speculating in this way. However, this is not such an easy way to El Dorado as it might seem. It requires *knowledge* of the market, *capital* with which to speculate, and an *organisation* that can make and put into effect quick decisions.

2 By carrying cargoes in ships or, as in the case of time charters, to hire them out to someone else who will. Since 1973, this has not been very profitable and there have been times in the 1980s when most owners were running at a loss – if they were running at all, that is.

It is important to realise that there are different types of market and that there is really no such thing as 'the shipping business'. The world of shipping is an enterprise made up of many different markets and, in most cases, each market is made up of two or more sub-groups. Technically, a VLCC has many design points in common with a small high-speed inter-island ferry, but their commercial operation has little in common.

As an example of commercial differences, if the relatively slow growth of British shipping after the Second World War is compared with that of Norway, it should be noted that the demand for liner shipping services was less than that for tramp services. The obvious choice for British shipowners was to turn to tramp shipping. This in effect they did with some success for several years, but with commercial change – as in physical change – there is 'inertia'.

The contribution of a nation's shipping to the balance of payments

There seem to be two common misconceptions concerning balance of payments or foreign currency earned by shipping. One is that if the nation has its own ships, these will automatically bring in foreign exchange, and the other is to confuse possible profit with foreign currency earned. If a national shipowner has to buy his ships abroad with foreign currency, and also maintain, store, crew and bunker them – all using foreign currency – the chances are that there will be a net outflow of foreign currency even if the shipping line itself makes a profit.

We need to note that there is a difference between foreign currency earned and foreign currency saved, eg:

- Foreign currency *earned* is the net inflow/outflow of foreign exchange into the *state* due to the ship being a national carrier.
- Foreign currency *saved* is to consider what extra foreign exchange would have been spent *if* there were no national carrier.

Earning foreign exchange has been one of the most cogent reasons for developing countries wanting to own their own fleets. Consider therefore a national shipping line trading from its own country – eg to the USA.

Note the foreign exchange saved should also be calculated – ie you should consider how much foreign exchange would be saved by not having to employ a foreign ship to carry the cargo and this *might* bring a positive bottom line to the balance of payments contribution.

If the figures for different ship types were analysed in detail, we would note that they make different contributions. Container and passenger ships will usually make a significantly greater contribution to the balance of payments, though often making less profit than tankers and bulk carriers.

Those in developing countries might also note that the services generated in London for shipping, such as broking, insurance, banking, etc, produce more foreign exchange (over £1 billion (GBP) in 2002) than the ships themselves.

Political constraints

- Wars cause losses of ships and a need for rapid rebuilding and produce a considerable stimulus to research and shipbuilding capacity. During the First World War, the UK lost 50 per cent of its pre-war fleet, and in the Second World War, it lost 60 per cent.

  The effect of war on trade can be colossal, as artificial demands are created and routes lengthened, as in the closure of the Suez Canal.

  Blacklisting can occur, and ships trading to one country may not be allowed to visit another – eg ships visiting Cuba were not allowed to trade with the USA for quite a long period.

  Also, because of the possibility of war, nations do not like to be dependent on the ships of other nations for the delivery of essential supplies. The withdrawal of British ships from the liner trade routes during both world wars made countries aware of their dependence on foreign ships and thus the need to develop their own fleets.
- Changes of government, political ideology, colonialism, political align-ments and international agreements drafted by the WTO (World Trade Organisation) all cause changes in trading patterns.
- Forms of taxation and government restrictions (ie manning scales) can have their effect, as with the growth of flags of convenience.
- Governments can protect their own fleets and thus exert influence.

These points are of considerable importance and are normally considered as *policy*.

> *Whosoever commands the sea commands the trade;*
> *whosoever commands the trade of the world*
> *commands the riches of the world*
> *and consequently the world itself.*

This quote is a famous policy statement made about four centuries ago, but is it true today? As a slogan, it is very persuasive and seems to be in the subconscious of many of the world's shipping policymakers. Personally, I would say that in a world of over-supply of ships, it is better to have the cargo than the ships, and that the first line should read:

> *Whosoever commands the trade commands the sea.*

Maritime policy

What is this?

National Shipping policy, an element of overall economic policy, expresses the attitude of the State to Shipping. Shipping policy can be understood as the totality of economic, legal and administrative measures by means of which the State influences the position of its national fleet, that is, its place and role in the national economy and in international freight markets...The attitude of the State to its own merchant marine as a rule reflects indirectly its attitude to the fleets of other countries.

Shipping policy has then two aspects – foreign, expressing the attitude to other fleets, and domestic, to own merchant marine.

The above quote is given by Chrzanowski in his book on maritime economics (*Introduction to Shipping Economics*, Fairplay, 1985). This is a very comprehensive definition, but the meaning of 'maritime policy' can take a wider compass. It *does* concern government – but a government has many departments, eg the USA has the FMC, Maritime Administration, US Department of Justice, Coastguard, Customs, etc. Each bureaucrat or official may also have his own interpretation of a national policy.

In addition, it is not only governments that have policies – organisations such as the IMO and UNCTAD have policies, as do conferences. Therefore we could say:

Policy is a course of action adopted for the sake of expediency to achieve a certain goal or offset a danger.

A policymaker is therefore an administrator who is trying to solve a problem. A person can usually find some sort of solution to a problem, but in the quest for 'the truth' or the real solution, the fundamental difficulty lies in asking the right question or identifying what the real problem is. For example, in the 1960s, governments and shipowners wasted a great deal of time trying to formulate a policy to stop crews smoking in bed, after a survey showed that this was the greatest hazard to shipping. It was many months before anyone seemed to realise that the crucial question to ask was, 'How do we make mattresses non-inflammable?' Once this question had been identified, the solution was easily found.

Many in the maritime field want to establish such policies as 'How we can help our merchant fleet' or 'How we can privatise our ports' without stopping to consider whether these are the right questions to ask.

Once the policymaker has identified the problem, the solution lies in a variety of options – all with good and bad effects. (For further information on this, see E Frankel, 'Hierarchical logic in shipping policy and decision-making', *Marit. Pol. MGMT*, 1992, vol 19, no 3, 211–21.)

Important points to note on policy

- Nearly all policies, no matter how good, will have some *bad* effects.
- There is no definitive solution, nor will a sound working policy necessarily remain so.
- There are dangers in changing policy – should it be implemented quickly or slowly?
- Are internationally agreed policies better than national unilateral policies?

Also with regard to planning, a centrally planned economy can have a plan and enforce it – but a liberal democracy can have a plan but will have greater difficulties in enforcing it. It can introduce penalties, financial incentives, etc, but the results of this manipulation may not always be as predicted, eg tax incentives.

Furthermore, having a policy is one thing, but enforcing it through the various agencies whose interpretation of its various points may differ widely is another, eg port state control.

Why do governments *need* a policy?

- To protect some aspect of national interest – usually jobs or foreign currency investment. This is usually only necessary during periods of low freight rates.
- To increase efficiency, eg privatisation.
- To put pressure on another country.
- For political or ideological reasons.

Policymakers need to know what is happening and why – therefore they need data. They must also pursue the right goals.

How can governments achieve this policy?

A government has really only one of two options: it can either help its own national industry, or make things difficult for its foreign competitors.

1 Helping a country's own national industry by subsidies or some other form of financial assistance

Such help can take many forms:

- *Operating subsidies*. This is where direct financial assistance is given to help the nation's ships compete on the international shipping markets. In the USA, operating subsidies are paid to liner ships operating on what are considered to be essential routes. With these subsidies, certain conditions are usually attached – such as that the ships must be built in the home country.

- *Construction subsidies*, or some form of financial help to meet the high capital cost of building the ship. This can take several forms, such as building grants, long-term loans with easy terms, custom duty exemption or rebates on imported material or parts, or financial help with expensive research.

- *Indirect subsidies* such as various forms of tax concessions like free depreciation. This type of subsidy has the merit that it encourages successful and resourceful management. With direct operating subsidies there is the danger of encouraging inefficient management. The upsurge in British tonnage shown in Fig 9.1 for the late 1960s was almost certainly due to British owners being given this assistance. However, as they were the only British industry enjoying this benefit, there were many takeover bids from profit-making organisations, who tended to lose interest in the shipping side of the business when this benefit was removed.

The indirect subsidy can also be used to stimulate new growth in the industry by having the profits reinvested rather than just dispersed to the shareholder.

State-owned fleets must inevitably enjoy all these subsidies or at least have the comfort of knowing that the resources are there to help them in these ways when times are bad.

The motives for subsidies are the same as those for any other form of protection for shipowners previously described.

The arguments against subsidies are that they encourage inept management and upset the rules of 'fair play' in the cut and thrust of international competition, and various examples indicating the pros and cons of subsidies are often cited.

One popular example indicating the dangers of subsidies is the effect of the repeal of the Navigation Laws in 1850 which protected British shipping. It is argued that once this protective shield was removed, British shipping had to make itself efficient and competitive and that it was this stimulus that caused it to grow steadily to become the greatest merchant navy in the world. It could, though, also be argued that this growth was due to a cheap and plentiful supply of coal, the steam engine and the shortage of wood – making it necessary to build iron ships. There was also the fact that the major competitors of the British – the Americans – were involved in a bitter civil war.

A second popular example indicating the dangers of subsidies is that the French fleet became dependent on such subsidies at the end of the nineteenth century; and, instead of modernising, the subsidies enabled them to continue building large wooden sailing ships long after such ships had ceased to be an economic proposition.

As a counter-argument to this, the success of the German and Japanese merchant fleets during the interwar years was undoubtedly partly due to the prudent use of subsidies.

It is also worth noting that subsidies to shipbuilding at times of low freights will increase the supply of ships, and therefore worsen the situation for shipowners.

At an international level, such as the EU, the administrators will continually try to ensure a 'level playing field for all its members'. However, if any national shipowner or port operator in the EU is asked what financial help they receive, they will shake their heads sadly and say they receive no help at all, but that if only they had the assistance that their colleagues in other member states received, all would be well. The reason for this type of response seems to be that the help each country receives is not perceived as a subsidy. For instance, British ports consider that the state financing of dredging and navigational light operation that happens in Continental ports is a subsidy, whereas the Continental ports do not consider it to be such.

One of the most comprehensive analyses of maritime subsidies throughout the world is made annually by the US Department of Transport Maritime Administration. In the executive summary at the beginning of their 1993 edition, they list the subsidy measures publicly known throughout the world as:

- Operating and construction subsidies.
- Financing programs whereby governments allow cheap loans for ships built in national shipyards.
- Export credits.
- Tax benefits.
- Social or economic programs, such as government-paid training.

This publication gives a country-by-country account of the financial help each one receives but I am not sure that I can agree with what it says about the UK! This same publication also considers protectionism, something that we will now go on to examine.

2 Protection offered to a nation's home shipping industry (protectionism)

Since the Second World War, major trading nations have reduced the barriers to trade in goods that had intensified during the interwar years. During recent years, however, an increasing number of countries have introduced various forms of protection for their own national fleets.

The reasons for this may be many and varied, as in the case of a developing nation wishing to build up its own fleet. At the other end of the scale, in the USA, the high operating costs of American ships make it difficult for USA ships to compete in an open market with other maritime nations.

Other nations may feel justified in helping their fleets for military or strategic reasons, or because it is felt that this is a useful way of earning foreign currency. Protectionism will almost certainly increase during periods of low freight rates.

Types of protection

As we will see, there are various types of protectionism, and it may be helpful to divide this into *unilateral action* and *bilateral* or *multilateral action*.

Unilateral action taken by a nation to protect its shipping:

- *Cabotage*, or the reservation of the coastal trade either to ships flying that nation's flag (eg France) or to include also ships owned by nationals, but perhaps operating under a flag of convenience (eg the USA).
- Reduced customs dues on goods imported on own-flag ships.
- Restriction of credit if goods are not carried in national ships.
- Various forms of import/export licence control.
- Priority in loading and discharging for nationally owned ships and the reduction in harbour dues, light dues, etc.
- Preference on inland transport charges.
- Reservation of types of cargo, ie government-sponsored, or a percentage of the amount of cargo to national ships. Quota systems are invariably difficult to monitor, control and enforce and often lead to an extra layer of bureaucracy.
- Encouraging or insisting that exporters sell CIF (cost, insurance and freight) and that importers buy FOB (free on board). The result of this is the control of transport of goods entering or leaving the country.

Although these measures will undoubtedly protect a nation's shipping, the overall effect on the country's economy may not be so advantageous. Shipments may have to wait for a suitable ship, costs may increase, and probably other participants in the trade will retaliate.

One measure that can be adopted by those you are protecting your fleet against, is to tranship cargo to a nearby foreign port. This again not only increases the cost and time, but also increases the danger of cargo getting lost, broken and pilfered.

The International Chamber of Commerce has observed that developing countries would do better to invest money in trying to establish good modern ports and inland transport systems rather than in shipping.

Bilateral or multilateral agreements between countries:

Many countries enter into an agreement with one or more others to mutually protect the shipping engaged in trade between the two countries. For instance, the USA has a bilateral maritime agreement with China that provides for parity in bilateral liner-cargo carriage and ensures vessels of each nation at least one-third share of such cargoes.

Note also that the 40:40:20 provisions of the UNCTAD Liner Code can be considered a multilateral shipping agreement.

So how do you enforce a policy and measure its success?

Both enforcement and measuring the success of policies can be a problem. Many policies such as quota systems increase bureaucracy and reduce efficiency, and the question of enforcement should be one of the first aspects an administration should consider before launching into a new policy.

Is your fleet or port stronger because of your policy or because of a lucky change in market forces? Also, does it really work, or is it like an aspirin – just reduces the pain!

Creating a 'commercial' policy for developing countries

This is a problem because:

1 The 'game rules' have already been established (eg network planning) by the developed countries.
2 Developing countries have less money (less money equals more policy could be considered as a basic rule).
3 Developing countries have less shipping management know-how, or perhaps cultural differences, in:
● the critical path;
● decision-making, ie high up rather than low down.
4 Developing countries have more reasons for being in shipping.
5 There is more government control.

A summary of policy dilemmas

If an administration does nothing, national flag shipping may die. If it does take positive steps, then there is a danger of retaliation, loss of efficiency, increased costs, and reduced freight rates. The final result of government help can be creeping government control in the long run, and could perhaps be the end of free market shipping. Finally, if the policies are successful and the national shipping line becomes profitable and strong, it will then in all probability denounce the policies that restored it to health!

Much of the problem could be reduced if there was more international co-operation to reduce long periods of low freight rates, by keeping the *supply* of ships in step with the *demand* for ships.

One of the effects of administrations, unions and other organisations having policies is that the shipowner becomes inundated with regulations and a variety of cost and time constraints. The ship operators will therefore then be tempted to seek for an avenue of escape, to avoid some of these regulations. One such method of avoidance is the use of flags of convenience – the topic discussed in the next section.

Flags of convenience

Flags of convenience are also known as *flags of necessity* or *open registries*. The outstanding example is Liberia (see Fig 9.1), which, as can be seen from this graph, has a merchant fleet that has grown from virtually nothing in the early 1950s to one of the largest fleets in the world. Other examples are Panama, Bermuda and Somalia. Honduras was a flag of convenience, but is no longer of any significance.

What are flags of convenience?

All ships must be registered somewhere, and the ship acquires the nationality of the state in which it is registered. It flies the flag of that state and is governed by its laws. Under the Geneva Convention on the High Sea (1958, art 5, para 1), 'Each state shall fix the conditions for the granting of its nationality to ships, for the registration of ships in its territory and for the right to fly its flag.' The same convention also states that there must be a *genuine* link between the state and the ship, but this seems to be open to a very vague interpretation.

A flag of convenience can therefore be defined as the flag of a country whose laws allow – and in fact make it easy – for ships owned by foreign nationals to fly their flag. This is as opposed to countries where the right to fly the national flag is subject to stringent conditions and involves responsibilities – hence the expression *open registry*.

In addition, a flag of convenience country may possess some or all of the following features:

- It may be a small country that is poor and has few resources with which to raise foreign currency. The revenue raised by registration may be quite small. In 1975, Liberia was reported as having obtained only $12 million in registration fees.

  As regards cost-saving, it is not entirely clear as to which flag offers the cheapest registration cost – as the table given in *Lloyd's List* in February 1997 illustrates (see Table 9.5).
- Manning by non-nationals may be permitted and no strongly developed trade unions may exist.
- There may be a very low tax levy.
- No adequate administrative machinery may exist to enforce international safety regulations.

(*Note*: Others, such as the ITF, would say that a flag of convenience situation exists if the beneficial owner (the one who gets the profits) does not reside

Table 9.5   Registration costs for a 98,600 GT tanker in $ (USD)

Flag	Initial registration fee	Total fees over 10 years
Panama	20,000	85,000
Marshall Islands	31,000	21,100
Bahamas	35,000	78,000
Liberia	28,000	180,000
Cyprus	?	102,000

(Source: Lloyd's List.)

Table 9.6   Top ten countries offering flags of convenience in 2000

Rank	Country	Percentage of total	dwt (millions)	Percentage of total 2002
1	Panama	32.9	133	36
2	Liberia	17.6	71	15
3	Malta	9.6	39	8.4
4	Bahamas	9.4	38	9
5	Cyprus	7.4	30	7
6	Marshall Islands	2.5	10	3.8
7	Bermuda	2.3	9	1.6
8	St Vincent	1.9	8	1.8
9	Antigua and Barbuda	1	4	1.3
10	Cayman	0.3	1	0.5

(Source: ISL.)

in the flag state or, perhaps more to the point, the profits do not remain in the flag state.)

Fundamentally, the term 'flag of convenience' tends to be a pejorative term, rather like calling someone 'ugly'. We are fairly certain there are ugly people about but no one will admit to it – the same is true with regard to flags of convenience!

Major suppliers of flags of convenience

For the purposes of the analysis given in Table 9.6, the ISL have taken into consideration the following flags: Liberia, Panama, St Vincent, Bermuda,

Marshall Islands, Vanuatu, Antigua and Barbuda. This choice of flags does, however, seem somewhat arbitrary. For instance, the Greek Co-operation Council states that Greek shipowners share their vessels among 27 flags, of which in 1996 the five most significant were Greek (42 per cent), Cypriot (20 per cent), Maltese (13 per cent), Liberia (9 per cent) and Panama (7 per cent).

It is interesting to note that different ship types do appear to show preferences towards certain flags. However, with the exception of passenger ships where the public perception of the Bahamas flag might be considered to be more 'up-market' and safer, the main reason is the probable ownership preferences. For instance, many of the general cargo ships will be owned by Greeks – who for patriotic reasons prefer the Cypriot flag.

The development of flags of convenience

The precise definition of a flag of convenience tends to be elusive; possible antecedents be found, some going back for centuries. However, it seems usual to date the modern practice back to 1922, when two American ships were registered in Panama in an attempt to 'beat prohibition'.

The figures in Table 9.6 are a conservative estimate, as I have only included the larger generally accepted flags of convenience. I have not, for instance, included the Norwegian International Ship Register; this is a relatively new, but growing, concept.

It is interesting to note that in 1979 UNCTAD proposed to reduce *open register* fleets and hoped that by 1990 they would have disappeared! However, at a conference in December 1999, Mr O'Neil, Secretary General of the IMO, said he could not see any reason to suppose a change in flag of convenience tonnage, as the factors that brought them into existence hadn't changed. He also reported a recent survey which indicated that 'a sub-standard operator had a 14 per cent cost advantage over his more regulatory-conscious competitor'.

Table 9.7   Flags of convenience as a percentage of world total

Year	Number	GT
1939	0.6	1.2
1950	2.4	4.9
1960	4.8	12.4
1970	6.9	19.3
1980	11.5	28
1993	15.4	38.9
2000	23	58

Why do some nations go into the business of open registry?

In 2000, Liberia received $18 million from its ship registry – a worthwhile contribution to its national economy. For developed countries, open registry may be a means of keeping some level of control over its own ships.

Why do shipowners use flags of convenience?

1 Freedom from taxation – an advantage only during profitable periods.
2 Greater operational freedom, ie few government-imposed restrictions.
3 Possible reduction in operating costs, particularly for American owners as a result of the high cost of American crews.
4 Avoidance of disadvantages, restrictions and the possibility of being discriminated against if operating under one's own flag.

Chief users of flags of convenience As Table 9.8 shows, Greece is the leader in the use of flags of convenience in absolute terms, but it is worth noting that the UK makes the largest percentage use of this facility in its fleet.

The effects of flags of convenience

- Because of tax avoidance, it is said that flags of convenience give their owners an unfair trading advantage and encourage the shipping entrepreneur, as opposed to the responsible shipowner. However, they are open to all!
- A large volume of tonnage without national traditional ties or international shipping involvement means that they do not carry their fair share of responsibility in the world shipping community. Most flag of

Table 9.8 Top ten countries using a flag of convenience

Rank	Country	dwt (millions) under flags of convenience 2000	dwt (millions) under flags of convenience 2002	Percentage of world flags of convenience tonnage in 2002
1	Greece	90.9	99.8	22
2	Japan	77.3	82.9	18
3	Norway	25.6	32.5	7
4	Germany	21.7	30.4	7
5	USA	35.2	26.7	6
6	Hong Kong	25.3	24.8	5
7	China	17	18.2	4
8	Korea (Rep)	17.9	18.0	4
9	Taiwan	12.4	11.3	2
10	UK	11.9	10.4	2

convenience countries are members of the IMO, but not noticeably active ones. Few are members of the International Chamber of Shipping, nor are they concerned with the expensive problem of training seafarers – as they can gain their crews by poaching from the traditional maritime countries. Again, when times are bad, they accept no responsibility for the crews – who then return to accentuate any unemployment or redundancy problem in their own native country.

- It is obviously better for the UK, for instance, if UK ships are registered there. To avoid the exodus of national shipowners to flags of convenience, many traditional maritime nations have instituted an International Ship Register. These enable owners to enjoy many of the flag of convenience benefits, while retaining their nationality – eg the Norwegian International Ship Register. For the UK, the Isle of Man flag serves more or less the same purpose.
- There may be difficulties in obtaining satisfaction in just legal claims, eg as with the disastrous effects of the *Torrey Canyon*.

  In many serious fraud cases, such as the case of the *Salen*, it was never possible even to establish who the real owners of the vessel were.
- It would be wrong to assert that all flag of convenience ships are relatively unsafe compared with ships operating under a traditional maritime flag. Many shipowners operating under flags of convenience take their responsibilities seriously, and there is a growing awareness by flag of convenience governments of the necessity to improve safety standards. The casualty record of flag of convenience countries is, however, worse than the world average.

  One of the recognised safety problems of flag of convenience vessels is their tendency to use multi-racial crews who are, to a great extent, monolingual. For ordinary day-to-day work, they soon learn sufficient words to get by, but in moments of crisis communication may completely break down. Furthermore, the thoroughness of the investigations carried out by some flag of convenience countries into casualties is not always as rigorous as it might be.
- Finally, shipowners who do not use a flag of convenience probably enjoy better tax concessions and with more consideration from their governments, who to avoid an exodus of their ships to these flags.

Curtailing the worst aspects of flags of convenience

This could be done by Introducing legislation to:

1 Ensure that the crew does not have too many different language groups and that they can communicate with one another when under pressure.
2 Establish clearly who is the 'real' owner.
3 Deposit capital or assets by the owner in the flag state.
4 Increase port state control as regards safety standards.

10 SHIPPING FINANCE

by Dr H Leggate

Shipping is generally recognised as being a low-margin business. In the day-to-day trading activities, income is derived from the movement of cargo, which is dictated by the freight rate. Expenses comprise voyage costs, port dues, administrative costs and wages, which may be substantial, leading to a low operating profit. Financing costs in the form of interest can further reduce the 'bottom line' and must therefore be taken very seriously. The extract in Table 10.1 shows the components of an income statement in terms of operations and financial items. While this chapter will focus on the financing element of this statement, it is important first to make some observations about the operating profit margin.

The operating profit

The operating profit margin can be calculated as operating profit as a percentage of operating revenue. In Table 10.1, the operating margin is 80/525 × 100 = 15.2%. It has already been stated that such margins are low in

Table 10.1 Extract from a shipping company income statement	
	$ (millions)
Operating revenue	525
Voyage expenses	−136
Other operating expenses	−234
Net gain on sale of vessels	32
Depreciation	−107
Operating profit	80
Interest expense	−23
Gains/losses on sale of investments	1
Other financial items	−12
Profit before tax	46

	Operating profit					
	Japan			Norway		
	Mitsui OSK	NYK	K Line	Bergesen	Leif Hoegh	Wilhelmsen
1990	4.43	3.1	4.9	21.05	16.44	9.16
1991	2.48	3.46	3.06	27.48	20.75	8.13
1992	4.31	3.8	3.77	7.69	14.8	6.89
1993	3.35	4.17	2.59	9.23	14.76	4.36
1994	2.42	2.36	1.4	−3.4	3.75	1.4
1995	2.95	3.8	2.49	6.35	9.51	6.45
1996	4.26	3.92	5.35	12.72	9.77	7.84
1997	4.95	4.74	4.89	21.51	15.71	16.49
1998	5.65	4.29	5.2	19.95	16.82	14.98
1999	6.62	4.41	4.19	12.5		

Table 10.2 Operating profit percentages in the shipping industry

(Source: Leggate and Carbone, Financial Characteristics of the Shipping Industry, 2001.)

the shipping industry. This fact is illustrated by Table 10.2, which examines the major shipping companies in Japan and Norway during the 1990s. It can be seen that for the 'Big 3' Japanese companies, the margin is particularly low over the period for all companies, barely averaging 4 per cent. For the Norwegian businesses, the profit percentages are higher – although more volatile.

Financing the activities is a key element of any business, and given the huge capital requirement of the shipping companies in terms of vessels, this cost can be significant. Typically, the industry has used substantial amounts of debt to finance its activities, and therefore have what is known as high gearing or leverage. (These terms will be explained later in the chapter.) The financing cost or interest is deducted from the operating profit to give the profit before tax.

The financing requirement of the industry is a reflection not only of the capital intensity of the industry, but the ageing fleet. Aggregate figures for the world fleet show that the average age of vessels is 16 years. On analysis of the data by sector, the age distribution is concentrated on the older vessels. Of these, the general cargo ships are the oldest, with the tanker sector not far behind.[1] Estimates of these financing requirements for the world fleet, based on age and future predictions for the industry, are shown in Table 10.3. For newbuild, the financing is based on 80 per cent of the total purchase price, and for secondhand vessels it is 60 per cent, in line with the industry averages.

Table 10.3 Financing requirements 1998–2002 (world fleet)		
Type	Sub-type	Newbuild $ (USD) (billions)
Tankers	Crude oil	27,480.0
	Chemical	3,436.0
Gas	LPG	5,801.8
Dry bulk		30,807.8
Reefers		4,784.3
General	'Tweendeck	5,873.8
	Singledeck	6,971.5
Containers		31,646.3
Ro/Ro		8,650.0
Total	Newbuild	125,451.3
	Secondhand	33,000.0
TOTAL		158,451.3

(Source: Ship Finance: Choices, Competition and Risk/Reward Equations, Drewry Shipping Consultants.)

Table 10.3 shows a total world fleet newbuilding finance requirement of $125 billion (USD) from 1998 to 2002, and secondhand of $33 (USD) billion. These are, of course, substantial amounts of money. It should also be noted that even more finance may be needed to cover operating activities of the business.

There are numerous sources of finance available to companies, but they essentially fall into two categories: debt and equity. Both equity and debt have a cost, and companies strive to minimise this cost in the establishment of their capital structure. Debt theoretically has a lower cost than equity, because it carries less risk. If this is the case, then why do companies bother with equity finance? The answer is that the financing decision is based on a number of factors – not merely the costs of capital, but control of the business, cash flow, and access to funds. It could be argued that financing is principally a marketing problem. The company tries to split cash flows generated by its assets into different streams that will appeal to investors with different tastes, wealth and tax profiles. Such elements will be explored throughout this chapter.

Equity

Equity represents the permanent capital of a business. The equity holders, or shareholders, are the owners of that business and have ultimate control of the company's affairs. In practice, this control is limited to a right to vote on appointments to the board of directors and a number of other matters. They hold the equity interest or residual claim, since they receive whatever assets or earnings are left over in the business after all the debts are paid. However, shareholders have limited liability in that the maximum amount they can lose if the company goes bust is their investment in the shares. None of the other assets of the shareholder is exposed to the company.

The cost of equity

Shareholders derive return in the form of dividends and capital gain, and this represents the cost of equity capital. Dividends are usually paid annually or half-yearly out of earnings or profits. They are discretionary in that the company need not declare them, even if profits have been made. Indeed, a business may decide to retain earnings to reinvest in the business. These retained earnings are in fact a major source of finance for a company. Capital gains or losses may arise from fluctuations in the share price and may be realised if the holder sells his shares. Since both dividends and capital gains are uncertain, shareholders require a high rate of return to compensate them for this risk or uncertainty, which can make equity a costly form of finance.

The issue of share capital is also more costly than the issue of debt, due mainly to the exacting compliance procedures relating to stock markets, particularly on the established exchanges. There are, however, cheaper ways of doing this through the issue of shares to existing shareholders, known as rights issues, or by the placement of shares to known investors.

Apart from the relatively high cost of equity, another reason why shipping companies have avoided equity finance is that it may mean relinquishing control of the business. This is a particular problem for the smaller companies where the shares are owned by family members. An increased number of shares distributed to new investors will dilute the overall voting power of existing shareholders, and one way of avoiding this situation is to make what is known as a 'rights issue'. Here the shareholders are offered additional shares, often at a discount on the market price, in proportion to their existing holding. If the 'rights' are taken up, the percentage holding remains unchanged, but the company still manages to raise the required finance.

Debt

Debt finance is a non-permanent source of finance in that it must eventually be paid back to the lender. The variety of corporate debt instruments is almost endless. These instruments are classified by maturity, repayment provisions, seniority, security, default risk, interest rates (fixed or floating), and issue procedures. Lenders are not the owners or proprietors of the business and therefore have no voting power. From the investment perspective, debt carries less risk than equity because interest and principal must be paid before there can be any distribution to the shareholders. Debtholders are entitled to a fixed regular payment of interest and repayment of the principal according to an agreed schedule. Interest may be fixed over the period of the loan regardless of what happens to the prevailing rate of interest, or may be variable. Floating interest rates are often tied to the LIBOR (London Interbank Offer Rate), which is the interest rate at which major international banks in London lend dollars to one another. If the company fails to make these payments, it defaults on the debt and it can file for bankruptcy. The usual result is that debtholders then take over and either sell off the company's assets or continue to operate under new management. Default is therefore the most important risk for lenders.

Default risk

Credit rating agencies assess default risk of debt instruments via a rating system, and Table 10.4 illustrates the ratings given by the two main agencies, Standard and Poor's, and Moody. Standard and Poor's ratings go from AAA (the best) down to D. The higher rated debt from AAA to BBB are known as investment grade, and the remainder, from BB to C, are known as speculative grade. D is reserved for debt with a history of default. These categories are further defined by 'plus' and 'minus'. Thus within each category there are three subcategories: plus, equals and minus. The Moody's ratings are similar, but use a different notation, from Aaa to C, again with three subcategories: 1, 2 and 3. It is interesting to note that the much talked about 'junk' bonds or debt is not a term defined by the rating agencies, but is a term that has been colloquially applied to the lower-rated bonds.

These ratings are based not only on historical information, but on an impression of the future. Both these rating agencies see the industry as high risk because of its economic sensitivity, capital intensity and competitive structure. The key factors in the analysis are capital structure, age, size and diversity of the fleet, and management ability.

Capital structure relates to financial gearing, or the proportion of long-term debt finance. The industry has traditionally relied on loan finance and as such has high levels of gearing, often in excess of 70 per cent. Clearly, this factor contributes to the possibility of default in periods of recession.

The age of the fleet has already been discussed in terms of capital requirements, but it is also an issue for the investor since, without detailed knowledge, it is an indicator of quality. The running costs are also higher for older vessels, which has a cash flow implication.

The size of the fleet affects the rating. Companies with larger fleets tend to achieve a higher grade than those with smaller fleets. Associations with other companies, for example, a highly rated parent company, or a highly rated charterer, also affect the decision.

Table 10.4 Default ratings		
Standard and Poor's	Moody's	
AAA	Aaa	
AA	Aa	Investment
A	A	Grade
BBB	Baa	
BB	Ba	
B	B	Speculative
CCC	Caa	Grade
CC	Ca	
C	C	
D		Default

(Source: Standard and Poor's and Moody's rating agencies.)

The diversity of the fleet in terms of the operating sector is a further issue for the reduction of market risk.

Finally, sound management and industry expertise is examined in considerable detail to determine the future prospects for the company. These are the factors that affect the perception of the company for both the rating agencies and the investor, and ultimately determine the cost of the finance to the company. Historically, the grades achieved by the shipping issues have been poor.

The cost of debt

The cost of debt is determined by the interest rate or coupon on the debt instrument. As previously explained, debt should be cheaper than equity because of the certainty of return. From a corporate perspective, the cost is further reduced by taxation, since tax authorities treat interest payment as a cost. That means that the company can deduct interest when calculating its taxable income. Thus interest is paid from pre-tax income and dividends from post-tax income.

Currently, interest rates are at a 40-year low and lenders are queuing up to throw money at the shipping industry. Furthermore, the consolidation among the large industry players – such as Wallenius Wilhelmsen and Hyundai Merchant Marine car carriers, Bergesen, Teekay Shipping and Navion – has created the need for bigger and bigger debt.

Bank finance

Bank finance remains the most important method of raising capital in the shipping industry, and financial institutions provide loans in varying forms to shipping companies. At the simplest level they are term loans, under which the bank lends a certain amount to the shipping company to acquire a vessel over a specific period. The loan is repaid over the period using the income generated by the vessel, and sometimes its residual value. These repayments are made up of the loan principal and interest. Such loans can be customised to the requirements of the user. This can include equal or unequal instalments, and even periods of moratoria whereby the capital element of the loan is suspended. Such flexibility can be helpful in deteriorating market conditions since the shipping industry is very cyclical, leading to volatility in earnings. Interest is normally paid at a variable rate based on LIBOR (London Interbank Offer Rate). LIBOR is a base line rate and the company will typically pay a percentage in excess of this rate. Fixed rate loans are less common.

In order to minimise their risk, banks may ask for collateral, which may take various forms. Such security may be direct in the form of a mortgage on the vessel itself, or indirectly in the form of guarantees. Syndicated loans are also becoming more widespread as a method of diversifying risk. In this situation, a number of financial institutions will share the loan and thereby share the accompanying risk. The number of participating banks can be very large, but in the shipping industry it is generally four to eight banks, all having shipping expertise and experience.[2]

The cost of a bank loan is the interest payable on the debt, which will depend on the particular deal struck with the financial institution.

Bonds

Bonds represent an alternative form of debt finance, and they are increasingly used by the industry. The debt is essentially carved up into small bundles and sold to a number of investors on the capital markets in a similar way to shares. The fixed amount of interest paid to the lender is known as the coupon and the loan is said to 'mature' on a specified date. Table 10.5 gives examples of various shipping bonds.

Table 10.5	Examples of shipping bonds (quoted May 1999)					
Company	Issue date	Issue price $ (USD)	Coupon %	Maturity	Size $ (USD) (mill)	Price $ (USD)
Gearbulk	23/11/94	100	11.25	2004	175	104.5
Amer Reefer	27/02/98	100	10.25	2008	100	63
Cenargo Holdings	12/06/98	98.45	9.75	2008	175	92.5
Enterprise Shipholdings	22/04/98	99.77	8.875	2008	175	70

The price of a bond fluctuates over its life and is inversely related to the prevailing rates of interest. At any stage an investor can sell his or her bond at the prevailing market price, and in so doing make a capital gain or loss.

For example, Table 10.5 shows that, in 1994, Gearbulk issued bonds to raise $175 (USD) million. The issue price for each bond was $100 (USD) which paid a coupon of 11.25 per cent for 10 years to 2004. This means that an investor in this bond would receive $11.25 each year up to and including 2004. On the maturity of the bond he will receive his original investment of $100. However, if he should decide to sell the bond today, he will receive a price of $104.5, which means a capital gain of $4.50.

Bonds can have a number of advantages over both traditional bank finance and equity. First, in comparison with a bank loan, there is a positive cash flow effect because the principal is not amortised. In other words, the company only has to pay the 'interest' element of the loan during the life of the bond. Repayment of the principal is held over until the end. The coupons themselves are typically paid on a half-yearly basis, which again can ease cash flow. Furthermore, the company has the option to roll over the debt at the end of the life of the bond – eg issue more bonds or shares to cover the repayment. Another possibility would be the use of convertible bonds, which, if converted, become permanent equity capital, which does not have to be repaid at all. In comparison with equity, debt finance should cost less, as it is a less risky form of finance. Coupon payments are fixed and there is a guaranteed maturity value. Furthermore, the tax deductibility of debt makes it even more cost effective.

The industry's initial flirtation with the bond market in the late 1990s proved difficult, with investors demanding high coupons reflecting low credit ratings. Since then there has been a marked improvement, with the industry raising $1.3 (USD) billion worth of new issues since 2001. The total for 2003 alone was more than $550 million, including the CMA-CGM issues of the first shipping junk bond denominated in euros. The position in the bond market stems from the high liquidity – ie the large amount of trading.

Capital structure and gearing

The attractiveness of debt was illustrated by Peter Stokes in *Ship Finance, Credit Expansion and the Boom-Bust Cycle*.[3] In terms of percentage points above LIBOR, bank loans are cheaper than other forms of finance for the industry. Subordinated loans, which have a lower standing in the event of bankruptcy, are up to 6 per cent more expensive, with equity being a massive 15 per cent above LIBOR (see Table 10.6).

The evidence suggests that the industry should stick to loan finance. In practice, however, businesses employ a mixture of debt and equity in their capital structure. The main reason for this is that debt, although relatively inexpensive, increases the financial risk of the business. This financial risk stems from the fact that interest payments on the debt must be made before

Table 10.6 The attractiveness of debt	
Type of finance	*Cost*
Bank loan	LIBOR + 1%
Subordinated loan	LIBOR + 4–6%
Equity	LIBOR + 10–15%

(Source: P Stokes, Ship Finance, Credit Expansion and the Boom-Bust Cycle.)

the shareholders can receive a dividend. This obligation increases the risk of default and bankruptcy, such that when debt is high, companies will find it difficult to raise their borrowings. The extent of debt finance is known as *gearing* or *leverage*. This is measured by taking long-term debt as a percentage of total capital. The extract from the balance sheet shown in Table 10.7 shows that assets of their business are financed or balanced by equity and liabilities. The gearing ratio of the company is 38.4 per cent.

$$\text{Gearing} = \frac{\text{Long-term liabilities}}{\text{Long-term liabilities} + \text{equity}} \times 100 = \frac{821}{2{,}138} \times 100 = 38.4\%$$

Typically, the gearing levels are high in the industry for reasons already discussed, but there is a significant amount of variation not only between *companies*, but also between *countries*, as illustrated by Table 10.8.

Japanese companies show very high levels of gearing averaging nearly 70 per cent over the period. Norwegian companies, on the other hand, have less debt finance (53 per cent). High levels of gearing in Japan are common across industries due to the special relationships that companies have with their main bank and also the government-backed loans available. Frankel[4] discusses these characteristics at length in his survey of the Japanese cost of finance, in which he investigates the claim that business in Japan experiences a lower cost of capital than its US counterparts. Investigation of the reasons behind this focuses on the relationship businesses have with their 'main bank'. In times of financial difficulty, such an institution would continue to offer support and never cut off lending. Hoshi, Kashyap and Sharfstein[5] examined a sample of 125 Japanese firms that ran into financial difficulty between 1978 and 1985 and found that those who had this 'main bank' relationship were effectively shielded from their financial distress or bankruptcy and enjoyed a subsequent recovery of earnings compared with other firms. In addition, the existence of lending by government agencies that favoured firms in particular industries at subsidised rates was an important factor. The Japanese Development Bank and the Small Business Finance Corporation are noted for such large subsidies.

Table 10.7 Extract from a shipping company's balance sheet	
Assets	$ (USD) (millions)
Intangible fixed assets	8
Tangible fixed assets	2,036
Total fixed assets	2,044
Current assets	353
Total assets	2,397
Equity and liabilities	
Paid in capital	285
Retained earnings	1,032
Total equity	1,317
Long-term liabilities	821
Total equity and long-term liabilities	2,138
Current liabilities	259
Total liabilities	1,080
Total liabilities and equity	2,397

But what about the shipping companies? The annual reports of the 'Big 3' do indicate substantial loans from the Japanese Development Bank to these companies, which may explain the unusually high levels compared to other companies in the sector. In Norway, however, relationships with banks are of a much more commercial nature and subsidies are not available.

Summary and conclusions

Shipping is a highly capital-intensive industry with a huge financing requirement, and it is also an industry that is subject to rapidly changing fortunes. From the perspective of an investor or financier, this volatility of earnings creates the risk that the costs of finance will not be met. This risk is somewhat alleviated by the fact that the assets are of very high value and so provide security to the providers of capital. Shipping companies have traditionally looked to bank loans due to their relatively low cost. However, they are increasingly using more progressive sources of finance such as equity and bonds, in order to access higher levels of funding with cash-flow benefits. As consolidation in the industry continues, we can expect to see greater access to the capital markets by shipping business.

	Japan			Norway		
	Mitsui OSK	NYK	K Line	Bergesen	Leif Hoegh	Wilhelmsen
1990	68.54	61.97	72.05	24.30	58.45	63.97
1991	73.57	64.48	72.05	21.90	54.41	57.81
1992	74.99	67.78	70.32	31.70	47.40	58.47
1993	77.56	64.49	72.89	36.07	39.47	66.61
1994	78.09	69.47	71.06	28.49	51.25	62.64
1995	81.65	70.79	67.28	43.12	51.84	66.28
1996	82.52	71.57	44.37	36.68	48.08	70.17
1997	83.20	69.52	41.68	36.51	57.40	70.97
1998	83.20	71.08	55.84	32.29	56.65	70.86
1999	80.81	73.25	59.50	34.66		

Table 10.8 Gearing in the shipping industry (in percentages)

Further reading

Drewry Shipping Consultants, *Ship Finance: Choices, Competition and Risk/ Reward Equations*.

Grammenos, C, 'Credit risk, analysis and policy in bank shipping finance', in *Handbook of Maritime Economics and Business*, edited by Grammenos, C, Lloyd's of London Press, 2001.

Leggate, H K, 'A European perspective on bond finance for the maritime industry', *Maritime Policy and Management*, vol 27, no 4, 1999, 353–62.

Leggate, H K, and Carbone, V, 'Financial characteristics of the shipping industry: challenging the preconceptions', *IAME Conference Proceedings*, Hong Kong, July 2001.

Stokes, P, *Ship Finance, Credit Expansion and the Boom-Bust Cycle*, 2nd edn, Lloyd's of London Press, 1999.

Notes

1 UNCTAD *Review of Maritime Transport*.

2 Grammenos, C, 'Credit risk, analysis and policy in bank shipping finance', in *Handbook of Maritime Economics and Business*, edited by Grammenos, C, Lloyd's of London Press, 2001.

3 Stokes, P, *Ship Finance Credit Expansion and the Boom-Bust Cycle*, Lloyd's of London Press, 1999.

4 Frankel, J A, 'The Japanese cost of finance: a survey', *Financial Management*, Spring, 1991, 95–127.

5 Hoshi, T, Kashyap, A, Sharfstein, D, 'The role of banks in reducing the costs of financial distress in Japan', *NBER Working Paper* no 3435, Oct. 1990.

11 CHARTERS

As mentioned earlier, anyone wishing to send small amounts of cargo between A and B would almost certainly use a liner ship. A merchant wishing to send a large amount, particularly if in bulk, would charter or hire a suitable ship. Such a merchant or organisation is referred to as the *charterer*. As a great deal of money is involved (it can cost several thousands of pounds a day to hire a VLCC), each of the parties, the shipowner and charterer, will usually employ a specialist, called a shipbroker and charterer's agent respectively, to survey the market and conduct the negotiations for him.

The charter market for ships is a highly competitive one and the cost of chartering a vessel fluctuates from day to day in response to the variations in the supply and demand.

The formal contract drawn up between the shipowner and the charterer is known as the *charter party*, perhaps from the Latin *charta partita* (divided document). In Roman times the contract was written out in duplicate on a piece of parchment. This was then torn in two and the charterer and the shipowner each had a copy of the contract. If there were disputes, the two parts had to be matched together to test if they were the original genuine documents.

That this is a long-standing method of operating ships can be appreciated by the fact that the earliest written voyage charter party in the British Museum is dated AD 236. Somewhat surprisingly perhaps, it contains all the basic elements of a modern voyage charter party.

Different ways of chartering a ship

These are summarised below (and also in Table 11.1):

1 The ship can be chartered just as a hull. The charterer then supplies the crew and in fact operates the ship as if he were the shipowner. Such a charter is referred to as a *bareboat* or *demise charter*.
2 The ship can be chartered as a functioning operating unit for a period of time. The charterer pays the hire money and the bunkers, and the ship trades where the charterer wishes. This is a *time charter*.
3 The ship can be chartered to carry so much cargo between A and B. This is known as a *voyage charter*.

	Bareboat charter	Time charter	Voyage charter
Table 11.1	**Different ways of chartering a ship**		
Period	Usually long	Long-medium trip	One or more voyages
Points of difference	Considerable ship details	Ship details, bunker consumption, start and finish dates, exclusions – geographical and cargo	Laytime (dem-des) Spot
Problems	Charterers	Charterers/shipowners	Shipowners
Forms	Specific	Standard but clauses negotiable	Standard but clauses negotiable
When to use	Often type of financing or accounting method	Shipowners, before market turns down	Shipowners, on a rising market

Note: *COA, or 'contract', is a variation of consecutive voyage chartering. It is a contract between owner and charterer to move so much cargo on a regular basis. No ship is named, which is an advantage to owners with large fleets or in 'pools'.*

The bareboat or demise charter

As with all these types of charter, the conditions and responsibilities can vary to suit the needs of the two interested parties – in fact more so, for until Bimco produced the demise charter party forms Barecon A and Barecon B in the early 1970s, there were no standard demise charter party forms for sale, as there has been for time and voyage charter parties since about 1890. This means that most demise charter parties are negotiated afresh each time and therefore the contents of such contracts may vary considerably. Where it is used, for instance, as virtually a 'hire purchase' contract between a shipowner and a financier, it will be drawn up before the ship is built and contain considerable technical detail as to how the vessel is to be constructed. In this particular example, the ship will probably also become the 'charterer's' property at the end of the charter period.

Basically, the shipowner's only costs are depreciation, the survey to establish the actual condition of the ship before the charter, and the fees of the broker (*brokerage*) – who usually gets a percentage of the hire money (which is normally paid monthly in advance by the charterer).

The charterer is responsible for all the daily running costs, the bunkers, and all the port costs. He also usually has to pay for the survey before handing the vessel back to her owners.

This charter is generally for a longish period – say from about five years to perhaps the whole life of the ship.

This system was used quite extensively after the Second World War when shipowners with sadly depleted fleets were anxious to fill the gaps as quickly as possible. It is also used now by financiers who wish to invest in shipping, but don't have the desire or 'know-how' to become practising shipowners.

A variation on this charter includes a management clause whereby the shipowner, for a fee, crews the ship and generally attends to the ship's husbandry, leaving the charterer free simply to operate the ship.

The time charter

This can be for any period of time and may be for a few weeks (short time charter) to 15 years (long time charter). However, because of inflation over the last couple of decades, few owners in general trading have wished to commit themselves for periods much longer than two years. The hire charge may be expressed as a rate per day or as a rate per month per ton dwt. The hire money is usually paid two weeks in advance.

Shipowner's account	Charterer's account
Depreciation	Hire money
Insurance	Bunkers
Survey (if required)	Port charges
Overheads	Canal dues
Crews' wages and victualling	Stevedoring
Running costs	Ballast
Some cargo claims	Some cargo claims
Brokerage	Water

It is obvious that the vessel's speed and bunker consumption must be disclosed accurately by the shipowner. The charterer must, however, realise that between annual dry-dockings the vessel's speed can be reduced by 1–2 knots, depending on how growth on the hull increases the skin friction.

Who pays for the crews' overtime and what happens if there are any delays – such as the ship breaking down – are points that vary from charter to charter. The shipowner may also put trading limits on where the ship can operate. For instance, a few years ago he may not have wished it to go to Cuba and thus risk it being blacklisted by the USA. An owner might also want to exclude certain cargoes for political, technical or moral reasons.

Complications may also arise if the vessel is in mid-voyage when the charter expires.

A variation of the time charter that relates it to voyage chartering is the *trip time charter*. Here the charterer hires the ship to carry the cargo from A to B, but pays on a daily basis rather than a tonnage-moved basis.

The voyage charter

In this case, the shipowner pays for virtually everything, except perhaps the loading and discharging costs. Parties have to agree on laytime (cargo-handling time).

The charterer pays the freight. This is normally assessed at so much per ton of cargo carried or alternatively as a 'lump sum' for the voyage. The charterer also usually has to pay for any delays in the loading or discharging of the ship. This is known as *demurrage*. On the other hand, if he can turn the ship round faster than agreed, the shipowner usually shares the financial gain with him. This is referred to as *despatch*. The rate for despatch is usually half that for demurrage.

Ships can be chartered for a series of consecutive voyages, or perhaps a series of consecutive voyages followed by a period on time charter. Charterers may also charter not a specifically named vessel, but a certain size or class of vessel to do so many voyages. This may be of some financial benefit to the shipowner, who can take advantage of the various positions of his ships. This type of charter is sometimes referred to as a *contract of affreightment*. Such 'contract' arrangements can be used for all bulk cargoes and they form an important element in coastal shipping employment.

To take advantage of large COAs over the last two decades or so, owners have gone into joint ventures with colleagues to form *bulk shipping pools*. These have usually been owners with 'handy-size' tonnage, and the pool has had a central administration and been marketed as a single entity; the revenues earned have been pooled and distributed. By so pooling their resources, the owners have been able to reduce their ballast legs, reduce idle time, and enjoy higher load factors. Also, by being a larger unit they are spreading their risk and hopefully enjoy better income stabilisation. The pool also to some extent reduces the competition and, as the majority of the pools have been in Western Europe, this is obviously something the EU administration will continue to monitor with care. During 1994, there were somewhere in the region of 60 such pools operating in the 'handy-size' bulk-carrier market, gas carriers, reefers and car-carrier markets.

Should you use time charter or voyage charter?

The advantages to the shipowner of time charters is the security of an assured income over a known period of time. With large ships that have been paid for with borrowed money, the financial risks in not having the ship earning are such as to deter the shipowner from speculating on the spot voyage market and to look for a time charter. In fact, in the past, the long-term time charter often had to be obtained before the shipowner could get the loan of the money to buy the ship.

However, because of inflation and the difficulty of agreeing on acceptable 'escalation' clauses, long-term charters of the length used in the 1960s (15 years) are now seldom sought by shipowners.

The charterer, on the other hand, looks to meet his known requirements with time charters and to cover his fluctuating peak demands with voyage charters.

With some cargoes, such as iron ore, the long-term supplies and demands are known – so this type of cargo lends itself to long-term time charter. Grain, on the other hand, is seasonal and depends on the success of the harvest. Both the supply and the demand therefore fluctuates. A large percentage of grain is therefore carried on voyage charters. In practice, of course, some shipowners and charterers prefer voyage charters and some prefer time charters, and so they charter accordingly.

From an economic perspective, the ideal from the shipowner's point of view is to charter his vessel on a series of voyage charters on a rising market and to use a time charter to keep his ship employed when the market becomes depressed. This is, of course, easy to say with the benefit of hindsight. In fact, it is a question of luck or good judgement in estimating when the freight rates will stop rising and how long they will remain depressed.

The charterer will obviously try to do the opposite; in fact, a shipowner's first indication that the market might be improving could be when a charterer suggests a time charter! Which to use will obviously depend on many factors. In 1992, for instance, 57 per cent of the tonnage was voyage chartered, 0.5 per cent was consecutive voyage chartered, 2.8 per cent was on COA, 34 per cent was on trip time charters, while the remaining 5.7 per cent was on time charter. However, in 1998 in the tanker market, owners settled 40 per cent for time charters and 60 per cent for voyage charters.

Fig 11.2 is an actual example from 1970 showing how, for tankers, various types of chartering predominate depending on the level of freight rates.

The situation in 1970 was rather unusual in that the rates went up continuously for a period of about nine months. After about May, many shipowners were losing heart and switching to time charters, but come September many of the charterers lost their nerve and started to offer long-term time charters – many for 15 years. This should have been wonderful for those shipowners, and it *was* for a couple of years – until inflation turned these charters into a disaster.

Standard forms for charters

A printed standard form of charter party is not essential, but it makes the negotiations concerning the contract so much easier if the basic format and clauses are known and their legal interpretation understood by both sides. One of the unfortunate side-effects of this universal legal understanding is

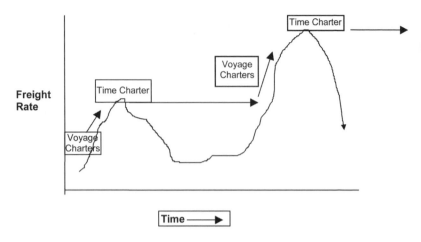

Fig 11.1   Which to use – time or voyage charter.

that once a standard form is accepted, those concerned are very loath to modernise and update the form. Many still contain verbal relics from the days of sail.

Charter party forms are drawn up either by shipowners' organisations such as Intertanko or large chartering organisations. Although the authors of these charters, in order to get the charter party accepted, have tried to be fair to all parties, they are invariably biased in favour of their own interests. However,

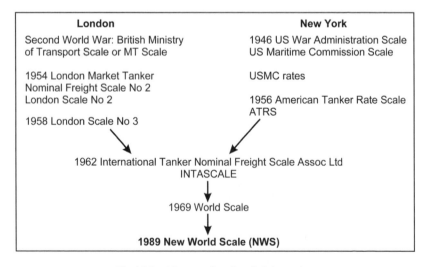

Fig 11.2   History of tanker freight scales.

clauses can be amended and additional clauses written in, depending on the circumstances of the case and the needs of both parties.

Norgrain (the North American Grain charter party), which was issued in 1973 and amended in 1989 to replace the Baltimore Form C, was however produced by a committee of all interested parties.

Typical standard forms (the date refers to the latest edition)

Time charters

- *Gentime 1999* Offers the market a realistic alternative to NYPE 1993.
- *New York Produce Exchange* (NYPE) 1993. The version introduced in 1981, known as Asbatime, was little used in comparison with the 1946 version, which has been the most commonly used dry-cargo time charter. It was originally introduced in 1913, with other amendments in 1921 and 1931. This is a general-purpose time charter. A charterer's charter party, the difference between this and the Baltime is noticeable in the 'off hire' conditions.
- *Baltime 1939 (amended box layout 1974)* This is a general-purpose time charter produced by Bimco (the Baltic and International Maritime Conference, a shipowners' and shipbrokers' organisation). It should be replaced by Gentime.
- *Linertime 1968 (amended box layout 1974)* This is a deep-sea time charter for chartering in liner tonnage, devised by Bimco. It should be replaced by Gentime.
- *Coasthire 1954* Chamber of Shipping coasting and short sea daily hire charter party.
- *Supply time Time charter for oil rig supply vessels.*
- *Sinotime 80* Time charter used by Chinese charterers.
- *Barecon 89* A Bimco-approved standard *bareboat* charter.
- *Oil time charter parties* tend to be oil company forms and are simply named after the company, eg BP time, Shelltime, etc. They usually have a number after them to indicate which version they are, such as Shelltime 5. There are also Bimco-approved oil time charter parties.

Voyage and general charters

- *Multiform 1982 (revised 1986)* A multi-purpose charter party. It was meant to replace – and be an improvement on – the old-fashioned, all-purpose Gencon. So far, the Gencon seems to have retained its popularity.
- *Gencon (as revised 1922, 1976 and 1994)* For carrying anything anywhere. This is the basic general charter – probably the most popular of the dry cargo charter parties.
- *Amwelsh 93* This has proved itself to be one of the most popular coal charter parties. It is also one of the oldest in origin as it was adopted in 1953 from the Chamber of Shipping Welsh Coal Charter of 1896.

- **Centrocon 1914** One of the 'classics'. Used for shipping grain homewards from the River Plate.
- **C ore 7** Popular ore charter party; basically for Mediterranean use, but it has been adopted for worldwide trading.
- **Sovorecon** Devised by the Moscow Ship Chartering Bureau. To be used for shipping ore and ore concentrates from the USSR.
- **Nubaltwood 1964** Timber charter party drawn up by the UK Timber Trade Shipowners' Mutual Association Ltd.
- **Synacomex 1962** Grain charter party drawn up by French charterers.
- **Saltcon 1937** Salt from Mediterranean to Norway, but can be used for all salt cargoes.
- **Sugar 77** For sugar charters.
- **Slothire 1993** Standard slot charter party.
- **Incharpass 1967** Drawn up by the Institute of Chartered Shipbrokers for chartering passenger ships.
- **Volcoa 83** Standard volume contract of affreightment for the transportation of bulk dry cargoes.

Tanker voyage charter parties

- **Intertankvoy 1971**, revised as **Tankervoy 86**. Drawn up by Intertanko (Association of Independent Tanker Owners) for use when chartering to large oil consumers who have no standard form of their own.
- **Shell Voy 5, Bee Pee Voy, etc**. Voyage charter parties used by major oil companies.
- **Biscoilvoy 86** Standard charter for vegetable/animal oils and fats.

Structure of standard forms

Time charter form

- Date, name and address of shipowner and charterer.
- Description of ship – name, where registered, tonnages, capacities, draft, horsepower, speed, fuel consumption, cargo gear, pumps, and heating coils, etc.
- Condition of ship and classification society.
- Trading limits.
- Hire money, how paid, what currency to be used, and when payments to be made.
- What breakdowns or delays cause the vessel to come off hire.
- Date hire commences and date completed; *where* hire commences.
- Charterers to have the right to complain and perhaps remove master or chief engineer. There will probably also be clauses concerning strikes, war, ice and how bunkers onboard on delivery and re-delivery are to be paid for.
- How arbitration should be organised in the event of a dispute.
- How general average claims should be settled.

- How the annual dry-docking will be fitted in.

Voyage charter party form

- Date, name and address of shipowner and charterer.
- Description of ship – name and where registered, tonnages, capacities, draft and cargo gear relevant to the cargo in question.
- Nature of goods to be shipped and in what manner; name of loading and discharging ports.
- Date vessel is to arrive at the loading port and date after which charter party may be cancelled.
- The laytime allowed, when it is to start and what holidays, if any, will be allowed; the freight rate and currency.
- The demurrage and despatch rate; whose agents are to be used.
- How the problems of strikes, ice, congestion in ports, shortage of cargo, etc to be settled.
- There will also be clauses on arbitration and general average, as in the time charter, and perhaps details of the route to be followed and under what conditions the vessel might be allowed to deviate from it.

Voyage estimating

Before going out into the 'market' to charter his ship, the shipowner must first be able to assess which 'offer' is going to give him the best rate of return. As voyages are of different length and involve different costs, it is not enough to compare only freight rates; he must prepare a *voyage estimate* for any of the 'offers' that seem to him to have possibilities.

Preparing a voyage estimate entails four separate steps:

1 How long will the voyage take: sea time + port time?
2 How much cargo can the ship carry, and therefore how much freight will the ship earn?
3 How much will the voyage cost the shipowner?
4 What is the ship's daily profit? (We must note that it is the daily profit that is important for comparing voyages of different lengths.)

1 How long will the voyage take?

The following factors need to be taken into account:

- The distance ... derived from distance tables.
- The speed ... must be a speed you can expect the ship to be able to maintain on this particular voyage. Therefore the sea time = distance/ (speed $\times$ 24).
- The port time is difficult to assess without experience of the trade. If in doubt, fax your agent at the port for an estimate. Your estimate must include the effects of any congestion and/or holidays. Are there liable to be delays from strike action?

Having established the total time, calculate the bunker consumption:

> Total bunkers required = time at sea × daily fuel consumption
> + time in port × port fuel consumption

2 How much cargo/how much freight will be earned?

- What is the limiting loadline? (See the calculation at the end of Chapter 1.) What is the maximum dwt the ship can carry at this draft?
- The ship will have to carry enough bunkers for the voyage plus a safe reserve. However, if at the loading port bunkers are cheap (say £Bc a ton) and at the discharging port they are expensive (say £Be a ton), then you will have to consider taking extra.
  This will occur if: Be − Bc is greater than the freight rate per ton.
- The ship will also consume a few tons of stores and water each day. Therefore the cargo dwt = maximum dwt − (bunkers + stores + water).
- However, the ship may be full before it is down to its marks, so the limiting factor will be the ship's 'cubic' capacity. This will occur if: 'ship's cubic'/'cargo stowage factor' is less than the cargo dwt.
- Therefore the freight earned for the voyage will be:

> Freight earned = tons of cargo × freight rate per ton

3 How much will the voyage cost the shipowner?
(see also Chapter 8)

DRC (daily running costs) × total time	=
Bunkers requirements (at sea + in port) × cost per ton	=
Cargo-handling costs (if not paid for by the charterer)	=
Other port costs	=
Canal costs (if any)	=
Other, ie extra insurance	=
TOTAL COST	=

4 What is the ship's daily profit?
Profit per day = (total freight − total cost)/total time

Most shipowners now have computer programs that actually do the calculation, providing the necessary 'inputs' are made; however, the following example shows that it is not difficult. (Appendix B shows how the calculation can be done using an XL spreadsheet.)

Example of a voyage estimate for a bulk carrier with a dwt of about 26,000 tons and a speed of 14.5 knots

The vessel at the moment is at Rotterdam and is to load at Tampa for Vancouver. The cargo is phosphate and the freight offered is $14 a ton. The loading and discharging cost will be paid for, ie it is FIO.

From–to	Distance	Time (days at sea)	Time (days in port)
Rotterdam–Tampa	4,558	13.5	–
Tampa loading			4
Tampa–Cristobal	1,212	3.5	
Panama transit		1	
Balboa–Vancouver	4,150	12	
Vancouver discharge			7
TOTAL TIME		30	11 = 41

Total cargo = dwt tonnage less stores and bunkers on board

= 26,000 − (300 + 700)

= 25,000 tons

Total freight = 14 × 25,000 = $350,000

Commission at 6 per cent = $21,000

TOTAL EARNINGS = **$329,000**

At sea the vessel consumes 34 tons of fuel oil for her main engines and 2 tons of diesel oil for her generators. In port she needs just 1 ton of diesel.

Cost of fuel oil is $97 a ton. Cost of diesel oil is $132 a ton.

Cost of fuel oil for trip = 30 × 34 × 97	= $98,940
Cost of diesel oil for trip = 132 × 11 + 132 × 30 × 2	= $9,372
Running cost of $3,000 a day for 41 days	= $123,000
Port charges:	
Rotterdam (leaving)	= $1,000
Tampa	= $10,000
Panama Canal	= $50,000
Vancouver	= $11,000
TOTAL COST	= $303,312

Total earnings = $329,000

TOTAL COST = **$303,312**

Profit = $25,688

PROFIT PER DAY = **$626.54**

Notes: 1 To give an accurate assessment for comparing the profitability of different offers, the shipowner should include any ballast run and/or other costs incurred before loading the next cargo.

2 It is not usual to include administration costs and capital repayment costs in these estimates, perhaps because, as stated earlier, these are often difficult to quantify. However, they are both 'fixed' costs and therefore do not affect the 'profit comparison', which is the purpose of this calculation. It does mean, however, that the profit figure is too large and, when it is considered that for a modern expensive vessel the capital repayments may be the largest single cost, this distortion to the 'profit' figure may be considerable. In fact, in the example given, if the administration and capital costs had been included, such a voyage would be shown to be making a loss, not a profit.

How shipowners get 'offers' for their vessels

The shipowner may entrust his ship to just one broker, who can discreetly 'sound out the market' to determine the most lucrative employment for his principal's ship. In fact, if the owner has a house broker, such a broker would know when his principal's ships would next be open.

The shipowner may, on the other hand, decide to advertise his vessel to several brokers, who will then compete with one another to find the best employment for the ship. This latter method will certainly mean a more comprehensive assessment of the market. However, by making his interest public knowledge, the shipowner might, at certain states of the market, tend to lower prices.

Shipbrokers work and operate at major shipping centres such as London, New York, Hong Kong, Singapore, Shanghai, Oslo and Tokyo. London, though, is still perhaps the most important chartering centre and it has one unique feature, the *Baltic Exchange*. In 1993, the total world dry-bulk cargo was estimated to be 2,600 million tons, of which more than 50 per cent was at some stage handled by the 'Baltic'. For tanker chartering, London brokers have an even bigger share of the market; and for sale and purchase, London dominates entirely.

In the late 1960s, a Norwegian company explored the obvious possibilities of using computers to match up cargoes and ships, but the idea did not succeed. In 2000, Sealogistics and OneSeaDirect announced that they would be combined to create an internet-based chartering service, mainly for tankers.

The Baltic Exchange

- Like Lloyd's and the Stock Exchange, the Baltic grew up from the coffee houses frequented by men with a common interest – which, in the case of the Baltic, were shipowners and merchants. Two of the more famous coffee houses used for this purpose were the Jerusalem Coffee House and the Virginia and Baltic.

- By 1810, the volume of business caused a move to be made to the Antwerp tavern in Threadneedle Street, which was renamed the Baltic.
- In 1823, the Baltic became a club with a membership limited to 300.
- In 1891, a second shipping exchange was formed in London, but in 1899 a joint committee was formed between the two and, in January 1900, the Baltic Mercantile and Shipping Exchange was incorporated as a public limited company.
- In 1903, the building in St Mary Axe was opened and an extension into an adjoining bomb site after the Second World War was inaugurated in 1956 by Her Majesty Queen Elizabeth II.
- In 1982, the name was officially changed to the Baltic Exchange Ltd, when it was re-registered as a private limited company.
- In 1992, the historic building was severely damaged by a terrorist bomb after which, until it took up residence at 38 St Mary Axe in 1995, it operated at Lloyd's of London for a year before moving back to an extension in its old building.

The function of the 'Baltic' The Baltic is a centre for chartering ships or, to be more accurate, a meeting place or market where shipbroker and charterer's agent can meet, exchange information, and negotiate quickly and informally. Business is conducted verbally and members are proud of their motto – 'Our word is our bond'. In fact, this is more than a motto, as the member companies see it as a commercial necessity to maintain high business standards.

It is a forum where those concerned with the chartering of dry cargo ships can physically meet to conduct business. Many have argued, especially those located outside of London, that in this modern age, with all its high-tech efficient communication systems, there is no longer any need for the Baltic. It is true that its daily sessions are not as crowded as they used to be, but London can still claim to be the world's major chartering centre and the Baltic provides a focus and a readily identifiable centre where ideas and information can be exchanged and standards policed, maintained and monitored. In addition to the floor, the Baltic has – together with the traditional bar, coffee room and restaurant – the availability of meeting rooms. It is in these facilities that the work of the brokers is extended as they mingle with maritime lawyers, ship financiers, arbitrators, insurance brokers, P&I club representatives and the world of shipping in general.

The Baltic now has a website which, among other things, shows four daily dry indices and 24 individual routes which are published at 1300 London time, and 11 individual tanker routes which are published at 1600 London time. A list of dry bulk fixtures concluded over the past 24 hours is gleaned from the market and published on a daily basis at 1300.

In 1999, it was estimated that the Baltic was involved in 50 per cent of all tanker fixtures, 50 per cent of all S&P fixtures, and 30 per cent of all dry cargo fixtures. In *Our Mutual Friend*, Charles Dickens describes St Mary Axe as 'the heart of the City'. As regards shipping, this sentiment can probably still be considered true.

Many dry cargo shipbrokers still have their offices within easy walking distance, though the high office rents in the 1980s in the City forced many to relocate to cheaper areas of London.

The broker, having surveyed the market, will advise the shipowner of the various possibilities, perhaps recommending one particular line of action.

The fixture

The freight rate is not the only consideration for shipowners. Some cargoes, like scrap iron, may damage the ship and the future employment at the end of the charter must also be considered. Will a long ballast journey be necessary, or can a cargo be picked up from the discharge port? Should the shipowner be looking for a quick voyage charter, or is this the time to consider a time charter? Much will depend on his and the broker's future expectations of the market.

On receiving the suggestions from the broker, the shipowner can go ahead and make a *firm offer*. This offer will have a time limit, eg 'offer open to 1500'. The owner may not offer his ship elsewhere until the time expires, or the charterer rejects his offer. The following tabulates the typical components with an example of a firm offer:

Ship details m.v. Fred s.dk B.C. Br fg built 1981 38,000 dwt
Cargo details 36,000 lt 5% MOLOO bk wheat
Load port / Discharge port OSB New Orleans to OSB Hamburg
Freight rate USD 10.40 FIOT (perhaps going rate 9.50)
Arrival and cancelling dates 15/31 July 1995
Laytime 12000/9000 WD 24 Consec WP SHEX
Demurrage and despatch Dem USD 8,200 pd pro rata D1/2D Laytime saved
Charter party Norgrain
Total commissions
Any other points Subject Details

In this example the owner is offering his ship called *Fred*, which is a single-deck bulk carrier, registered under the British flag, built in 1981, having a total dwt of 38,000 tons. The rest of the offer you should be able to interpret, using the following list of abbreviations. However, a special mention should perhaps be made concerning such conditional expressions as 'subject details'. These expressions have been used quite frequently, but organisations such as Bimco have on many occasions warned against their use. They are illegal under American law and a source of possible dispute between parties not used to doing business with one another.

Having received the above fax, the charterer may then accept, reject or counter offer.

If the charterer were interested, one would expect him to *counter offer*, saying 'accept except....' and then try to reduce the freight rates and tighten up on the arrival and cancelling dates which are rather wide. Perhaps the charterer is looking for two or more safe discharge berths.

Offers and counter offers would continue between the two until hopefully they come to an agreement and have a *fixture*. Charter parties would then be drawn up, signed and exchanged.

Important chartering terms and abbreviations

Chartering will nearly always involve communication by e-mail, fax, etc where, in order to save time and money, abbreviations are often used. These savings were considerable in the past, but the abbreviations are now an established part of the chartering culture. These abbreviations may appear almost spontaneously as a frequently needed phrase appears, and very often one abbreviation can mean many things (BSC can be British Shippers' Council, British Steel Corporation, British Sugar Corporation etc), so it is often necessary to know the context in order to determine the meaning.

Below, some of the more widely used and better established phrases and abbreviations are explained:

Abbreviations concerning despatch

- D1/2D. Despatch rate to be half the demurrage rate.
- DDO. Despatch discharge only.
- DLO. Despatch loading only.
- DBEAT. Despatch payable at both ends on all time saved.
- DBELTS. Despatch payable at both ends on laytime saved.
- FD. Free of despatch.

Abbreviations and phrases concerning laytime

- Notice of Readiness. This is the declaration given by the master to say that the ship has arrived and is ready to load the cargo. The start of laytime is usually related to this time.
- SHINC. Sundays and holidays inclusive, ie they are included in the laytime.
- SHEX. Sundays and holidays excluded.
- WWD. Weather working days, ie if there is bad weather, deductions can be made from the laytime.
- Working days – weather permitting – is similar to the above, but deductions are only allowable if work would have taken place had the weather been fine.
- PWWD.SSHEX. UU. Per weather working day, Saturdays, Sundays and holidays excepted unless used.
- PWWD. SSHEX. IUATUTC. Per weather working day, Saturdays, Sundays and holidays excepted. If used, actual time used to count.
- FAC. Fast as can, ie ship to be loaded as quickly as possible.

Abbreviations and phrases concerning chartering

Concerning who pays for what:

- CPD. Charterer pays dues.
- FIO. Free in and out, ie charterer pays cargo-handling costs.
- FIOS. Free in and out and stowed.
- FIOT. Free in and out and trimmed.
- FIOSPT. Free in and out — spout trimmed.
- 4,000 gross/2,000t free. This is an example stating that the ship should load at 4,000 tons per day (ie laydays = cargo dwt/4,000) and the shipowner has to pay for the loading. At the discharge port, the cargo should be handled at 2,000 tons per day and the charterer will pay the cost.
- Gross terms or liner terms. The shipowner has to pay for the cargo handling.

Abbreviations and phrases concerning the ship and cargo

- BIBO. Bulk in, bags out.
- DLOSP. Dropping last outward sea pilot — usually for when time starts or stops in a time charter.
- DWCC. Dwt cargo carrying, ie the weight of cargo the ship can carry.
- ETA. Estimated time of arrival.
- ETD. Estimated time of departure.
- ETS. Estimated time of sailing.
- MOLOO. More or less at owner's option. When agreeing on the cargo dwt, the owner usually likes to allow himself a small percentage more or less, as he may not be certain of the bunker and stores situation. Alternatively, they may agree on 'max–min' dwts.
- MOLCHOPT. More or less at charterer's option.
- aa. always afloat.
- naabsa. not always afloat but safely aground.
- FOW. First open water. This usually refers to ports closed by ice in the winter.
- SWAD. Salt water arrival draft.
- IWL. Institute (of insurance) Warranty Limits. There are certain areas that the underwriters exclude from their normal cover. If the charterer wishes to send his ships to these regions, extra premiums would have to be negotiated.
- HHDWS. Heavy handy dead-weight scrap.
- Sous Palan. This is French for 'under the hook' and is usually used with reference to where the shipowner's responsibility for the cargo starts and finishes, ie when he lifts it on, to when he lifts it off.
- SPOT. A term used for a vessel that is so positioned that it can start loading immediately.
- YAR. York Antwerp Rules (see section on general average).
- WIPON. Whether in port or not.
- WIBON. Whether in berth or not.

Abbreviations concerning the range of ports the charterer has the option of sending the ship to

- A/H. Antwerp to Hamburg.
- BCNS. Barry, Cardiff, Newport, Swansea.
- CH&H. Continent between Havre and Hamburg.
- HH. Havre to Hamburg.
- HA&D. Havre, Antwerp & Dunkirk.
- LHAR. London, Hull, Antwerp or Rotterdam.
- UKHH. UK or Havre or Hamburg.
- USNH. United States North of Cape Hatteras.
- Northern Range. US ports of Newport News, Philadelphia, Baltimore, New York, Boston, Portland.
- OSP. One safe port.
- BB. Below bridges.
- BNA. British North Atlantic.
- BBB. Before breaking bulk — ie freight payable BBB.

Other abbreviations

- L/A. Lloyd's Agents. These are usually ship's agencies who also act on behalf of Lloyd's of London. They form a major part of the worldwide information service that keeps Lloyd's informed. They assist ships that are damaged and insured with Lloyd's to get good repairs at a fair cost to the underwriter.
- FONASBA. Federation of National Association of Shipbrokers and Agents. The ICS (Institute of Chartered Shipbrokers), representing the UK, has played a leading role in this organisation since its inception a few years ago.

Charter party laytime definitions

- *Port.* This means an area within which ships are loaded with and/or discharged of cargo and includes the usual places where ships wait for their turn or are ordered or obliged to wait for their turn no matter the distance from that area.
    If the word 'port' is not used, but the port is (or is to be) identified by its name, this definition will still apply.
- *Safe port.* This means a port which, during the relevant period of time, the ship can reach, enter, remain at and depart from without, in the absence of some abnormal occurrence, being exposed to danger that cannot be avoided by good navigation and seamanship.
- *Berth.* This means the specific place where the ship is to load and/or discharge. If the word 'berth' is not used, but the specific place is (or is to be) identified by its name, this definition shall still apply.
- *Safe berth.* This means a berth which, during the relevant period of time, the ship can reach, remain at and depart from without, in the absence of some abnormal occurrence, being exposed to danger that cannot be avoided by good navigation and seamanship.

- *Reachable on arrival*. This means that the charterer undertakes that when the ship arrives at the port there will be a loading/discharging berth for her, to which she can proceed without delay.
- *Time lost waiting for berth*. To count as loading/discharging time or (laytime) means that if the only reason why a notice of readiness cannot be given is that there is no loading/discharging berth available to the ship, the laytime will commence to run when the ship starts to wait for a berth and will continue to run, unless previously exhausted, until the ship stops waiting.

  The laytime exceptions apply to the waiting time, as if the ship were at the loading/discharging berth. When the waiting time ends, time ceases to count and restarts when the ship reaches the loading/discharging berth subject to the giving of a notice of readiness, if one is required by the charter party, and to any notice time if provided for in the charter party, whether or not the ship is then on demurrage.
- *Laytime*. This means the period of time agreed between the parties during which the owner will make and keep the ship available for loading/discharging without payment additional to the freight.
- *Customary despatch*. This means that the charterer must load and/or discharge as fast as is possible in the circumstances prevailing at the time of loading or discharging.
- *Per hatch per day*. This means that laytime is to be calculated by multiplying the agreed daily rate per hatch of loading/discharging the cargo by the number of the ship's hatches and dividing the quantity of cargo by the resulting sum. Thus:

$$\text{Laytime} = \text{quantity of cargo}/(\text{daily rate} \times \text{number of hatches})$$

$$= \text{days}$$

A hatch that is capable of being worked by two gangs simultaneously shall be counted as two hatches.
- *Per working hatch per day or per workable hatch per day*. This means that laytime is to be calculated by dividing the quantity of cargo in the hold with the largest quantity by the result of multiplying the agreed daily rate per working or workable hatch by the number of hatches serving that hold. Thus:

$$\text{Laytime} = \text{largest quantity in one hold}/(\text{daily rate per hatch}$$

$$\times \text{number of hatches serving that hold})$$

A hatch that is capable of being worked by two gangs simultaneously shall be counted as two hatches.

- *As fast as the vessel can receive/deliver.* This means that the laytime is a period of time to be calculated by reference to the maximum rate at which the ship in full working order is capable of loading/discharging the cargo.
- *Day.* This means a continuous period of 24 hours which, unless the context otherwise requires, runs from midnight to midnight.
- *Clear day or clear days.* This means that the day on which the notice is given, and the day on which the notice expires, are not included in the notice period.
- *Holiday.* This means a day of the week or part(s) thereof on which cargo work on the ship would normally take place, but is suspended at the place of loading/discharging by reason of either the local law or the local practice.
- *Working days.* This means days or part(s) thereof that are not expressly excluded from laytime by the charter party and that are not holidays.
- *Running days or consecutive days.* This means days that follow one immediately after the other.
- *Weather working day.* This means a working day, or part of a working day, during which it is or, if the vessel is still waiting for her turn, it would be possible to load/discharge the cargo without interference due to the weather. If such interference occurs (or would have occurred if work had been in progress), there shall be excluded from the laytime a period calculated by reference to the ratio which the duration of the interference bears to the time which would have, or could have been, worked but for the interference.
- *Weather working day of 24 consecutive hours.* This means a working day, or part of a working day of 24 hours, during which it is or, if the ship is still waiting for her turn, it would be possible to load/discharge the cargo without interference due to the weather. If such interference occurs (or would have occurred if work had been in progress) there shall be excluded from the laytime the period during which the weather interfered or would have interfered with the work.
- *Weather permitting.* This means that time during which weather prevents working shall not count as laytime.
- *To average.* This means that separate calculations are to be made for loading and discharging and any time saved in one operation is to be set against any excess time used in the other.
- *Reversible.* This means an option given to the charterer to add together the time allowed for loading and discharging. Where the option is exercised, the effect is the same as a total time being specified to cover both operations.

The final reckoning

The total earnings for a voyage charter will consist of the freight plus any demurrage that has been incurred. The deductions will consist of the fixed costs for the period of the voyage, the running costs, the port dues and disbursements, and any despatch that has to be paid.

To calculate what demurrage or despatch has been incurred, it is necessary to complete a time sheet. There follows a time sheet for *MV Reed* at the load port:

Relevant extracts from the charter party

- Laytime to commence at 1300 if notice of readiness given before noon, at 0700 next working day if given after noon: notice to be given in ordinary office hours.
- Laytime shall not commence to count before holds are passed as clean by shippers' inspector.
- Cargo to be loaded at the rate of 5,000 metric tons per weather working day of 24 consecutive hours.
- Time from 1700 Friday or the day preceding a holiday to 0800 Monday or next working day not to count unless used (but only actual time used to count) or unless vessel already on demurrage.
- Demurrage $4,000 (USD) per day and pro rata/despatch at half demurrage rate on laytime saved.

Statement of facts

Arrived	*0600 Thursday 9 February*
NOR given	*0900 Thursday 9 February*
Holds passed by inspector	*1400 Thursday 9 February*
Loading commenced	*0700 Friday 10 February*
Ship worked from 0700 to noon	*Saturday 11 February*

(Note ship was not worked during any other excepted period.)

Rain stopped all work in port	*0700 to 1130 Tuesday 14 February*
Loading completed	*1515 Wednesday 15 February*
Sailed	*0600 Thursday 16 February*

Cargo loaded 22,000 metric tons

Repairs to vessel's main auxiliary engine delayed sailing after completion of loading.

Normal port working hours are 0700–1700 Tuesday to Friday

Normal port working hours are 0800–1700 Monday and days after a holiday

Time sheet

Date	Day	Time allowed			Total time used			Remarks
		d	h	m	d	h	m	
9 Feb	Thur		10			10		Laytime commences 1400 hrs
10 Feb	Fri		17		1	3		Laytime stops 1700 hrs see C/P
11 Feb	Sat		5		1	8		Worked from 0700 to 1200 see C/P
12 Feb	Sun		0		1	8		A holiday – no work done
13 Feb	Mon		16		2	0		Laytime continues from 0800
14 Feb	Tues		19	30	2	19	30	Rain stops work from 0700 to 1130
15 Feb	Wed		15	15	3	10	45	Loading completed 1515

Total laytime allowed	= 22,000/5,000 = 4d 9h 36m
Total laytime used	= 3d 10h 45m
Total laytime saved	= 22h 5m (22.85 hrs)
Despatch payable	= 2,000 × 22.85/24 = **$1,904.2**

Notes: 1 The delay caused by the repairs to the auxiliary engine has no bearing on the time sheet. The cost of the delay is for the shipowner's account.
2 The despatch or demurrage is calculated by compiling a time sheet at the loading and discharging ports.
3 The shipowner will have to pay despatch on 22.85 hours for the above conditions, but in practice the amount will depend on the terms of the charter party. Is despatch, for instance, to be paid on laytime saved or all time saved? If the laytime is termed reversible, the total laytime for the round voyage is considered as one calculation. If the laytime is to be averaged, you would calculate the days on despatch or demurrage incurred at discharge and then add to or subtract from the time saved in loading.

Arbitration in charter party disputes

Occasionally, due to exceptional or unusual circumstances or the careless-ness in the wording of an additional clause that has been inserted into the charter party by either the shipbroker or the charter's agent, a dispute arises. If it is an important issue and the parties concerned wish to establish a precedent, it may go to court. This, however, is a lengthy and expensive procedure and most charter parties contain an arbitration clause, usually stating that any disputes should be settled by either arbitration in London or New York. The following is an arbitration clause from Intertankvoy:

'Any dispute arising out of this charter party shall be referred to arbitration in London, one arbitrator being appointed by each party, in accordance with the Arbitration Act 1950 or any statutory modification or re-enactment thereof for the time being in force. On receipt by any one party of the nomination in writing of the other party's arbitrator, that party shall appoint their arbitrator within 14 days failing which the decision of the single arbitrator appointed shall apply. If two arbitrators properly appointed shall not agree they shall appoint an umpire whose decision is final.'

A list of arbitrators is kept at the Baltic. The arbitrators, whose qualifications and experience are listed in full, are commercial men with shipping experience.

The 1925 Federal Arbitration Act governs the arbitration of all maritime disputes in the USA. An arbitration clause from the New York Produce Exchange is reprinted here:

'That should any dispute arise between owners and charterers, the matter in dispute shall be referred to three persons at New York, one to be appointed by each of the parties hereto, and the third by the two so chosen; their decision or that of any two of them: shall be final, and for the purpose of enforcing any award, this agreement may be made a rule of the court. The Arbitrators shall be commercial men.'

Under both English and American law, an arbitration award can be enforced through the courts as though it were a decree of the court. Under American law, an arbitration award is final and cannot be challenged in the courts; but under English law, the aggrieved party can move a court to set aside the award on the grounds that the award was *ultra vires*.

Mediation

The Centre of Dispute Resolution also offers mediation services with regard to charter party disputes.

The tanker market and chartering

The tanker market and its chartering practice tends to differ from the dry cargo market in that it has a different history, different technology, fewer players, and is forced by the nature of its cargo to display greater environmental awareness.

The market background

Although 'oil' had been found and used to some extent in the ancient Babylonian Empire, its real commercial potential only started to emerge at the end of the nineteenth century, particularly in the USA.

The USA, like the Middle East, is naturally endowed with large deposits of easily obtainable crude oil. This natural supply, coupled with the entrepreneurial genius of such men as Rockefeller, is the main reason for the American dominance of the oil market (until, that is, OPEC appeared on the scene in the early 1970s). This is also why most of the oil multinationals are American and why New York was for so long the main centre of tanker chartering.

The Dutch (through Shell) and the UK (through BP) enjoyed good concessions of oil in various parts of the world, though they lost most of these in the years following the Second World War. This shift in the political control of many oil sources led to a number of countries, for strategic reasons, refining the oil at destination rather than source. Others argue that the main reason for the change in the position with regard to refining was the rapid development of the chemical industry at this time. However, whatever the reason, the early 1950s saw significant changes in the tanker industry:

- A large growth in tanker cargoes in the 1950s and 1960s as the oil was now carried twice. First as crude oil from source to refinery, and then the refined oil had to be distributed.

  1950 – tankers carried 225 million tons of oil

  1960 – tankers carried 540 million tons of oil

  1970 – tankers carried 1,440 million tons of oil

- The above development saw the increase in tanker size in general, as at the end of the Second World War 16,000 dwt was the largest tanker, whereas by the end of the 1950s there were 100,000 dwt tankers, and by the end of the 1960s we had the VLCC. This general growth in size also saw the specific dedication of a class of tankers as *crude oil carriers*.

- The 16,000 dwt tankers, built in their hundreds by the Americans during the Second World War, were known as T2s. The T2 was so commonplace at this time that it became the unit of measurement for refineries, which would measure their requirements in the number of T2s per month.

  Another different unit of measurement in the oil industry is the barrel. Because of the American dominance of the market, crude oil price and quantity is often quoted in 'barrels'. As it is a measure of volume, its conversion to tons depends on its density. Approximately, it is 7 barrels per ton, eg Valdez crude is 7.054, Kuwait crude is 7.253, Bonny crude is 7.410.

- This growth in the global tanker fleet also saw the growth in what are called *independent tanker owners* – ie owners who are independent from the major oil companies. Before the Second World War the oil companies owned 70 per cent of the tanker fleet and the independents owned 30 per cent. By the mid-1970s, the situation had reversed – with the oil companies only owning 30 per cent of the tonnage, and since then this percentage has been steadily decreasing. This growth of independents has of course meant a growth in tanker chartering.

The year 1973 and the rise of oil prices saw an increase in the power of OPEC, with a consequent reduction in the power of the large oil companies in oil trading and the growth of oil traders speculating in the market. These oil traders now form a large proportion of the tanker charterers, and as such have affected tanker chartering in several ways:

- They buy the oil, charter and load a tanker and then try to sell the oil at a profit during the voyage. This explains why much tanker chartering is 'open-ended', ie the precise destination is not stated when the fixture is made. This is one of the advantages of using *scale rates* (more on this later).
- As the cargo may be sold several times during a voyage, care must be taken to deliver the cargo to the right owner. In this context, masters are well advised not to discharge without sight of the bill of lading (B/L). This can create problems if the ship and cargo arrive before the documents. Also, although oil companies can be considered 'blue chip' as charterers, the same may not be said of all oil traders, so it may be worth checking the financial credibility of unknown charterers. For this sort of service, the IMB (International Maritime Bureau) can be very helpful.

The rise in oil prices also caused an increase in indigenous oil sources being developed all around the world, eg North Sea oil. In its turn, this has had a great impact on oil trading patterns, tanker requirements and the power of OPEC.

Technical constraints in tanker chartering

A quick comparison between a dry cargo charter party and a tanker charter party will show that the tanker charter party involves a great deal more precise technical information and knowledge than its dry cargo equivalent. It is therefore important to become familiar with the more important of these technical matters.

Tank cleaning Tanks have to be cleaned to avoid contaminating the next cargo. Even if the next cargo were the same, without some cleaning there would be a build-up of sludge that would hinder the draining and the pumping of the oil.

The problem of the build-up of sludge has, since the early 1980s, been reduced by the introduction of *crude oil washing* (COW) on crude-oil tankers, which have the greatest sludge problem. This is a technique where the tanks are washed with crude oil during discharge. From a commercial point of view, it should be noted that COW can increase the total discharge time. Also, to do it well, it is necessary that the crew members concerned with this task are well trained and highly motivated.

The main problem concerning tank washing has been the problem of dirty ballast. This has almost certainly in the past been the main cause of pollution of the oceans by tankers. Traditionally, after discharging its cargo, tankers had to take in ballast to make them seaworthy for the return trip to the load port. This ballast was loaded into the cargo tanks where it became contaminated by the oil left behind. When this ballast was discharged, pollution occurred. Over the years, various precautions were taken to reduce this, such as *load on top* (LOT). Following this came the MARPOL/SOLAS Convention, which requires COW and *segregated ballast tanks* (SBT) for most tankers. The consequence of this was that the carrying capacity of tankers of a particular size was reduced, as about 30 per cent of the tanks are now used only for ballast.

A further major reason for removing the oily residues in the tank was that if they were not removed they evaporated, and the gas air mixture in the tank became highly explosive. This problem has been largely removed by *inert gas systems* (IGS), whereby the tanks are filled with an inert gas when discharging. However, the IGS system costs money to operate and the apparatus is subject to failure and misuse, so it is not always working or working correctly.

To facilitate cleaning and to reduce corrosion, the tank sides (bulkheads) are often coated with special paints or coverings. These coatings are often mentioned in the charter party as the charterer may be worried that his cargo could be contaminated by the coating. On the other hand, charterers like to load the cargo hot, as in this state it is easier to pump. If the cargo is too hot — say, above 135 °F — it may damage these coatings, hence a maximum temperature is often given in the charter party.

Pumps and pipelines   The oil is usually pumped into the tanker through pipelines. The 'plumbing' and pipeline arrangements can be complex, particularly for a product tanker, so charterers may wish to see and inspect a copy of the pipeline system before chartering.

The ship's pipeline system is connected to the shore system by a flexible pipeline and the connection is made at the manifold, usually in the centre of the ship. So here the tanker will need a derrick or crane to handle this flexible connection.

Tankers use their own pumps for discharging and ballasting, and tankers of all sizes are nearly always allowed the same laytime for loading and discharging, ie 72 hours. This means that larger tankers must have larger pumps, and in general when designing a tanker the pumping capacity is made about 10 per cent of the dwt — ie a 100,000 dwt tanker should be able to pump at about 10,000 tons per hour. This doesn't mean that tankers can discharge in 10 hours, as the final draining and stripping of the tanks can take considerable time. Much also depends on how far the oil has to be pumped and the diameter of the pipelines. This problem is measured as *back pressure*, a term that may appear in the charter party.

To facilitate pumping heavy oils, the oil may need heating before discharge. It must not be assumed that all tankers have equal heating facilities and charterers may require the oil to be kept at, or brought to, a certain temperature. Heating cargoes can also be expensive.

How is the amount of oil in a tank measured? The distance from the surface of the oil to the top of the tank is known as the *ullage*. Each tanker will have a set of tables for each tank; so once the ullage is known, the volume of the oil is known.

To convert the volume into a weight, the density and temperature of the oil must be measured with great care as, particularly on a large tanker, a small error in any of these readings will lead to a large error in the final assessment. Charter parties will contain clauses on measurement and the penalties to be exacted if the tanker does not deliver the required amount.

Verification of technical details Most charterers cannot afford to risk the financial liabilities or the bad media publicity if the tanker they charter is found, after causing some pollution, to be in poor technical shape. To ensure therefore that the ship is in reality in a satisfactory state, the OCIMF (the Oil Companies International Marine Forum) has introduced *SIRE* (Ship Inspection Report programme). SIRE maintains a readily accessible pool of technical information and operational procedures for tankers. This information is obtained by a physical inspection of the ship and is readily accessible to charterers (even if they are not OCIMF members), as well as other organisations such as port and canal authorities and government authorities. The owner's response to the report is also part of the same data base.

Differences regarding chartering tankers

It is often the custom in tanker chartering for only one broker to be involved. Furthermore, as most of the oil companies' offices are not in easy walking distance of the Baltic Exchange and much of the chartering is initiated in New York, tanker chartering is conducted over the telephone rather than on the floor of the Baltic.

As well as being more technical, tanker charter parties tend to be less archaic in appearance and more precise in their wording. In time charters, for instance, instead of saying 'about' when defining the contractual speed, the actual speed is given and the charterer will expect it to be precisely adhered to, though the same consideration will be given to bad weather, etc as with dry cargo vessels.

In tanker voyage charters there is usually no despatch paid and, as the laytime conditions are more uniform (being usually determined by World Scale), the time sheet calculation becomes much simpler.

Tanker freight scales Another difference in tanker chartering is that instead of quoting the freight in actual cash terms, it is quoted in scale values that reflect the profitability in freight per ton miles of the charter. For instance, if you are quoted $14 per ton for a voyage from A to B and $15 a ton for a voyage from C to D, separate estimates have to be calculated to determine which of the two offers is the more profitable. On the other hand, if one is offered 120 World Scale for a voyage between E and F, and 110 World Scale for a voyage between G and H, the higher scale value for the voyage between E and F indicates that it is the more profitable offer. (The history of tanker freight scales is given in Fig 11.3.)

The World Scale is calculated and kept up to date by the World Scale Association, which has offices in London and New York. It is non-profit making and obtains its money from the subscribers to the World Scale tables, which convert the scale numbers into cash values when entered with the loading and discharging ports. The USD rates given for the load discharge situation are for New World Scale (NWS) 100. If for a specific voyage your tanker were offered NWS 80, then you would consult the World Scale Book for the 100 rate and then take 80 per cent of this rate.

The scale values are calculated by taking the cost for a standard vessel which is a 75,000 summer dwt tanker having an average speed of 14.5 knots and a daily fuel consumption of 55 tons of 380 cSt. Port costs and any other costs − such as canal dues − are included. The scales also include laytime and demurrage rates for all sizes of tanker.

The reason that scales are not used for cargo vessels is that the variety of cargoes and loading ports is so great that any scale tables would be too large, complicated and expensive to be worthwhile.

12 THE LINER MARKET

The distinction between 'liners' and 'tramps' is not absolute, nor has it always existed. It started halfway through the nineteenth century when steamships appeared and started offering scheduled services between ports. They eventually offered a faster and higher-quality service at a higher price, which naturally tended to attract those shippers with high-value cargo who were prepared to pay extra for speed and predictable delivery dates.

The distinction became clearer from the technical point of view in the 1950s when the typical tramp ship became a bulk carrier and specialised in ship loads of raw material, and from the 1960s when the conventional general cargo ship was increasingly being replaced by the container ship.

Thus at the present time liner ships and tramp ships are different types of ship, operated in different ways by increasingly different forms of management. They carry different types of cargo, which are governed by a different pricing mechanism.

Liners should have most of the following characteristics:

- Cargo – general
- Ships – general (conventional), container, Ro/Ro, etc
- Fixed schedules – hence arrive with steam vessels
- Fixed routes
- Fixed tariffs – many administrations require five to six months' notice of change
- Operators responsible for *all* costs
- Contract is the bill of lading – (not usually negotiated)

However, some of the major differences between liners and tramps will lie in their company organisation.

Typical company organisation

The function of some of the more important departments in a shipping company (those not considered elsewhere) are discussed in the text that follows. (See also Fig 12.1.)

The function of *husbandry* – in other words, keeping the ships seaworthy – will be common to all shipowners and ship managers and forms the major component of the 'costs' in the 'profit = revenue − costs' equation.

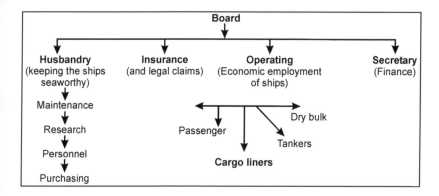

Fig 12.1   Some of the important departments in a shipping company.

The *operating* function, on the other hand, is concerned with the 'revenue' and its purpose is to maximise the economic employment of the ship. As part of this, it has a function of co-ordination, not only among the other departments of the company, but also with the ship and the agents, who will have to attend to the various and many problems that may arise at the ship's port of call. Where to bunker and the amount to take is one of its continuing problems, as the varying price of bunkers in different ports of the world means that careful planning can make substantial savings in this direction.

The major area of concern for this unit is *finding cargoes* for the ships, and it is here that the major differences in type of operations for tramp ships and liners becomes apparent. For the *liner* operator, this becomes a large labour-intensive function involving advertising and organising the thousands of items that make up a general cargo. However, it is in the documentation area that the liner operator becomes so much more labour-intensive than a tramp owner. For a tramp ship, there may be just one charter party and bill of lading, whereas for a liner vessel the bills of lading may run into thousands.

Other specific activities of this department include *scheduling and marketing*. Scheduling concerns where to send the ships and when.

For cargo liners, this is a twofold problem:

1 The decision to open up a new route or line. This is fundamental and will require a special research team. Not only has the supply and demand on the new possible routes to be considered, but also the strength of the competition, the conference involved, and whether they will accept, reject or tolerate someone joining the trade.

   If it is decided to join the conference, many of the questions concerning scheduling – such as sailing dates, ports and frequency of service – will be determined by the conference.

2 Once the run is established, the line manager must maintain schedules and combat the problems of delays, strikes, breakdowns and the annual dry-dock.

Marketing

Marketing in shipping, as in any other business, involves product analysis, traffic and market development and promotions and product development. Product analysis means assessing:

- The supply and demand for the particular shipping service in question.
- The costs of such a service.

Traffic and market development is concerned with how to deploy one's resources. Others directly involved with the ship's operation:

Forwarding agents Some 75 per cent of liner cargoes are obtained through forwarding agents. Although not essential, their expertise in the handling, routeing and documentation of consignments makes them a useful and much used intermediary, particularly for the small shipper. With containers, for instance, they can fill a container with part loads from many different shippers (*groupage*).

Ship's agents Whenever and wherever a ship comes into port, the owner will need an agent to act on his behalf to:

(A) Advise him on various details of the port such as changes in charges, the depths of water, or the possibility of any strikes.
(B) Make preparations on his behalf, such as reserving a berth, notifying the Customs and Immigration, ordering stores, ordering stevedores, tugs, pilots, etc.
(C) Meet the ship on arrival and report at the Custom House with or for the master. He will also pay the dues, give the master the necessary cash to meet the crew's requirements, arrange for the crew to visit the doctor or dentist if necessary, note protest if required, collect any outstanding freights, and hand in the notice of readiness to the receivers.
(D) Keep in constant touch with the ship and advise the company of progress and any delays, etc.

Loading brokers If the shipowner doesn't have sufficient sailings from a port to employ his own staff fully, he will use a firm of loading brokers to advertise his sailings, advise shippers as to when and where to bring their cargoes to the docks, and when the cargo is loaded to sign the bills of lading on behalf of the master.

The International MultiModal Transport Association The International MultiModal Transport Association (IMMTA), a worldwide trade and transport non-governmental association working in the interest of efficient trade and transport, has decided to respond positively to the global concern regarding the trustworthiness of companies involved in trade and transport. From 1 January 2003, IMMTA members could apply for certification as an IMMTA-approved MTO (multimodal transport operator). The IMMTA has taken this step in order to assist MTOs and NVOCCs that may not otherwise be considered reliable or trustworthy partners in today's transport world.

Three levels of certification are offered: Silver, Gold and Platinum, each corresponding to a certain number of predetermined benchmarks. While the IMMTA cannot certify the performance of its members, the intention is to allow governments, shippers, consignees, banks and insurers to know that an IMMTA-approved MTO complies with a certain level of minimum benchmarks.

The World Shipping Council This was formed to provide an industry voice in Washington and in 2003 the European Liner Affairs Association (ELAA) was formed as a liner shipping lobby to the European administration.

Demand and the liner market

As can be seen from Fig 12.2, the container demand, which reflects much of the liner market, shows a healthy growth, almost doubling itself, every decade. However, as the graph shows, this growth varies from region to region and 'Far East Asia' can be seen to have been the fastest-growing region.

Table 12.1 shows how on the three main liner routes in the 1990s – transatlantic, transpacific and Europe to the Far East – the vessels' capacity

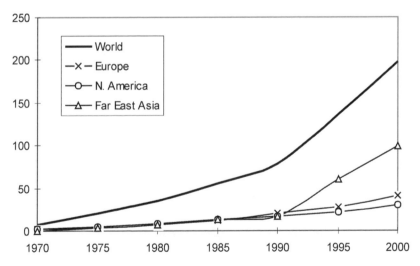

Fig 12.2 Growth in major containerised trades.

The increasing size of the modern liner in response to the growing demand.

utilisation (load factor) is not the same in each direction. This imbalance of trade is a greater problem for the containerised trades as it is not so easy to work 'triangular routes' as it was with the previous breakbulk liners. This imbalance in load factors is perhaps the major cause of the development of 'round the world services'.

In 2000, profits in liner trades were: transpacific 7.8 per cent, Europe to Far East 6.9 per cent, transatlantic 1 per cent.

What do liner shippers want?

Table 12.2 shows the results of two shipper surveys published in the *American Shipper* in March 1990. Survey A shows 'What shippers want most', while survey B indicates the standards used by Fords when picking its carrier.

Consortia, alliances and conferences

Legally, these carrier agreements are carefully monitored by many national administrations. The Federal Maritime Commission (FMC) – the main US

Table 12.1 Vessels' load factors in percentages					
Transatlantic		Transpacific		Europe – Far East	
Eastbound	Westbound	Eastbound	Westbound	Eastbound	Westbound
62.7	56.4	78.5	65.1	50	81.4

body concerned with monitoring the activities of liner companies – has long taken strict views, but these have been modified by the Ocean Shipping Reform Act (OSRA) 1998. The EU has tended to give exemption to most liner agreement practices, though like other administrations it has worries about liner agreements concerning inland transport. Canada has the Shipping Conferences Exemption Act of 1987, and Australia has its Trade Practices Act of 1974. In 2001, the OECD issued a report on *Competition Policy in Liner Shipping*.

Consortia

Consortia were developed in the early 1960s and were formed by liner companies to meet the demands of large capital investments required to set up the new containerised transport systems.

These consortia took a variety of forms. Some liner companies merged to form new larger organisations. Others formed a separate 'marketing' company and then bareboat chartered their ships to the company. However, over the course of time they have tended to evolve into separate companies. Normally, members of a consortia are members of a conference.

Alliances

One of the trading developments brought about by containerisation has been the steady globalisation of the major container shipping routes. This has meant that the old regional conference patterns have had to be adjusted. Some conferences have ceased to exist or have merged to form larger, more flexible units. Many of the major players have formed themselves into alliances, such as the Grand or the Global. Many of the new developments would not have been possible until the 1984 USA Shipping Act allowed *slot sharing*.

The first alliance, the Global Alliance, was formed in 1994 between APL, OOCL, MOL and Nedlloyd. The term itself is a generic one, although in some countries it may have a specific meaning in law. The purpose of participants in strategic alliances is to establish co-operative agreements on a *global* basis. Participants include national and cross-traders and may embrace conference and non-conference lines with Asian, European and US lines

Table 12.2 Two shipper surveys – surveys A and B

A	What shippers want	B	Fords' picking criteria
1	On-time delivery	1	Safety records
2	Overall responsiveness	2	Price-competitiveness
3	Price	3	Financial stability
4	On-time pick-up	4	Transit performance
5	Transit time	5	Handling of damage claims
6	Service territory	6	Equipment availability and suitability
7	Billing accuracy	7	Equipment condition
8	Correct equipment	8	EDI capability
9	Degree of control	9	Ease of doing business
10	Claims processing	10	Innovation initiative
11	Tracing capability		

(Source: American Shipper, March 1990.)

being partners. The agreements are not regional or restricted to one route, as with conferences, but global in character. In 1999, there were five such alliances: Grand Alliance, New World Alliance (Global Alliance), Maersk/Sea Land, United Alliance, Cosco/K Line/Yang Ming. In 2000, the first four of these alliances accounted for 65 per cent of slots deployed.

- The top 20 liner carriers controlled 26 per cent of world slot capacity in 1980
- The top 20 liner carriers controlled 41.6 per cent of world slot capacity in 1992
- The top 20 liner carriers controlled 72 per cent of world slot capacity in 2000

Conferences

A long-established feature in the liner trades is the conference system.

Liner shipowners engaged on the same trade usually operate with some measure of agreement among themselves. This agreement may be informal or formal and usually covers such items as freight rates, the number of sailings in a given time, working conditions, etc. In fact, in many cases the only factor left open to competition is the efficiency and quality of service offered. These associations of liner shipowners are known as *conferences*.

In 1540, there was an agreement on tariffs and services in the trade between Britain and Denmark, though the first officially recognisable conference was formed in 1875 when the UK Calcutta conference was organised. This was about the time when shipowners were starting to offer frequent reliable steamship services. It was almost certainly triggered off by the opening of the Suez Canal in 1860, which halved the distance to India from the UK and caused a surplus of tonnage on this route. The conference could, therefore, at this stage, be considered as a supply-regulating mechanism operated by the shipowner.

There are now some 150 conferences on paper, though not all of them are active, with membership ranging from two upwards. One of the largest conferences at the moment is the Far Eastern Freight Conference, which has 22 members and controls some 40 sailings a month between Europe and the Far East.

Conferences can be open or closed. A closed conference is one with restricted membership and, like any other club, the members reserve the right to vote on the eligibility of new entrants. The purpose of this is mainly to avoid too many ships being employed on the run with the consequent loss of profitability. This will, of course, seem very unfair to those shipowners who wish to join and find their entrance blocked.

Some countries, like the USA, do not allow closed conferences as this violates their laws on monopolies. Conferences trading to these countries are then open and any shipowner is free to join.

The 2001 OECD *Report on Competition Policy in Liner Shipping* estimated that conferences accounted for approximately 60 per cent of the TEU capacity in the major trades.

Why are conferences necessary? It is inevitable that a scheduled liner service cannot offer such a low freight as a chartered tramp ship that can pick the cargoes, sailing times and ports that give the greatest profits. With the tremendous capital outlay required to operate specially designed, fast, modern tonnage, shipowners argue that some protection of their investment is necessary. Furthermore, if there were a continuous freight war, the shipper would be the eventual loser as the inevitable effect of uncontrolled competition would be to reduce the frequency of the service.

Advantages offered by the conference system

1 Relatively fixed stable rates. A known rate that can be budgeted for is often of greater use to the shipper than the wildly fluctuating tramp rates.
2 Regular services.
3 Ships of the optimum size and speed, and best equipped to deal with the trade concerned.

Against these advantages, it is held that the conference system suffers from the usual monopolistic failings:

1 Excessively high freight rates.
2 Complacency and reluctance to accept change and greater efficiency.
3 High-handed bureaucratic attitudes.

It is important to realise that conferences have changed considerably since they were first set up over a century ago. In their early days they exercised considerable power, and in fact on some trades they enjoyed virtually absolute power concerning the cargoes entering and leaving certain ports. Much of the severe anti-conference propaganda goes back to this period. Since the Second World War their power has been declining, but even in the early 1970s they still controlled perhaps over 80 per cent of the global liner trade. Now, however, it is probably only half this.

Shipowners argue that conferences are not monopolies for the following reasons:

1 They claim that there is adequate competition from tramp shipping and non-conference liner ships. Many would argue, basing their arguments on the 'theory of contestable markets', that as shipping is a relatively easy business to get into and escape from, it is difficult for a monopoly to now exist in shipping without government legislation.

To overcome this competition, the shipowner encourages loyalty to the conference by:

(A) deferred rebates – ie if the shipper uses only conference line ships over a period of time, usually three to six months, then the shipowner will offer him a 5 per cent to 15 per cent rebate (not allowed in the USA).
(B) dual rates, where the lower rate can be used by any shipper who signs a contract to the effect that he will use only conference line ships.

2 If the conference rates become too high, large shippers can build and operate their own ships. The Blue Star line was originally created by large meat importers for just this purpose.
3 There is ever growing competition from the air. This can pose a serious threat, for although the amount carried is relatively small, it is the valuable cargo and the cargo from which the liner ships have traditionally made their profits. (Even in 1971, the UK trade figures showed that, by value, some 24 per cent of trade to the USA and Canada was carried by air.)

Developments to improve the less desirable features of conferences In the last few decades or so there have been several moves to improve upon some of the less desirable features of conferences.

In 1955, the British Shippers' Council was set up so that shippers could negotiate collectively with the conferences rather than individually. Soon after this, similar councils were set up in Europe and throughout the world, and subsequently the European Shippers' Council (ESC) was formed.

Following a resolution of European Ministers of Transport in 1963, the European shipowners formed CENSA (Committee of European and Japanese National Shipowners' Association) and in 1964 a joint meeting between CENSA and the ESC took place in London. From this meeting, a 'Note of Understanding' between the European conference lines and European shippers was drawn up. This established consultative procedures between the two parties.

These two bodies met in Genoa in October 1971 and succeeded in producing an agreed Code, which was accepted by these governments as a satisfactory answer to their requests. The base was consultation and the method was self-regulation. The Code was subsequently adopted and operated by 46 conferences covering the major trades, either openly or, where there was political opposition, by fact rather than by announcement.

Almost coincidentally, the developing nations through UNCTAD were promoting their ideas for a Code, but their approach was different. They sought a Code with special advantages for their national shipowners by way of an increased share of the trades and the control of the freight rates.

The date for formal signature closed on 30 June 1975, at which time only 30 nations (representing some 26 per cent of world shipping) had signed, some subject to reservations. By 1977, only 22 nations (representing some 3 per cent of world shipping) had ratified the Code – however, at the Fifth Triennial Session of UNCTAD that took place in Manila in 1979, there was general acceptance of the Code, and on 6 October 1982, the UNCTAD Liner Code came into being.

This Code contains:

- A cargo-share system on a 40:40:20 basis – 40 per cent for the nationals at each end, and 20 per cent for the non-nationals.
- An elaborate method of conciliation for resolving the differences between the shippers and the conference.

It is important to realise when considering the Code that:

- It was designed and put together before the 'container era' when there were many breakbulk vessels on the trade. It was never designed to cope with fourth-generation container vessels and 'slot-chartering'.
- It was conceived in a period of profitable freight rates and a period of expansion for national fleets.
- The USA is not a signatory.
- Many 'western' countries have signed the 'Brussels Package', which indicates that such countries will only refer to the Code in their trade with developing countries.
- The Code as such concerns a code of conduct for liner conferences, but some countries – such as India – have seen it as a code for liner shipping.

  The advantage of limiting the quota system to the conference ships is that this is a piece of administration that the conferences have the ability and experience to do. One of the problems of a general quota applying to a trade lies in the practical and efficient administration of the allocation. In most countries, this will involve government officials, growing bureaucracy, delays and increased costs.

Table 12.3   Details of conferences and the EU

Date	Comments
1986	Regulation 4056/86 exempts liner conferences from EU competition law.
1992	Transatlantic carriers form a new conference, the Trans Atlantic Agreement (TAA).
1993	European shippers seek TAA suspension.
1994	TAA replaced by Trans-Atlantic Conference, with more flexible rules. EU Commission finds Taca infringed EU anti trust rules by managing capacity and fixing inland transport rates. Taca lodges an appeal. FEFC found guilty of collective inland price fixing.
1995	EU Commissioner threatens huge fines on Taca members for inland price fixing. EU Commission removes Taca's anti trust immunity.
1997	Taca Lines fined 273 mn euros for abuse of their dominant position.
1998	Container Lines promised clear set of regulatory guidelines that would end legal disputes.
1999	Efforts to form a new conference on the North Atlantic, collapse. Taca membership declines. In 1999, it had seven member lines – Hapag Lloyd, Mediterranean Shipping Co, NYK, OOCL, P&O Nedlloyd, Sea Land (Maersk). In 1998, westbound it carried 1.25 mn TEUs and eastbound it carried 950,000 TEUs.
2000	Court of First Instance in Luxembourg hears appeals lodged by Taca and FEFC against Brussels.
2001	Commission provisionally approves Taca and invites comments.
2002	Decision on appeal cases.

Liner freight rates – see Chapter 8

Logistics and/or intermodal transport

With the advent of containers and other intermodal devices, liner shipping should no longer be considered just as sea transport – but instead as an integral part of a systems approach to transport. The introduction of intermodal devices, such as the container, not only involves new technology but also the need for new legislation, new documents, new information systems but, perhaps above all, a new way of looking at the transport problem. The liner ship now becomes just one of the modal carriers as the container moves between modes on its hopefully uninterrupted journey from source to destination.

Once the cargo arrives at a port it will be moved on by other modes. In Europe, the approximate modal split has been:

77% moves by road

12% by rail

8% by barge and water

3% by air and pipelines

Table 12.4   Comparison of transport modes (ie which form is best suited for what)

Mode	Energy efficiency	Speed	Average haul (USA)	Deaths per 100 million passenger miles	Date introduced	Vehicle life (years)
Air	1	400*	1,000	0.23	1958 (Jet)	22
Truck	15	55*	265	2.4	1920	10
Rail	50	20 (200)	500	0.1	1830 (1970)	20
Barge	64	5.5	330	very small	17thC	50
Pipeline	75	4.5	300	negligible	1856 (1970)	?
Ship (Liner)	100	16.5	1,500	small	1870 (1970)	15

The * in the speed column indicates that the figures are specific to the USA.

The figures in Table 12.4 are not only very approximate, but could vary depending on a number of circumstances. They do, however, enable us to make rough comparisons and draw general conclusions – such as that ships are very energy efficient and safe. I have found, though, that few students are prepared to accept that aircraft are ten times safer than road vehicles! Where I have put two dates – eg rail, etc – I am trying to indicate that a transport *mutation* took place about that time and that modern high-speed block trains present different transport opportunities to the previous systems.

Logistics is an even more refined transport concept and can be defined as 'an optimisation process of the *location*, *movement* and *storage of resources* from the point of origin, through various economic activities, to the final consumer'. Not all processes are sufficiently integrated to be optimised over the total process from start to finish, though the banana would seem to be a good example of one that is. The JIT (just in time) concept does, however, apply logistical thinking to at least part of the process.

Regionalisation to globalisation

The impact of intermodalism (containerisation) on liner shipping

- *Ships* Container ships are larger, faster, and with a quicker turn-around than the ships they replace. Therefore, fewer ships are needed – eg one modern fourth-generation container ship can replace perhaps 15 of the traditional 15,000 dwt vessels.

- **Ports** Fewer berths are needed, but more space to park the containers that the ship can load and disgorge in a day. There is also deeper water and better access to other modes. In London during the early 1970s, when both old and new terminals were operating side by side, 60 conventional berths handled 1.8 million tonnes a year, while the 7 new container berths handled 3 million tonnes a year. Fewer stevedores are required, but it must be remembered as regards labour that the containers have to be stuffed (filled) and stripped (emptied). In the port of Gothenburg it takes two stevedores about 1.5 hours to strip a container and from 2 to 5 hours to stuff one. Containerisation doesn't do away with labour to stow the cargo — it simply provides a method of pre-stowage that can now be done in warm and dry conditions.

- **Trading patterns** Because of the economics of big container ships, the cargo now comes to the ship, whereas in the past the ship went to the cargo. This has resulted in large ships trading between large 'centre' ports with smaller feeder vessels distributing the containers to smaller feeder ports. It is worth noting that it is the big liner companies who are the decision-makers as to which port becomes the area's centre port. In 1985, Evergreen started round the world services.

- **Shipping companies** The larger capital investment required to containerise a trade means that many liner companies have either been joined together into consortia or that smaller companies have been taken over by larger ones.

  In 2001, the 20 leading liner companies accounted for about 72 per cent of the world's container-carrying capacity and it is anticipated that this trend to fewer, larger liner companies will continue (see also Table 12.5).

- **Competition** The unit load meant that competition now came from other forms of transport as well as other ships. Landbridges such as the Trans-Siberian Railway have seen changes in developing trading patterns as well as a loss of market share to other modes. Ro/Ro ferries, bridges and tunnels have also brought about the demise of many short sea liner companies. In 2001, it was estimated that transhipment containers made up about 25 per cent of all container port throughput. (In Singapore, it is about 70 per cent.)

- **Documentation** As the cargo moves faster, so must the documentation. It seems to be an unfortunate fact that it is easier to change technology than well-established legal/commercial practices!

- **Computerised systems** Computerised systems are needed both to help improve documentation and also to keep track of all the containers in the world. Containers are expensive, and unless they are kept working their owners are going to lose money. It has been said that a containerised system of any size would be virtually impossible without a computer.

Table 12.5 Liner companies carrying quantities of containers

Rank	Company 1981	TEUs x 1,000	Company 1993	TEUs x 1,000	Company 2003	TEUs x 1,000
1	Sealand	41.7	Evergreen	128.8	Maersk/ Sealand	727
2	Hapag-Lloyd	40.5	Maersk	105.5	MSC	550
3	Maersk	36.6	Hanjin	85.0	P&O Nedlloyd	388
4	OCL	35.2	Sea Land	84.3	Evergreen	
5	NYK	29.0	NYK	74.8	Hanjin	
6	OOCL	27.7	Yangming	64.5	Cosco	
7	CGM	22.7	MOL	63.7	APL + NOL	
8	Evergreen	20.8	P&OCL	55.3	CP Ships	
9	APL	19.7	OOCL	46.7	CMA-CGM	
10	USL	19.3	APL	45.0	NYK	

Useful facts concerning containers Technically, containers are governed by the ISO (the International Standards Organisation) and the CSC (the Container Safety Convention). In 1968, the ISO defined a container as an 'article of transport equipment' that:

- is of permanent character,
- is intermodal,
- is easily handled,
- is easily filled and emptied,
- has an internal volume that is greater than 1 cubic metre.

An ISO container has therefore standard size, standard strength and *standard lifting facilities*. It is this latter characteristic which, to my mind, is the really significant factor that differentiates the present container revolution from previous attempts at putting things into standard-sized units.

The CSC was set up by the IMO in September 1977. The reason for this was probably that by 1977 many containers had been around for several years and accidents were starting to happen. Container doors were falling off, bottoms falling out during lifts, etc. In 1984, the *CSC safety plate* came into force. This is a plate fitted to the container door, showing its initial approval and plating, and when it was last surveyed. Under the CSC, containers have to be regularly surveyed in a similar manner to ships.

The life expectancy of a container depends on many factors, but it is approximately 8 years. However, on average one of those years will be spent out of service for repairs.

Standard containers (all lengths) amount to over 5 million, or about 87 per cent of the total (details of container ownership are given in Table 12.6).

Table 12.6 Details concerning container ownership

Container ownership	Length	Height	Cladding	Percentage share
Carriers				51
Lessors				45
	20 ft			48
	40 ft			50
		8 ft		3
		8 ft 6 in		89
		9 ft 6 in		7
			Steel	87
			Aluminium	11
			GRP	1

Container costs and prices In 2003, a general-purpose container built in China was priced at $1,350 (USD) per TEU and $2,160 (USD) per FEU. A 40-foot-high cube container had a price of around $2,270 (USD). Containers themselves attract costs, as shown in Table 12.7.

We need to remember, though, that containers are not the only form of unit load. When containers first appeared on the scene, many thought that palletisation, with special pallet ships, was where the future lay.

Ro/Ro ships do largely roll on and off containers, but they are more flexible as to the units they can use. There are also the barge-carrying ships, integrated tug barges, and several specialised units for specialised trades. However, with the enormous amounts of capital now invested in the containerised system, it is difficult to anticipate any radical change in the near future, though the system is continually evolving.

Table 12.7 Container costs

Container costs	Percentage share of total costs
Capital	32
Repair and refurbishment	25
Imbalance	22
Cleaning and maintenance	11
Insurance	10

13 SAFETY

Four separate spheres of risk

1 The ship itself.
2 The cargo.
3 The persons on the ship, ie crew, passengers, stevedores, visitors.
4 The environment.

There are also three separate spheres of interest:

1 The government interest in analysing casualties and keeping a watchful eye over bad practices, criminal negligence, etc. This is done in the UK by the Marine Accident Investigation Branch (MAIB), which holds investigations into certain casualties, where it feels there has been negligence or that there is something to be learnt in reducing the possibility of a similar casualty occurring.

   Governments can also co-operate through the IMO in improving safety standards internationally, eg routeing to avoid collision.
2 The technical aspect of safety in the design and construction of equipment.
3 Responsibility for payment for the damage or loss.

How serious a problem is this?

Table 13.1 gives a breakdown of the causes of ship casualties in the period 1989–2001. These statistics of casualties only consider total losses and it is interesting to note that, even in this modern age, the *weather* still poses a serious threat to safety. Freak waves are now an accepted hazard, and this caused the loss of the *MV München*, a LASH vessel, in December 1978. However, modern research shows that rapidly spreading cracks are also a very big threat and can cause fatal structural failure in bulk carriers which, if loaded with high-density cargo, can sink in seconds. On average, 150 lives a year are lost on bulk carriers. Contact damage is where a ship causes damage to something other than a ship, such as striking a dock wall or crane.

Of the casualties in Table 13.1, 16.2 per cent involve tankers, 50 per cent concern bulkers, and 60 per cent of the casualties happen to ships under the flags of the major open registries.

A 70,000 dwt tanker that broke her back in April 1994 during a storm off the coast of Mozambique. The subsequent salvage operation did not save the vessel, but did prevent massive coastal pollution.

The P&I (Protection & Indemnity) club analysis (see page 242) shows the rather surprising fact that 56 per cent of collisions take place in good visibility and in calm seas, though the report also indicates that only 19 per cent occur in open water. In fact, 60 per cent of grounding and collisions take place in pilotage waters.

Fig 13.1 shows the 'smoothed out' values of the percentage of GT totally lost by the merchant fleets of Greece, Liberia, the UK and the world.

Table 13.1 Causes of annual casualties (1989–2001) concerning ships greater than 500GT

Type of casualty	Average no 1993–7	1998	1999	2000	2002
Weather damage	35	18	21	19	21
Foundering	0	1	2	18	20
Stranding	8	16	11	20	18
Collisions and contact	12	14	15	12	12
Fire and explosions	20	13	8	13	23
Missing	0	–	–	1	1
Damage to machinery	5	5	3	4	2
Other casualties	27	18	13	12	
TOTAL	107	85	73	99	97

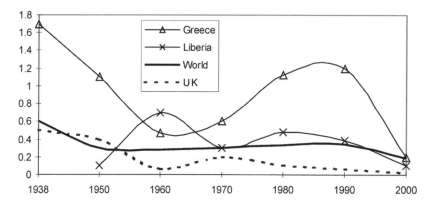

Fig 13.1   Percentage of GT total losses, 1938–2000. (Source: Lloyd's Register of Shipping.)

It is, of course, necessary to be very careful in drawing any conclusions from such a graph, but a few general observations may be made:

- The average world casualty rate remains remarkably constant.
- A long-established maritime nation operating a fleet of relatively modern ships has a consistently better safety record than a flag of convenience country.
- Greece is undeniably a long-established and responsible maritime nation, but a large percentage of its ships are old. In 1994, the average age of the Greek fleet was 24 years so Greece obviously has an exceptionally high proportion of old ships. Operating old ships can be very profitable because of their relatively low capital cost, but when they are involved in a serious collision or grounding, they are more likely to be considered a technical total loss than a modern ship in a similar situation because of the very high cost of repairs. It is, for instance, worth spending half a million pounds repairing a ship that is worth four million pounds, but not one that is worth only a quarter of a million pounds. In times of high freights, such as the early 1970s, total losses will decrease as the value of ships increases.

For the same reason, all old vessels will tend to show a worse safety record than new vessels (see Fig 13.2). One does, of course, hope and expect that newer ships are safer than older ships, but one should be cautious about making any exaggerated claims with regard to this.

Flag state conformance index (Flasci)

Factors considered when compiling the Flasci score include: port state control detentions, casualties, accidents, deaths and injuries, crew records, ownership of the register, and corruption rating of the government. In 2003,

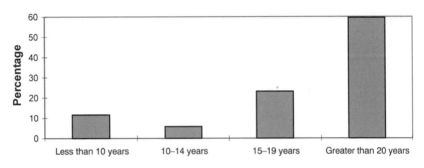

Fig 13.2 Percentage reported total losses in 2001 by age of ship. (Source: SSMR.)

under the *Paris Memorandum* criteria, some 11,000 ships worldwide are regarded as medium to high risk (see Table 13.2).

Lloyd's Register flag state audit

In 2003, Lloyd's Register developed a classification of flag safety, and under this system flags are rated as Poor, Modest, Good or High. Some examples from this classification are listed here:

- Poor – Cambodia, St Vincent
- Modest – Malta, Liberia, Panama
- Good – HK, Russia
- High – most EU flags

Table 13.2	Flag state conformance index (Flasci) (Source: Cardiff University's Seafarers International Research Centre)				
Country	Flasci score	Country	Flasci score	Country	Flasci score
Norway	84	Bermuda	63	Philippines	46
UK	80	Cayman	62	Vanuatu	44
DIS	77	Canary Islands	60	Bahamas	43
NIS	77	Latvia	60	Liberia	43
Netherlands	76	Estonia	58	Antigua and Barbuda	42
GIS	75	Singapore	58	Barbados	42
France (K)	72	Cyprus	50	Panama	41
Hong Kong	64	Malta	49	Turkey	41
Isle of Man	64	Neth Antilles	48	Marshall I	36
Madeira	64	Russia	48	Ukraine	36

Table 13.3	Losses of different types of vessel (Source: Lloyd's Register of Shipping)		
Ship type	Annual average (% of ships lost (1987–92))	Average loss ratio (% of type of ship lost)	Average age of type (in years)
Tanker	7.3	0.16	16
Dry bulker	10.1	0.24	14
General cargo ships	69.7	0.58	20
Ro/Ro cargo	5.2	0.48	14
Container ship	1.8	0.17	11
Ferry/passenger	5.9	0.18	18

Table 13.3 looks at the total losses of different types of vessels. As can be seen, the tanker is one of the safer types of ships in that it has a lower average loss ratio, in spite of its relatively high average age. The higher loss ratio for general cargo ships is perhaps largely explained by the higher average age, while many would argue that the loss ratios for the dry bulker and the Ro/Ro cargo ships are due to the large floodable spaces between bulkheads. From 1993 to 1997, the overall loss rate improved. By 1997, the percentage total loss rate by numbers for all ships was 0.22 per cent and by tonnage was 0.16 per cent. We need to note that in 1997 major losses were running at over twice the level of total losses, and small losses at around ten times the level of total losses.

Collisions

Table 13.4 shows where collisions are most likely to occur. The peak time for collisions is between 0400 and 0600 hours, and collision costs make up 17 per cent of P&I club payments.

See also Nautical Institute webpage: www.nautinst.org.

Cargo claims

The UK P&I club has somewhere between 20 to 25 per cent of the world's ocean-going fleet entered with it. The ships entered with the club are broadly representative of the world fleet overall, so the statistical analysis of their claims could be considered representative of the world fleet.

Table 13.5 shows that the cargo category most often involved in major claims is dry bulk, accounting for some 38 per cent of claims and involving nearly 50 per cent of the total value of all bulk carrier claims.

The P&I club list of contributory causes for the claims in Table 13.5 is interesting in that the causes do not seem to have changed much over the

Table 13.4 Location of collisions

Location	Percentage
Coastal water	32
Open water	19
In harbour	14
River/canal	13
Separation zone	11
Anchorage	10
Other	1

(Source: 'Managing risks', Seaways, June 1999.)

Table 13.5 Bulk carrier cargo claims

Bulk carrier cargo claims	Percentages of number of claims	Average value in $ (millions)
Dry bulk	38	0.4
Steel products	22	0.29
Bagged bulk	10	0.31
Timber	4	0.21
Containers	5	0.52
General	3.5	0.21
Grain	3	0.42
Others	14.5	0.1–0.6

(Source: UK P&I club – Analysis of Major Claims, 1993.)

last century, and could be found in any basic textbook in the days of sail, ie leaking hatchcovers, bad stowage, condensation, leaking hull, fire, lashing failure, bad handling, shore terminal, poor tally, pipe failure and, finally, damage prior to loading.

An industry estimate made in the year 2000 was that 2,000 or so containers are lost overboard every year. Of the 20 million container transits a year, this represents a loss of 0.01 per cent (see also Table 13.6).

Loss of life and injury

During the first half of the period shown in Table 13.7 (1983–8) Lloyd's Register of Shipping showed that over 3,300,000 seamen suffered accidental

Table 13.6	Cargo losses in transit and in storage 1998 (percentages)	
Type of loss	In transit	In storage
Theft	4.8	29.8
Damage in transit	3.8	
Accident to conveyance	91.4	
Warehouse incidents		59.3
Natural hazards ashore		10.9

(Source: The Institute of London Underwriters.)

Table 13.7	Loss of human life as a result of shipping casualties
Between 1983 and 1992, 10,013 lives were lost.	
Type of casualty	Percentage
Foundered	39.5
Missing	5.3
Fire and Explosion	4.7
Collision	41.8
Wrecked/Stranded	6.6
Contact	0.6
Lost etc.	1.5

(Source: Lloyd's Register of Shipping.)

injuries. However, research undertaken at the Department of Maritime Studies, University of Wales College of Technology, would indicate that these official statistics are an underestimate, and the report suggested that the published figures showed only one-tenth of the problem worldwide (see Table 13.8).

Pirate activity

Between 1991 and 1995, over 500 incidents of piracy or armed robbery on ships and seafarers were recorded by the IMO; in 1992, the International Maritime Bureau set up a piracy centre.

Pirate attacks on ships increased by 40 per cent in 1999 from 1998 (202 to 258), according to the IMB report issued in January 2000 (469 in 2000 and 335 in 2001). This report indicated that a typical pirate attack took the form

Table 13.8 Worldwide estimate of seafarers' lives lost at sea each year	
Cause of death	Estimated no of fatalities
Maritime disasters	1,102
Occupational accidents	419
Illness	921
Missing at sea	74
Homicide/suicide/other	91
TOTAL	2,207

(Source: ITF, Seafarers' Bulletin, no 12, 1998.)

Table 13.9 Areas of most pirate activity	
Country	Percentage
Indonesia	45
Bangladesh	10
Malaysia	8
India	6
Singapore Straits	6
Somalia	5
Nigeria	5
Others	21

of around ten men in a speedboat trailing and boarding a cargo ship. These attacks were usually violent, and some of the incidents indicated that the pirates knew what they were looking for and which containers to plunder. Lloyd's List in 2002 suggests that the annual bill for piracy now exceeds $25 (USD) billion (see also Table 13.9).

Security

The problems caused by security in shipping will almost always involve delays and expense, with seldom the possibility of increase in revenues and few customers will be enthusiastic to pay more for what seems to be a less efficient service. In 2003, a consultancy paper reported in Lloyd's List suggested that security costs per TEU was probably between $5 (USD) and $10 (USD).

The IMO on security SOLAS now includes an *International Ship and Port Facility Security Code* (it came in as an amendment in July 2004). Its 85 pages include the provision of security officers on board ships, ports have to complete a Port Facility Security Assessment, and contracting governments have further responsibilities.

The environment

The pollution analysis in Table 13.10 is for all ships and it is interesting to note that in 1993, tanker groundings accounted for only 5 per cent of tanker pollution claims for the UK P&I club. For tankers, the most common causes of pollution were valve and shell plate failure, though the greatest expense was for incidents caused by grounding, fire and sinking.

Of the 13 million tonnes of oil carried by tankers during the years 1969 to 1970, 0.00192 per cent was spilled as a result of tanker casualties (results of a sample survey conducted by the US Coast Guard). In 1977, 1.3 million tons of oil was estimated to be discharged annually into the sea. Of this, only a small percentage was a result of tanker accidents. These statistics are typical of those that appeared in the 1970s after the *Torrey Canyon* disaster in 1967, which raised public awareness of the oil pollution problem. Since then, such statistics abound and the following points should be noted:

- Tanker accidents account for a very small percentage of sea pollution. It should also be noted that none of the *notorious* tanker accidents seem to have had any serious long-term effect on the environment. In 2000, it was estimated that 12 per cent of all maritime pollution came from shipping activities. Of all the maritime pollution, only 11.3 per cent came from tankers and 14.4 per cent came from non-tankers.

Table 13.10   Pollution analysis

Pollution claims	Percentage 1993	Average value $ (USD) (millions)
Grounding	23	1.6
Bunkering	12	1.5
Collision	12	0.9
Valve failure	12	0.3
Shell plate failure	11	1.1
Wrong valve	8	0.6
Pipe failure	5	0.2
Fire/sinking	4	5.0
Other	13	1.3

(Source: UK P&I club – Analysis of Major Claims 1993.)

- The number of oil spills over 700 tons is reducing: between 1970 and 1979 there were, on average, 24.2 spills a year; between 1980 and 1989, 8.9; and between 1990 and 1999, 7.3.
- Many serious researchers have also produced data to indicate that nowadays most oil pollution of the seas comes from either natural causes or from discharges ashore.

In spite of its notoriety, the *Exxon Valdez* is only in double figures in the ranking of serious ship oil pollution incidents, spilling only 37,000 tonnes. The *Sea Empress* spilt 70,000 tonnes, and the *Braer*, which caused surprisingly little damage, spilt 86,000 tonnes.

Government and international action on safety

The history of governmental and international involvement in safety is very often the history of maritime tragedies. Governments will seldom act unless spurred on by public outrage at some recent catastrophe. It is not surprising, therefore, that much modern legislation on safety can be traced back to the loss of the *Titanic*. Here are some significant dates in relation to legislation:

- 1909 – the White Star liner *Republic* sank after a collision in fog after leaving New York. It was the first time a successful radio (CQD) distress message had been used. Virtually all the 1,500 passengers were saved, so the authorities did nothing following this collision – even though shortcomings in the system were apparent.
- 1912 – loss of the *Titanic* when 1,500 people lost their lives in the most tragic circumstances. The International Ice Patrol was formed almost immediately and the irregularities in the radio watch system resolved.
- 1913 – the First International Safety of Life at Sea Conference (SOLAS) took place, but its satisfactory completion was frustrated by the First World War.
- 1929 – the Second International SOLAS Conference.
- 1948 – the Third International SOLAS Conference.
- 1960 – the Fourth International SOLAS, now convened by the newly formed IMCO (now the IMO).
- 1967 – the stranding of the *Torrey Canyon* near the Scilly Isles brought international support for the routeing of ships, which had been under discussion for several years. It also inspired the 1969 Brussels Convention on Oil Pollution.

Shipowners, realising that there would be public demand for punitive legislation to prevent oil pollution, tried to remove the necessity for it by instigating a scheme known as TOVALOP (Tanker Owners' Voluntary Association for the Liability for Oil Pollution). Under this scheme, tanker owners would volunteer to clean up any pollution they caused. The oil industry also offered to increase the money available for this procedure by a scheme known as CRISTAL. These offers, however, were made too late, in that the mechanism for severe anti-pollution laws had been set in motion. TOVALOP and CRISTAL ended on 20 February 1997.

Many countries are now signatories to the 1969 Civil Liability Convention on Oil Pollution, and the public crusade against tanker owners following the *Torrey Canyon* disaster is a good example of how media reaction can form and create public opinion, which in turn can influence administrations' policy. The *Exxon Valdez* 20 years later showed yet again that no politician can afford *not* to take a firm stance against tanker owners.

The Civil Liability Convention (CLC) and the International Convention on the Establishment of an International Fund for Compensation for Oil Pollution Damage 1971 (1992 update in force from 2000) applies to ships carrying more than 2,000 tons of persistent oil in bulk as cargo. Such a ship must obtain a Government Certificate testifying that there is available, in respect of the ship, adequate insurance or other security to meet the convention liabilities. This applies at all times to ships registered in contracting states, and to all other ships when calling at ports of contracting states. Liability is strict – the only defence being an Act of God, deliberate damage by a third party, or sole negligence on the part of a government or other authority regarding the upkeep of lights or other navigational aids.

Following the *Exxon Valdez* oil spill, the US administration introduced OPA 90, which greatly increased shipowners' liability concerning oil spills when trading to the USA. These regulations came into force in 1995 and ships trading to the USA require Certificates of Financial Responsibility (COFRs). The existing insurance market was reluctant to issue these COFRs, so new insurance organisations were rather hastily set up, eg Shoreline Mutual and Firstline.

When chartering a tanker it is therefore necessary to ensure that she has a Civil Liability Certificate. Most oil company charter party forms will include clauses to this effect. If trading to the USA, the ship will also need the necessary COFR.

The International Oil Pollution Compensation Fund (IOPC) came into existence on 16 October 1978. It is financed by the receivers of crude oil in contracting states, and its purpose is supplementary to the CLC.

Some significant dates are listed below:

- On 7 October 1985, the *Achille Lauro*, a cruise vessel in the Mediterranean, was taken over by terrorists. One person was killed and it had a huge effect on the Mediterranean cruise market. It also caused the passenger ship industry to take stock concerning its security measures.
- On 6 March 1987, the *Herald of Free Enterprise* disaster took place. This was the tragic loss of a cross-Channel ferry (193 deaths), which capsized just after leaving port with its bow doors still open. This caused most Ro/Ro ferry operators to improve their safety procedures and to ensure that bow doors are closed/opened on the berth. It also caused the IMO to take

a long hard look at the potentially unsafe features in the design of this ship type. The loss of the Scandinavian *Star* in 1990 and the *Estonia* (900 deaths) in 1994 both emphasised the urgency for action in this area.

- On 15 February 1996, the *Sea Empress* grounded when approaching Milford Haven and lost 136,000 tons of oil.
- On 1 July 1998, the IMO introduced the International Safety Management (ISM) Code which became mandatory for passenger ships, tankers and bulk carriers over 500 GT. On 1 August, the International Convention of Standards of Training, Certification and Watchkeeping for Seafarers (STCW) came into force.
- Following 9/11 in New York, there were calls for wide-ranging security measures to counter terrorist threats, and in May 2002, the IMO proposed 12 measures to bolster ship and port security.
- In July 2002, the ISM Code became mandatory for all vessels over 500 GT.
- In October 2002, the VLCC *Limburg* was damaged by a terrorist bomb (boat) off the coast of Yemen. Also in October, the IMO floated a new protocol, came into force 12 months after it was ratified by 10 states. This protocol makes far-reaching reforms to the 1974 Athens Convention covering the carriage of passengers and their luggage.
- On 14 November 2002, the 70,000 dwt tanker *Prestige* spilt oil off the Spanish coast, and sank on 19 November in the Atlantic. It was built in Japan in 1975, owned by Greeks, chartered by Russians, registered in Bermuda, with a crew from the Philippines (Greek master), and bound for Singapore. Since 21 October 2003, single-hull tankers built in 1980 or before have not been allowed in European ports.

Enforcement of safety

The major practical problem of safety is not the lack of adequate legislation (see Fig. 13.3), but the enforcement of existing legislation. Traditionally this has been done by the flag state – but not all states have the will or the trained staff to enforce the legal safety requirements. To overcome this problem, the 1978 SOLAS Protocol extends this enforcement to port states. In 1982, 14 Western European nations signed the Paris Memorandum as a bid to operate port state enforcement in a uniform manner on foreign ships. Details of port state inspections are kept at the computer centre, which is located at St Malo in France.

In the 1994 *Bimco Review*, Mr W O'Neil, the Secretary General of the IMO, when writing on the implementation of safety, said, 'There is a two-pronged approach to ensuring this is done – by flag state control and port state control.... Port state control is designed as a secondary line of defence. Whenever a ship goes to a port in a foreign country it can be inspected to check that it complies with IMO requirements. In extreme cases, the inspectors can order repairs to be carried out before the ship is permitted to sail.'

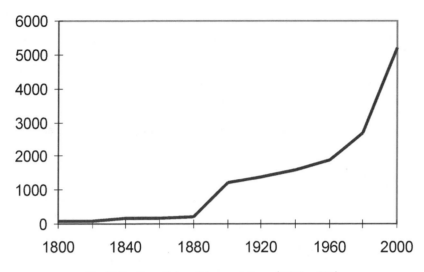

Fig 13.3 Growth in safety regulations (1800 = 100).

To put even more pressure on shipowners and flag states, some port state authorities are starting to publish lists of vessels that fail the port state inspection. The 25 per cent inspection regime established by the EU Port State Control Directives is guided by a targeting factor which, hopefully, will allow the authorities to focus on substandard ships. The targeting factor is made up of flag, age, classification society, when last inspected, and the levels of deficiencies noted on previous inspections (see www.equasis.org).

The very considerable increase in operators' liability, if found negligent in employing substandard ships, has also been a strong inducement to increase safety. A maritime accident – like any other accident – may involve those concerned in both criminal and civil litigation. In the past it was usually the master of the ship who bore the brunt of any legal retribution, but over the last few years there have been several occasions where the management and company directors have been brought before the courts.

Tankers trading to the USA must have a letter (renewed each year) from the USGC before loading and discharging. The purpose of the letter is to indicate that the vessel is both safe and environmentally sound.

The Maritime and Coastguard Agency This agency aims to:

- Promote and enforce high standards of marine safety. It inspects UK flag ships and carries out port control of non-UK vessels.
- Minimise loss of life among seafarers.
- Respond to maritime emergencies 24 hours a day.
- Minimise the risk of pollution.

MAIB (Marine Accident Investigation Branch) Department of the Environment, Transport and Regions and the MAIB is part of the investigates all types of marine accidents, both to ships and to the people on them. Its role is to determine the circumstances of an accident and its causes. The MAIB does not enforce laws or carry out prosecutions.

The International Commission on Shipping (ICONS) This is a fully independent body set up in 1999 by funding from the ITF and the Maritime and Port Authority of Singapore (see www.icons.org.av). Its broad terms of reference are to:

- Investigate the approaches by government, industry and other interested parties to safety, the environment and social requirements.
- Recommend appropriate strategies that encompass non-regulatory and regulatory methods of improving the enforcement and compliance to safety, environment and social requirements.

European Maritime Safety Agency (EMSA) This body was set up in 2002 to co-ordinate the activities of national EU safety agencies, and it is aimed that it will eventually have a staff of 60.

The economics of safety

Fig 13.4 shows that at the lower degrees of safety, a relatively small cost outlay will generally increase safety. However, absolute safety is unobtainable and at the higher levels of safety – say, 95 per cent plus – great cost outlays may be necessary to increase safety by even a fraction of 1 per cent.

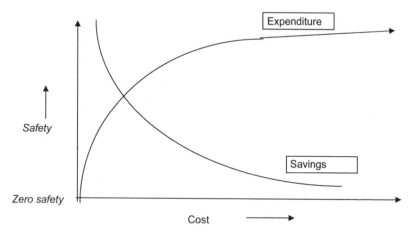

Fig 13.4   The economics of safety.

This can create a problem for the shipowner, for if he makes such a cost outlay with no corresponding increase in revenue, he may no longer be able to operate competitively and it is at this point that international legislation may be necessary, so that the cost becomes obligatory to all. In addition, we need to stress the significance of the two extreme types of accident:

1 The unexpected or very rare catastrophe – to what extent can anyone be expected to take precautions against all such possibilities. It must also be remembered that the ship's crew will very probably have no experience of how to cope with this novel situation and any realistic training, even if possible, is usually very expensive. For instance, when the *Titanic* sank it was obviously the first time the captain and most of the crew had been placed in this unusual and extreme situation!

2 The anticipated problem – like going aground in shallow water. For this type of accident, experience, training and technology can usually help for a relatively small extra cost. A well-trained crew on a well-equipped ship will be safer than a poorly trained crew on an ill-equipped ship, but both have an equal probability of grounding on an *uncharted* rock.

Formal safety assessment (FSA)

This methodology is designed to provide decision-makers with a comprehensive understanding of safety problems, possible solutions, and their costs and benefits. Built into this methodology are the concepts of stakeholders, and that the risk imposer pays.

This methodology introduces a more proactive and logical approach to the problem than the reactive policy that has traditionally been used. The methodology is based on comparing the different areas that could be targeted in terms of potential savings in life and the costs involved.

Steps that need to be taken

1 Assess risks and consequences.
2 Decide on priorities for action.
3 Analyse causes (human, technical and administrative).
4 Determine the *risk control options* (RCOs).
5 Calculate the cost benefits for all stakeholders.
6 Decide on strategies.

At discussions at the IMO, problems have arisen concerning how human life could or should be valued, nor has anyone yet defined the limit of acceptable risk; for example, it has been estimated that a helicopter on cruise vessels would add to passenger safety, but that the cost for each life saved would be £4 million. In 1993, the UK Marine Safety Agency (MSA) proposed to the IMO that FSA could be applied to the strategic oversight of safety and pollution prevention. FSA is the process of identifying hazards, evaluating risks, and deciding on a practical course of action to manage these risks.

In 2000, the IMO agreed for the MSA to apply the FSA principles to bulk carriers. At the end of 2002, the MSC of the IMO proposed extending SOLAS regulations for bulk carriers.

A breakdown of claims

Table 13.11 shows the main category of cause of all the major claims as a percentage of the total number of claims. The main cause is the cause that is most obviously linked to the incident giving rise to the subsequent claim. 'Where there is a direct human act or decision taken by an individual which is immediately causative of the incident leading to the claim, the claim will be attributed to human error even though there will be other factors present without which the human act would not have resulted in the loss.' This definition is the one used by the P&I club and by many authorities collecting safety statistics. In Table 13.11, if we include shore error, this would indicate that some 63 per cent of claims are caused by human error. This is quite modest compared with other sources, which often claim up to 80 per cent of maritime *unsafety* is caused by human error.

Human error   To define human error as widely as the above definition is, in my opinion, a mistake, as I have found it has caused many to focus on the wrong problem. The term *error* to me would indicate that an act or judgement has been made by an individual that is obviously grossly incompetent at that moment of time. For instance, for years Ro/Ro ferries left and arrived at their berths with their bow doors open. To do it now (after the *Herald of Free Enterprise* disaster) would be gross human error, but if done before that time, one could only call it a poor operating procedure. To

Table 13.11 Main cause of major P&I club claims (percentages)	
Structural failure	12
Shore error	13
Mechanical failure	7
Equipment failure	9
Deck officer error	27
Engineer officer error	4
Crew error	13
Pilot error	6
Under investigation	4
Other	5

(Source: UK P&I club – Analysis of Major Claims 1993.)

my mind, it is unfair to classify an act as 'human error' if the person performing the act does exactly what 95 per cent of his professional colleagues would have done in the same circumstances. However, this is perhaps just another example of the particular care that is needed when interpreting the bottom line in statistical safety data.

In fact, in the case of many shipping casualties, the cause is seldom one simple error or mistake. A casualty usually occurs when chance, often a very remote chance, brings together several dubious practices in one place at one moment of time. For that reason, I would rather consider the causes to be based on the points below:

1 *Failure in communications*

(A) Between shore and ship, as in the case of the ship that unwittingly stowed nitro-glycerine (not knowing it was nitro-glycerine) over a cargo liable to spontaneous combustion, not knowing that the cargo had these characteristics. There is, of course, legislation covering these circumstances, but it can arise when a commodity is passed from hand to hand on its way from factory to ship, that not all the relevant information is passed on with it.

(B) Between ship and ship: there have been many casualties because one ship has not anticipated correctly what the other ship was doing or going to do.

(C) Between persons on the same ship: there have been many cases of collisions and groundings because those on the bridge have misunderstood one another, or assumed that the other had seen the danger or would take the necessary evasive action. Misunderstandings again often arise when several people are involved with one piece of apparatus — such as radar or automatic helmsman.

2 *The speed of technological advance outstripping our realisation of possible dangerous consequences.* For instance, in December 1969 there were explosions on three VLCCs. Subsequent research indicated that they were possibly caused by an unexpected side-effect of tank-cleaning. A few years previously, methods of reducing corrosion in tankers were also suspected of having similar catastrophic side-effects.

3 *The speed of technological advance outstripping the ability of the training facilities to ensure that those involved know how to use their new equipment.*

It was possibly some 20 years after radar was introduced in the British Merchant Navy before an adequate number of men were trained to use this device competently. During this time, there were many collisions known as radar-assisted collisions, eg the *Andrea Doria/Stockholm* collision. Under many other flags, particularly under some flags of convenience, this problem has still not been eliminated.

4 *Miscellaneous*. Simple bad habits such as smoking in bed, carelessness, drunkenness, etc. To facilitate a more accurate analysis of casualties, the UK hopes to have 'black boxes' mandatory for ships in 1999.

The cure for many accidents/claims

1 Removal of the cause eg making beds non-inflammable to reduce the dangers from smoking in bed, or routeing ships to avoid collisions.

2 Reducing the risk by supplying sophisticated apparatus and the necessary training, eg radar.

3 Reducing the extent of the damage eg dividing the ship into watertight compartments so that if there is a collision and the vessel is holed, the danger of sinking is lessened.

The application of these principles

1 To the ship

- *Construction*: The government and classification societies lay down basic principles of construction. In passenger ships, for instance, the accent is on prevention much more than in cargo ships where the high cost of building a ship to be virtually non-inflammable would not be economic.
- *Equipment*: Radio to call for assistance – also EPIRBs (emergency position indicating radio beacon); radio auto-alarm to listen automatically for distress calls (see Chapter 5 re communications and the introduction of the GMDSS in 1992); internal communications within the ship; lifeboats with quick and easy ways of getting them into the water even when the ship is listed, and inflatable liferafts; lifejackets that can be easily put on by passengers (they should not be too cumbersome but at the same time give adequate buoyancy); good firefighting apparatus for both accommodation and cargo space.
- *Training*: This must be realistic, and – unlike most other shipboard activities – one cannot hope or even desire that the crew learn from experience. Possibly only one deck officer in twenty will ever have to abandon a sinking ship, so for any ship in this unfortunate predicament, the chances are very high that it will be a completely novel situation to those in charge.

2 Ashore

- *Management -- the ISM Code* (the International Management Code for the Safety Operation of Ships and Pollution Prevention). The ISM Code had been discussed by the IMO for several years and it was agreed in 1993–4 that it should become mandatory within the SOLAS convention. This took effect in July 1998 for some ships, and applied in 2002 for other ships. One important aspect of the Code is that every company should designate a person ashore who has direct access to the highest level of management. Part of this person's responsibility should include monitoring the safety and pollution aspects of the operation of the company's ships.

ISO 14001 environmental management system (EMS) is focused on environmental impacts. The idea is to identify significant impacts and, if negative, to reduce or remove them. Wallenius Lines embraced this system in 1998 and they claim it gave them several economic advantages. Many companies are going for or have gone to 'quality management systems', such as *ISO 9000*. This is important as safety is not an add-on extra, but a consequence of an efficient well-run organisation.

- *Research*. In October 1987, 'black boxes' or VDRs (vessel data recorders) were put on some British vessels as part of a research programme to assess their effectiveness. At that time they were expensive, each device costing around $150,000 (USD). However, the IMO recommended that VDRs should be put on all new ships and existing passenger ships from 1 July 2002. In July 2001, P&O had fitted them to all their ships. In 2002, an average price was around $70,000. A VDR consists of three basic functional parts: 1) Sensor interface; 2) Data acquisition and recording module; 3) Protective memory capsule.
- *Analyses of cause* (investigations). VDRs could help here.
- *Coastguard, lifeboat and helicopter rescue services*.
- *International co-operation* through the IMO and the ICS.
- *Organisations such as AMVER* (AMVER stands for automated mutual-assistance vessel rescue, which was started in 1958).

How the damage is paid for

1 Damage to the ship: by insurance and/or P&I.
2 Damage to the cargo: by the cargo owners' insurance or, if it is the shipowner's liability, then by his P&I club (1 and 2 could be the subject of general average payments).
3 Damage to the crew, stevedores or passenger liability: paid for by the shipowner's P&I.
4 Damage to the environment: IOPC, P&I, COFR, etc.

Of course, although the above organisations actually hand over the money, they are merely acting as 'bankers'. In most cases, these organisations will be paid by the shipowners – who will in turn collect the money from their customers. So, in the end, everyone pays for safety.

Marine insurance

London is still the most important centre in the world of the marine insurance market. Of this London market, about 44 per cent is conducted by the large marine insurance companies; the remaining 56 per cent of the underwriting is conducted at Lloyd's.

Lloyd's of London is a unique and interesting body. It started in Edward Lloyd's coffee house (the earliest record of it is in 1688), where shipowners and merchants met to discuss business. Individual merchants would accept part of the risk of the shipping adventure and underwrite their signatures on a policy of insurance.

In 1771, a committee was formed to regularise the transactions and in 1871 Lloyd's was incorporated by an Act of Parliament. In general, the system has changed little over the years. Even in their new building, the underwriters maintain their tradition by sitting in 'boxes' reminiscent of the old coffee tables of the original coffee house. Lloyd's is in fact a vast insurance market place, and an insurance broker engaged by the shipowner will move among the underwriters asking them to accept part of the 'risk'. If they will, they sign the 'slip' indicating what proportion of the risk they are prepared to accept. From the slip, the policy is eventually drawn up. Lloyd's is not a company, but a collection of individuals who have agreed to accept the commercial discipline and code of conduct laid down by the committee of Lloyd's. However, in the last decade Lloyd's has run into financial difficulties and possible future restructuring will be considered.

Over the course of years, a vast intelligence network has grown up around the world to assist the underwriter – such as Lloyd's agents, etc. *Lloyd's List*, London's oldest newspaper, started as part of this intelligence service.

There are many different types of policies, most of which are self-evident from their titles – eg voyage policies, time policies, fleet policies, port policies (to be used between voyages), builders' construction policies, etc. For large ships, the insurance may be the greatest of all her operating costs.

Protection & Indemnity (P&I) clubs

These are mutual insurance clubs that shipowners have formed (the first was started in 1855) to meet the financial liabilities that they could not insure with Lloyd's or with any of the large insurance companies. When they were formed originally, the shipowner's biggest worry was the one-quarter collision risk that the underwriter would not accept. Now his biggest financial liability is to his crew and cargo.

Of the total amount of money paid out by a large P&I club recently, the amounts were apportioned as follows:

- Cargo liability, 32 per cent
- Injury and illness, 25 per cent

- Oil pollution, 14 per cent
- Quarter collision liability, 24 per cent
- Removal of wrecks, 3 per cent
- Others, 2 per cent

P&I insurance covers claims made by the crew for loss of life, personal injury, hospital and medical expenses while abroad, and all repatriation expenses. There are also the extraordinary medical expenses – such as an outbreak of the plague.

It covers the shipowner for damage done by his ship to docks, piers and other fixed objects.

If his ship sinks, marine insurance will pay up on the value of the ship, but the shipowner is left with the responsibility of perhaps having to remove the wreck. This would be paid for by the P&I club. Many of the fines that might be imposed by governments can be covered, as also are claims for loss, short delivery, pilferage or damage to cargo. In other words, P&I covers claims and losses incident to the business of shipowning, which the committee of the club considers come within the scope of the cover.

The shipowner pays, usually by an advance call, so much per ton for his entered tonnage. If necessary, the club may have to make a supplementary

In severe weather, containers can become detached from their fixings and fall overboard. Not only will this cause loss of stability and financial loss, but loose containers are one of the greatest hazards to cruising yachtsmen.

call or, alternatively, offer a return of the 'call' – depending on the accuracy of their estimate.

To avoid the efficient shipowner having to subsidise the less efficient one, each shipowner is assessed for his calls on his past record.

In addition to P&I cover, many of the clubs offer the following cover if the shipowner requires it:

- War risk insurance cover on the ship's hull and machinery and/or on the freight to be earned.
- FD&D (freight, demurrage & defence). This covers the shipowner for legal advice and expenses relating to the problems that arise in the commercial operation of his ships.
- Strike cover against either strikes by his crew or in any of the ports that the ship is visiting.
  Further facts about P&I:
- As with insurance, London is the centre of P&I club activity.
- There are about a dozen British clubs, which handle about 70 per cent of the business.
- There are three Scandinavian clubs, which handle about 17 per cent of the business.
- There is one club in the USA, which handles about 2 per cent of the business.
- There is one club in Japan, which handles about 9 per cent of the business.
- The majority of the clubs work together in what is known as the London Pool, and all large individual claims go into the pool and are shared by them. The pool is in turn reinsured at Lloyd's for any large catastrophic claims.

General average

This is one of the oldest practices in marine insurance and is mentioned in Aristotle's *Nicomachian Ethics*. This practice, now codified and agreed to internationally under the York Antwerp Rules, states that if the maritime adventure is in peril and the captain decides to sacrifice the ship or cargo for the common good, then all parties who gain by the safe completion of the voyage make a contribution to reimburse the one who has suffered by the sacrifice.

For example, suppose a fire breaks out and the ship is in peril. If in the course of putting the fire out some cargo is ruined, then the owners of the cargo can be considered to have made a sacrifice for the common good and can therefore be reimbursed by a general average contribution from the shipowner and other cargo owners.

Another example might be a ship that has run aground. If it stays aground then an approaching storm may break the ship up on the rocks, and all the ship and the cargo would be lost. To pull the ship back into deep water, the engines may have to be used so severely that they are damaged. The shipowner can subsequently ask for a contribution from the cargo owners to make good this damage. It is only the loss that was voluntarily incurred for the common safety that can be claimed for. In the latter example, the damage incurred by the ship going aground is not a general average situation, only the financial sacrifices subsequently necessary to get her out of danger.

Although the idea is simple in theory, in a real situation the practical application of it can be complicated. Supposing there is a situation where there is a general average loss that amounts to £1 million. The shipowner appoints a general average adjuster, who has to establish the total cost of the ship and cargo – which in this case is £30 million. The proportion of the adventure lost in this case to the general average sacrifice was 1/30. Hence all participants in this adventure will have to pay 1/30 the value of their stake in the adventure, ie the shipowner will contribute 1/30 the value of his ship, and each cargo shipper 1/30 the value of his cargo to make good the loss. This does, of course, take time to calculate – it may well take several years. The shipowner is responsible for collecting all these contributions, so before he loses his lien on the cargo he may therefore ask his agents at the various discharging ports to collect a general average deposit or bond from the consignees before releasing the cargo.

By the year 2000, the headquarters for general average had moved to the Baltic Exchange and it was found that the number of times per annum that general average was being declared was reducing each year. In 2001, a further international conference was held to consider the future developments of general average.

Protest

In all cases of general average:

- Protests should be noted as soon as possible – within 24 hours of arrival in port – and, with cargo, a protest must be made before breaking bulk.
- A *note of protest* is simply a declaration by the master of circumstances beyond his control that may give, or have given, rise to loss or damage. Such a declaration must be made before a notary public, magistrate, British consul, or other authority. Usually, statements under oath will be taken from the master and other members of the crew and these will have to be supported by appropriate log book entries. At the time of noting protest, the master should reserve the right to extend it.
- Protests are admissible in evidence before legal tribunals (ie courts), and in many cases are therefore essential to the establishment of a claim. In many countries, particularly on the Continent, protests are received as evidence as a matter of course. In the UK, however, they are not accepted as evidence in favour of the party making the protest unless both parties consent.

In any of the following circumstances it is advisable for the master to note a protest:

- Whenever during the voyage the ship has encountered conditions of wind and sea such as may result in damage to cargo.
- When from any cause the ship is damaged, or feared to be damaged.
- When through stress of weather it has not been practicable to adopt normal precautions in the matter of ventilation of perishable cargo.
- When cargo is shipped in such condition that it is likely to suffer deterioration during the voyage (but, in this case, protest will not be effective unless the bill of lading was endorsed to show condition of cargo at time of shipment).
- When any serious breach of C/P is committed by the charterer or his agent (such as refusal to load, unduly delaying loading, loading improper cargo, refusal to pay demurrage, refusal to accept the bill of lading in form signed by master, etc).
- When consignees fail to discharge cargo or take delivery thereof, and pay freight in accordance with the terms of C/P and B/L.

Salvage

Salvage is the reward paid to those who save maritime property. For there to be a valid salvage service, the service must be voluntary, the maritime property must be in danger, and the service must be successful (no cure – no pay). Under York Antwerp Rules 2004, salvage is no longer part of general average.

Although most masters and ship operators would prefer to negotiate a fixed towage contract, if the vessel is in imminent peril, valuable time is saved if both parties agree to the Lloyd's Form of Salvage Agreement (Lloyd's Open Form – LOF). Under this agreement, the salvage is undertaken and an arbitrator appointed by the committee of Lloyd's subsequently decides what the 'reward' should be, taking into account the risk involved, etc. LOF 2000 includes the SCOPIC (Special Compensation P&I Club) clause, whereby salvers can claim compensation if they can reduce any environmental damage even if the vessel is not saved.

Place of refuge

Following the six-week search for a place of refuge by the stricken product tanker *Castro* in early 2001, the IMO has spent time considering the problems arising from 'places of refuge'. The following aspects are being considered:

- Action that the master of the ship in distress should take.
- Evaluation of the risks involved.
- Action expected from the coastal states.
- Compensation issues to be considered.

Under the Dangerous Vessels Act 1985 the harbourmaster of a UK port can prohibit the entry of a vessel in distress. However, under the MSA 1995 as amended in 1997, the Secretary of State's Representative (SOSREP) has the power to override a decision by a UK harbourmaster.

Safety and environmental issues

Although the environment has been with us longer than ships, a knowledge or study of this subject has not in the past been considered an essential part of a shipping person's education. Times have changed, though, so I have included the following section which has been prepared by Professor T Sampson of the World Maritime University.

Environmental implications of maritime transport infrastructure

Transport corridors

Environmental concerns over the infrastructure of maritime transport can relate to all activities that may disrupt existing ecosystems during the development and construction processes. This could include a road or rail right-of-way needed to connect hinterlands to ports – especially if cut through a stand of rain forest. Such development raises concern not just for the relatively small amount of forest that may be eliminated by the new or expanded right-of-way, but also for the potential for the increased use and ensuing destruction of rain forest bordering the right-of-way which, because of new or better access to the area, may naturally ensue.

Each country of course has a right to build or expand its transportation corridors, and this today is normally the result of careful planning. Such planning today most often includes an evaluation of the environmental impact that the corridor may present, and international funding sources for such projects are now most often contingent upon the proper addressing of environmental issues. An area of greater concern is related to infrastructure development or expansion that impinges upon waterways and wetlands. While road and rail rights-of-way may cut through or over waterways and wetlands, the development of greatest concern lies near the node that must tie waterborne transport to land transport.

Nodes connecting to waterborne modes

The node that connects with waterborne transport is by necessity in an environmentally very sensitive and ecologically important location. In the wetlands along the shore of an ocean, sea, lake or river exist the multitude of diverse species that lie at the base of the world's marine food chain. Even today the world is beginning to see the limits reached on the available harvests from the sea of the marine life that is in demand from mankind's existing population. The direct connection between quantities of harvestable seafood for man and the amount of wetlands available to support that harvest have been scientifically substantiated. In industrialised countries most of the wetlands surrounding population centres have been filled in or dramatically altered. As new or greater port facility capacity is needed, a way must be found to minimise the further impact on the world's shrinking wetlands.

Container stacking and handling areas should not be built or enlarged by filling surrounding wetlands. Connection corridors to road or rail modes should be planned without the need for elimination of wetlands. Similarly, the construction of longer or more berths for the vessels calling at a port facility needs to be achieved without the total bulkheading and filling of the needed area. The practice in many industrialised countries now is to require that any filling of wetlands can only take place if additional wetlands are created on a basis of equal area compensation. However, even this practice must be regarded as a questionable compromise. Destruction of one piece of the ecosystem is not immediately compensated by the formation of an 'equivalent' area. Wetlands develop over millenniums and a newly constructed 'wetland' may take millenniums before it compensates for the wetlands that have been altered or destroyed.

The concern for preservation of wetlands suggests that alternative approaches must be found to accommodate the pressure for expansion of maritime transport's needed port infrastructure. Site selection for new or replacement port facilities should not be made with the primary emphasis being the location's ability to expedite the flow of freight between modes to the exclusion of environmental concerns. A site with near-shore deep water may allow use of existing high ground for a terminal's supporting infrastructure, while minimising the amount of wetlands that need to be disturbed.

Expansion of a terminal facility through filling of wetlands should not be the right decision just because it is more cost-effective than rezoning and acquiring surrounding land that may currently be used for other industrial, business or residential uses. Some supporting terminal infrastructure needs may be provided with similar efficiency even if located at greater distances from the pierhead. Innovative use of technology to move containers away from the pierhead may reduce the need for access to the full length of a vessel and thereby the amount of wetland to be disturbed.

Run-off considerations

The construction of facilities to process the movement of intermodal freight nearly always entails the levelling of the land area and often the paving of this area. Such areas are often subject to intense vehicular traffic as quantities of freight are parcelled from one part of the facility to another. This means that these areas receive the constant drip of lubricating fluids and fuel as the result of normal operations, or maintenance and fuelling activities. There is also the constant possibility of a spillage of the freight that is in transit at the facility. Without proper pre-planning, any such polluting materials that find their way to the levelled ground will ultimately make their way into the environment – either the ground water below the facility, or to the ditches, streams, lakes, rivers or seas that surround the facility.

If the facility surface is not paved, there are some inherent advantages. A spilled material that is hazardous to the surrounding environment will not tend to drain off rapidly. The lack of pavement allows the time needed to make an effective and proper response with subsequent removal and replacement of the contaminated earth. However, the tendency is to allow spilled materials – including fuel and lubricants from the operating vehicles – to seep down into the soil where it shortly will be out of sight and out of mind. This material will slowly make its way to where it starts to damage the surrounding environment. An unpaved facility area requires a programme of inspections to detect unreported spills and periodic removal and replacement of the surface layers of the most heavily trafficked areas.

If a facility is paved it can prevent materials from soaking undetected into the ground and allow effective control of the slow but constant loss of fuel and lubricants from the vehicles. However, paved facilities must be designed with care to ensure that spills do not flow rapidly to the perimeter and then into surrounding waterways. This means that barriers may need to be constructed around the perimeter of the facility and/or that a drainage system that feeds to surrounding waterways must have a means for rapid closure or be channelled first through a separation reservoir or tank.

In the absence of an accident it may seem that run-off considerations are not so important. However, at a node in the transport system, huge quantities of hazardous materials pass over the same paths for a period of years or even decades. Some of these materials are extremely toxic and the gradual accumulation of these materials resulting from an almost undetectable but constant leakage can, over the course of years, lead to the sterilisation of the surrounding aquatic ecosystem.

Environmental implications of a maritime transport superstructure

Vessel emissions

The superstructure related to maritime transport of most notable environmental concern consists of the vessels that are involved – the ships and the barges. The scenario for future development in the movement of the world's goods implies that more vessels of greater capacity will come into use. This will bring with it the introduction of polluting air emissions into regions previously not contaminated and increasing volumes of these emissions along the corridors of transport that are already in use. This aspect of maritime transport's environmental impact will not be resolved in an independent fashion. Rather, it is directly linked to the overall development of technology to produce vessel propulsion systems that release fewer and fewer harmful emissions. However, until such time as non-polluting vessel propulsion systems are developed, it will remain an important area to be addressed. Alternative modes of transport must be considered where they hold the potential for a more sustainable alternative. In 2002, the ICS produced a code of practice on ships' bunker fuel to reduce toxic emissions.

At present, it is not possible to move goods in the marine, air or road modes without carrying a source of air-polluting emissions along with the cargo. But, for the movement by rail, much cargo is already moved along electrified rail totally without the problem of air emissions along the corridor. Admittedly, the electrical power must be produced somewhere, and if it is in an oil- or coal-fired power plant, the emissions problem merely exists at another location.

It is possible to generate the needed power for electrified rail without the air-polluting emissions. At present, nuclear power plant generation of electricity is the only practicable alternative, and it is often debated if this is an acceptable justification, given the potential of other environmental problems. However, in the not too distant future, increasing quantities of energy will be produced by wind and solar power and there is the potential for significant quantities to be produced from the energy of the sea – either from the motion of the waves or from the thermal differential between deep and surface waters.

As clean sources of electrical energy production begin to provide a greater share of the electrical energy demand, the emissions advantage of moving freight along rail corridors must be factored into the evaluation of modal choice. Until such time as technology can eliminate the emissions problem from the maritime transport mode, it will be important to ensure that expansion and new developments in freight movement do not contribute increasing levels of air pollutants to urban or regional areas that already have, or could have, air pollution levels harmful to residential and working inhabitants. From the environmental standpoint, it may be wise to choose locations for the nodes that connect the different modes at points outside of urban areas that lie along the transport corridors connecting population centres.

Dredging for vessel access

There is an additional environmental problem that might be considered an infrastructure issue, but it is linked directly to the superstructure requirements of the waterborne mode. For vessel access to the port or terminal facilities, a depth of water in excess of the draft of the vessel is required. In all ports but those favoured by naturally deep access, or where currents continually scour the bottom preventing the build-up of sediment, the dredging of the access, usually on a recurring basis, is necessary.

This process significantly alters the natural balance of the marine ecosystem over the length of channel or berth that must be maintained in this way. Recent studies in Northern Europe have suggested the virtual elimination of a region's eel industry from the process of dredging. As deeper-draft vessels are developed as a response to carry greater quantities of freight, and as the need is felt to allow such vessels to sail further up shallow estuaries or rivers, the issue of dredging takes on an increased importance. And, there are other aspects of dredging that are a cause for concern. The sediments that are deposited along the bottom of rivers that flow through industrialised regions have through the years been contaminated with toxic residue – most notably heavy metals. These residues in the past have been responsible for the contamination of the local seafood and even the elimination of marine life in many regions.

In many countries now, the contamination of the waterways has been curtailed by the elimination or control of point source discharges from industries that produce such harmful by-products. Over time, the natural sedimentation process at work in many waterways has buried these toxic materials at sufficient depths to shield the bottom-dwelling marine life from the toxic effects, allowing a natural recovery. To dredge up these areas now exposes the marine life in the area again to the same habitat-destroying toxins. Even though the sediment may be removed from the bottom of the waterway, the process releases this toxic material to the downstream areas that are not dredged.

The environmental problems associated with the dredging process extend beyond the concern for the bottom of the water course. Once this material has been removed, it must be disposed of in an environmentally acceptable manner. This material is normally used for land-fill applications ashore. However, when this material is contaminated with toxins and heavy metals, the leaching of the materials to ground water sources or inland streams, lakes or reservoirs spreads these persistent forms of contamination to new locations.

Marine growth on vessel hulls

Related to the problem of toxic materials in bottom sediments is the contribution from the materials applied to the bottom of vessels to retard or prevent the accumulation of marine growth. For maritime transport to be able to move efficiently and avoid the unnecessary burning of fuel, the build-up of marine growth must be avoided. Past practices have employed the use of paints that have included materials toxic to sea-grasses and barnacles. While these materials have proven rather effective in providing a clean underwater hull, they have contributed steadily to the accumulation of the toxins from the paint in the surrounding waters where vessels transit, moor and undergo repairs. The toxins from these paints steadily leach into the environment and are deposited wholesale into the surrounding waters when the adhesion of the paint to the hull breaks down or the bottom paint is mechanically removed without the collection of the residue. The result has been a steadily expanding plume in the water around port areas, rendering the water and sediments unable to sustain the basic components of marine life that are critical to the marine food chain.

Options are needed to reduce the introduction into the water of such toxins. Safe hull cleaning methods are needed as well as the introduction of coming technology to employ coatings that are naturally resistant to selected marine growth without the potential for overall harm to the surrounding marine ecosystem. The once popular TBT-based paints were banned from use in June 2003. They should finally be eliminated by 2008. The IMO has agreed that previous coatings of TBT can be sealed as many as five times cheaper than blasting.

Chemicals in portable tanks

Independent of the vehicle that moves the freight, there are other superstructure-related considerations for the environment that need to be addressed. Portable tanks that have been designed for maritime transport of hazardous materials present a significant concern. As the industrialisation process gathers momentum in the countries now regarded as having developing economies, there will be an increased need for a large variety of chemicals that pose significant environmental threats when transported by such tanks in concentrated forms. This includes the chemicals needed to support agricultural growth through pesticides, herbicides and fertilisers and the chemicals needed to support manufacturing and fabrication processes.

The safe and sensible use of such chemicals is beyond the purview of those who are supplying the means of transport. However, there is an obligation on the part of those supplying the means of transport to see that the transportation process does not stimulate harmful environmental practices. The cleaning of chemical tanks once they are emptied to reduce the hazard they present is a common practice. It is also done to allow the return shipment of a tank at a reduced rate if it does not contain a hazardous material. The prospect exists for tremendous numbers of such tanks to be cleaned in hinterland areas where there exists no means to dispose of highly toxic and polluting residues. In many parts of the world the common practice is already to dispose of the residues directly onto the ground or into the waterways. The transport system must find a way to discourage such practices.

Environmental implications of maritime transport operations

It is not the intent here to try to address all of the methods of operation of maritime transport that either endanger the environment or could be used to protect the environment. Volumes have been written on this and it is the subject of much of the global regulatory effort that is in place today. Instead, the focus here is upon the various environmental issues or problems that exist because of maritime transport operations that have the potential for correction if a systems approach is applied by the various entities engaged in intermodal freight transport.

Reception facilities for vessels

The movement of hydrocarbons and chemicals by the waterborne mode poses an inherent risk to the marine environment. This risk arises not just from the potential for a massive accidental discharge, but also from the more routine discharges associated with operational activities. It has been estimated that only one-quarter of the oil introduced into the water from ships is the result of accidental discharges. To address the pollution potential

With this type of ship, considerable care is needed to avoid environmental damage through spillage.

from operational discharges, an extensive regulatory system has been established. At the heart of the approach has been a prohibition for the discharge of hydrocarbons and chemicals into the water from vessels. They have been required to retain such accumulated wastes aboard until they can be discharged ashore.

Vessels that must have the permission of governments to operate have been forced to make the alterations to vessel design and equipment to comply with such regulations. However, these same governments that should provide facilities ashore for the reception of these accumulated materials have failed to make such facilities available in many port areas. Part of the reason for this is the failure of some governments to back voiced environmental concern with budget actions to support the key element of the environmental protection system they have established for vessel operators. Other approaches have been to provide facilities only in the port areas that receive large enough volumes of vessel traffic to justify the investment in reception facilities.

The result has been that a global mechanism to preserve the marine environment has actually worked to the environment's disadvantage. Hazardous residues that previously were discharged in open waters are now retained until the more environmentally sensitive near-shore waters are reached and, in the absence of adequate reception facilities, are often eventually discharged nearer to shore on the approach to or departure from many of the world's ports. As numbers and size of ships increase to meet future consumer transport demand, this lack of reception facilities becomes a problem of ever-increasing proportion. While the increasing traffic levels may mean that more ports will begin to justify the provision of facilities, this approach also ensures that newly developed ports, or small growing ports, will not receive the facilities to protect their environment until such time as vessel traffic levels have already increased to the point where they have sustained significant environmental degradation.

So far the reception facility issue has only been discussed in terms of residues of hydrocarbons or chemicals. While these substances may represent the issues of greatest current concern, the same reception facility mechanism and problems associated with these materials also applies to shipboard-generated garbage and sewage. For all of these materials a different systems approach is needed that will allow the preservation of the existing unpolluted and uncontaminated marine areas as they begin to develop in response to growing global transport needs. The operations of transport nodes must mesh smoothly with the operations of transport modes if sustainable development of intermodal transport is to be achieved.

Vessel ballast water

Another environmental threat presented by the waterborne mode is associated with disturbing the balance of localised marine ecosystems. Over the centuries the accidental transport of harmful insects, vermin and disease has been guarded against to protect a region's agriculture or the health of its population. What was taking place in the waterways went largely unnoticed. Now with vessels that carry large quantities of ballast water for a variety of operational purposes, the transport of unwanted marine organisms from one region to another has become a problem.

Some species live in a controlled manner in some regions only to disrupt the ecological balance by expanding rapidly in more conducive conditions or with the lack of a local predator, displacing other valuable marine species. This has perhaps been the result of such organisms now being relocated in larger and larger numbers due to the greater quantities of ballast carried and the increases in the volume of vessel traffic. As the demand for waterborne transport increases in the future, the potential for loss of critical or valuable regional species will increase as well. Recently, *Lloyd's List* carried a criticism of ballast water changing. Methods were suggested, such as cyclonic separation and other technologies that killed off invasive species. See www.globallast./imo.org

Containerisation of packaged hazardous materials

The growth in the movement of freight within containers has brought with it new environmental concerns. Very concentrated forms of toxins and other hazardous materials can be shipped in small packages and these move more and more frequently within containers. Detailed regulations have been developed to try to ensure that such materials are not stowed or stacked next to other materials which could have serious effects such as fire, explosion, or the release of poisonous vapours if the different types of materials become mixed. These regulations are very detailed, but also very complicated for untrained personnel to apply. The result has been a steady increase in detection of containers with improper stowage of such hazardous materials, and an increase in the number of hazardous material incidents that are taking place when such materials break free within a container.

As the demand for transport of such goods increases, so the potential increases for more and worse disasters that can have devastating effects on personnel and the environment. Response to these types of hazardous material incidents is most often by a local fire brigade; and even in industrialised countries today it is only in the larger fire response organisations where trained expertise is readily available to make a proper and effective response. Where training and equipment is lacking, the normal response of persons trained to fight fires is to hose the scene down with water. While in some situations this may in fact be the best response, in other situations it may in fact be the worst response. Some materials may react with the water, resulting in rapid oxidation of the material or the release of poisonous fumes. Perhaps the worst possibility for the environment is the tendency for such spilled materials to be flushed with fire hoses into the nearest ditch, stream or storm drain where, depending on the material, it can destroy any marine life over a large area for years. Persistent materials may infiltrate the human food chain and cause congenital problems that do not become apparent for decades.

The likelihood of containers, loaded as we now see them, reaching new distances into uncontaminated hinterlands, to be unloaded by untrained and unsuspecting persons, presents a significant problem. The system of intermodal containerised freight transport must accept the challenge of finding the solution to the threat that this poses. Within the facilities at the connecting nodes where such cargo is handled, there must be a provision for specialised areas to handle and store such materials such that any emergency situations that may develop can be handled in a manner to minimise the threat to personal safety and the environment.

This should be possible to accomplish by incorporating such plans for any anticipated new facility development or expansion at transport nodes. A more difficult problem will be to find a method to ensure the proper initial packaging of material and its stowage within a container at the supplier end of the chain. A still more difficult problem will be to find the means to ensure the safe unpacking of the hazardous material and the possibility for a trained response to any dangerous conditions or damage that are discovered at the customer end of the chain.

Even if the material has arrived at the customer end of the chain in an undamaged state, there remains the problem of the packaging materials for the hazardous substances. If the customer end of the chain is within newly developing hinterlands, it will not be likely that there exists an acceptable means of disposing of these contaminated and dangerous quantities of refuse. It may be necessary that the transport chain provides the pathway for such material back to an acceptable disposal facility.

Implications of competition and privatisation in maritime transport

In the past, providing the means for global transport of freight has been the domain of both government and private enterprise. In recent years, while governments continue to play an active role, the tendency is for the gradual relinquishing of the field to private enterprise, with governments remaining more as a player within the infrastructure sector and less so within the superstructure and operator sectors. Many studies have indicated that this is a positive change from the standpoint of economics for both national and private interests, as well as for suppliers and customers. But not much is written about the effect of this trend on the environment. Does this trend put us on the path to sustainable development?

On the surface, the answer to this question seems to be, no! Governments, by their nature, may make an investment in concepts that they deem to be in the best interest of their national security or the social welfare of their people, even though it may have a negative impact on both the economics and the competitiveness of the venture. Private enterprise will make such investments only if forced to by the government, or in some rare cases when the publicity of such investments will positively affect the bottom line. Even when such investments are made by private enterprise by the force of government regulation, the need to remain competitive exerts a pressure that drives compliance to minimal levels or defeats the intent of the regulation altogether. The reluctance of private entities to invest strictly for the benefit of environmental matters works against sustainable development.

Conversely, government control of transport systems tends to limit unnecessary investment or over-expansion of port or nodal facilities. Private competition among ports or facilities in a region can lead to many localities investing and creating over-capacity. In a global sense this can have a significantly negative environmental impact if such excess expansion is done in an environmentally detrimental manner, such as the filling in of more wetlands than is absolutely necessary to support the region's transport needs. In this case, the willingness of private entities to invest for competitive economic benefit works against sustainable development.

But, as seen in the case of reception facilities, the governments themselves are not always willing to make the needed investment to underwrite sustainable development. They are willing to pay only so much to effect the programmes that are needed to protect the environment from the hazards posed by the global transport system. And even governments' strong regulatory approach, which it is willing to work upon the private enterprise system, is lacking in its ability to accomplish its objectives. Regulation, without adequate enforcement, has always proved to be a weak remedy. And when governments must think of trying to effect enforcement on the entire global transport system, will any amount of enforcement be adequate? While there will remain a continuing need for regulation and enforcement, such an approach does not contain the total answer for achieving sustainable development of the global transport system and some of the answers may be found within the private sector.

Mechanisms must be found to achieve sustainable development that overcome the difficulties that have defeated past approaches of regulation and enforcement. Perhaps one of the greatest shortcomings of past regulatory approaches has been that the difficulties presented by the pressures of competition have been either inadequately addressed or ignored. While competition has proven to be wonderful in many ways — stimulating innovation, reducing costs of production, transport and operations — it also reduces market share and possibly bankrupts any business whose cost for product or service remains higher than the norm due to accepting costs for environmental preservation that are eschewed or avoided by others.

Misconceptions of the 'polluter pays principle'

As international accords and governmental actions have placed an increasing burden upon shipowners and operators to improve vessel safety and operations to preserve the environment, there has grown an increasing resentment towards the 'environmentalists'. It is often claimed, and can be seen to be true in many cases, that environmental proposals simply are not in tune with the realities of the global demand for maritime transport. An 'environmentalist's' response to the great concern over significantly greater needs for the transport of oil by 2025 might well be that consumers must simply be educated that they must do without increased supplies of oil. An 'environmentalist's' understanding of the 'polluter pays principle' has often been interpreted to mean that the vessel carrying the oil that might be spilled is the potential polluter. Remedies to make sure that this polluting shipowner pays have been many. There are regulations in place to make the shipowner pay for programmes for prevention and other regulations to make sure that the shipowner pays compensation for any environmental damage that might be sustained as a result of a vessel accident.

But this 'failure' of the 'environmentalist' to understand the perspective of the shipowner is only half of the problem. It is often true that the shipowner, the port operator, even the government regulators, do not understand the importance of the message of the 'environmentalists'. When the industrial revolution began in the middle of the eighteenth century, the damage that isolated industries could work upon a global environment was slight. Only a few industrial sites were trying to provide industrial goods for a relatively small number of persons and the harmful effects of pollution were of isolated local concern. Global population at this time was less than 800 million people. By 2025, hundreds of thousands of industries will be moving industrial goods through thousands of maritime transport facilities in an attempt to reach roughly 8,200 million people. In 2025, each isolated local pollution incident will have a global significance.

Environmentalists and maritime transport professionals must all find a better understanding of the environmental and developmental aspects of maritime transport. The application of the 'polluter pays principle' must be clearly understood and the mechanisms to make the polluter pay must in fact work towards sustainable development and not against it.

It must be understood by all parties that the polluter is really the consumer; and if the costs of dealing with the risks of pollution and the results of the pollution are borne by the consumer, then there is hope for sustainable development in the maritime transport field. It is an economic pressure that brings damage and risk of damage to the marine environment from the maritime transport system. This economic pressure is generated by the consumer. Pollution and risks of pollution will continue until they are economically unacceptable to the consumer. As systems and programmes are designed to reduce the threat of pollution from maritime transport, they can be expected to develop in comprehensiveness in proportion to the reality of the individual environmental threat. Costs of these systems and programmes will probably be proportional to their comprehensiveness. If the developmental need for the environmentally harmful product or service is great enough, the consumer/polluter will be willing to bear this expense. If the need is not great enough, the cost of the environmental protective mechanisms will diminish the demand for the product or service.

As mechanisms are developed to address the environmental risk of the product or service, their potential for effectiveness must be measured against their ability to bring this economic pressure upon the consumer. If a regulatory mechanism directs the expense of a programme or system at shipowners, the effectiveness may be defeated or minimised if some shipowners, under the pressure of competition, can find ways to 'legitimately', or practically, avoid the mechanism. The shipper of the product will likely choose the shipowner who has found this less costly way of operating. The consumer will be able to avoid the cost of environmental protection by choosing the shipper that uses the shipowner that avoids the mechanism. If instead the regulatory mechanisms could be directed at all shippers who pass all costs along to consumers, the shipowners would not be seeking ways to avoid such costs and the consumer would receive the full economic pressure arising from the environmental risks of the product or service.

Changing philosophical approaches

Most providers of transport services will not object to adopting environmental principles or regulated environmental standards, providing that these will be applied equally to all competitors and do not aggravate some natural disadvantage. If this can be done, competitive standing of an individual entity is not compromised; the cost of the environmental measure is merely passed on to the customer. This is the necessary result if sustainable development is to be achieved. It is the customer, the user of the products or services, that should be expected to incur the cost of protecting the environment from that product or service. Without this, alternative products or services that are less threatening to the environment cannot compete with or replace existing products or services. This approach, to have the consumer bear the cost of protecting the environment, goes to the heart of the 'polluter pays principle'.

From the aspect of the new or small businesses that are trying to find a way to increase market share against large or strong competitors, a better product or service must be provided at lower cost. Too often today, a lower cost alternative is found by limiting or avoiding compliance with environmental principles or regulations. It is in this sector that regulation and enforcement will remain a necessary ingredient to achieve sustainable development. However, the task of enforcement can be diminished if innovative and comprehensive approaches to government regulation are adopted.

A regulation that says that a vessel must discharge accumulated oily bilge waste to a shore-based reception facility is simply not effective if no reception facility exists. The regulation must contain the solution to the problem of providing the facility. Perhaps movement of cargo by any waterborne mode must include a volumetric or tonnage tax that can be drawn upon to provide the needed facilities. The regulation is still not effective if it costs the vessel to discharge at the facility. A competitive edge can be gained if the waste can be successfully discharged at sea. The vessel must gain a competitive edge, or at least retain its competitive standing, by using the facility. Perhaps the vessel must be paid to use the facility – or can only recover a 'pollution bond' if it can be shown that the facility is utilised on each port call.

More approaches are needed that contain such incentive mechanisms. Their use is beginning to be seen in some government actions. Pollution permits for aerial emissions are available in some countries to industries that face the cost of large capital investments for exhaust gas scrubbers. These permits for a prescribed amount of emissions can be sold to competitors on the open market. The amount received for the sale can be used to underwrite the cost of the investment in new equipment. The total amount of pollution is limited by the permits; and there is an incentive to be one of the first to sell the permit and purchase new equipment as the last to do so will have no market for the permit. An effective programme for the development of maritime transport needs to craft carefully within it such incentive related concepts.

Concluding remarks

Careful thought and planning on the part of all the entities involved in maritime transport is needed if the coming demand for increased transport capacity is to be met in a manner that supports sustainable development principles. Awareness of the problems and acceptance of the need for sustainable development of the global transport system form the basis for success. New and aggressive thinking can provide the right approaches. Co-ordination and co-operation among the diverse entities involved can bring together the sound principles of local actions into a comprehensive programme of global effectiveness.

With maritime transport systems being developed in a fashion that requires co-operation between private entities, and in concert with the support and co-operation of governments, the basis already exists for finding solutions to the many and varied environmental problems that stand in the way of sustainable development. A co-operation that can work to mesh effectively the various features and requirements of the different transport modes, and that can find solutions to the transport demands of both suppliers and consumers, has the capability to find the answers also to global environmental concerns – if it is recognised that this is a necessary and equally important part of the planning process.

Still, it must be remembered that there will be no single government entity that will oversee the growth in the maritime transport system and thus no single entity to examine the global environmental impact. As the company in which you work seeks to compete against the company of your neighbour, as the nation in which I live seeks development to the same extent as the nation in which you live, we have the natural impetus for non-sustainable development. Sustainable development of the maritime transport system will only happen if each of us, where we find ourselves working, places emphasis on the environmental considerations to the same extent as the developmental considerations.

14 DOCUMENTATION

Normally when considering documentation the accent is on the legal issues, as most of the important documents in shipping are either visible evidence of a contract or visible evidence that the condition of the ship and crew are satisfactory. However, there are economic and operational aspects of documentation that should be considered, and as the commercial cargo documents are the more interesting ones in this respect, we should perhaps start here.

The bill of lading (B/L)

As the most important and best known document in the commercial carriage of goods by sea is the *bill of lading* (B/L), it would make sense to use the B/L to illustrate certain aspects of the problem. Before doing this, though, we need to explain what a B/L is.

When a merchant or shipper has his cargo loaded on board a ship, the captain will sign the B/L to show it has been shipped on board and the condition it is in. This document can serve three functions:

1 As a receipt, to show the cargo has been received and the condition it is in. This is straightforward, and of course the sender would get such a receipt no matter what form of transport he used – whether it be road, rail, air or sea.
2 As evidence of a contract between the carrier and sender, and this too is common for all forms of transport.
3 It can also be a *negotiable* document, though – ie a document of title. So whoever rightfully owns the B/L is the lawful owner of the goods being sent. This is unique to sea transport and does not apply to any other form of transport. This feature is steeped in history, and we can find such documents in the British Museum that go back to Roman galleys carrying grain from Egypt to Rome. However, it does have one serious drawback, in that under the current state of the law, to maintain its negotiable status the *original* of the document has to be used. This means that it cannot at present be faxed or transmitted electronically and still legally retain this feature.

The B/L is also involved with the banking procedures concerned with the letter of credit. For instance, if A wishes to buy widgets from B, they must first agree on a price. If they exercise normal prudence, A will not wish to give B the money until he has the widgets, and B does not wish to part with his widgets without the money. As they may be thousands of miles apart, the banks have developed a well-tried system to solve this problem. A sends a letter of credit through his bank to B's bank with instructions to pay the money to B, as soon as B turns up with a B/L confirming that the cargo has been shipped and that when it was shipped it was in good condition, ie a 'clean' shipped B/L.

In most cases, though, the bank will not pay if:

- There is any mistake in the B/L. This is why traditionally the shipowner has wanted the shipper or his freight forwarder to fill in the bill and send it to him. As this document may contain long and complex consignment numbers, mistakes are easy to make.
- The bill is 'dirty' – ie if the bill has been claused to the effect that the cargo was not in every way in good order and condition.

With individual cargoes having values of millions of dollars, any delay in payment could cause serious cash flow problems for the shipper.

Fig 14.1 illustrates the physical movement of the *letter of credit* from the consignee's bank to the shipper's bank. When the shipper knows all this is set up, he instructs his forwarding agent to arrange shipment. The freight forwarder collects a blank B/L from the shipowner and fills all the details and returns it to the shipowner's office. The shipowner then instructs the shipper, via the freight forwarder, as to when to bring the cargo down to the port of discharge. When the cargo is received at the port terminal, the cargo will be inspected and the shipper's driver will present a *standard shipping note* – (SSN), which is similar in layout to the B/L, which the authorities in the terminal will sign and give the driver a copy.

When the cargo is loaded, a tally clerk will note the event and a further copy of the SSN will be signed and sent to the shipping company's office. Eventually the SSN will arrive on the desk of a loading broker who will compare the details on the SSN with the B/L received from the shipper. If all is in order, the B/L will be stamped SHIPPED and signed by the loading broker 'for and on behalf of the master'. Two or three signed Bs/L will be sent with several copies (about ten – one for each of the 'hands' it will pass through, so they can file it away) to the freight forwarder. The B/L will then be sent to the shipper who will take it to his bank, where hopefully he will receive his money for the goods. This bank will send it on to the consignee's bank, who will pass it on to the consignee. When the ship arrives with the cargo, the owner's agent will notify the consignee who will bring the B/L down to the agent's office. The agent will then give the consignee a release note to go down to the import terminal to collect the cargo.

In the above description the scenario was kept simple to illustrate the basic principle. However, various problems can arise with this documentation – such as with a claused B/L.

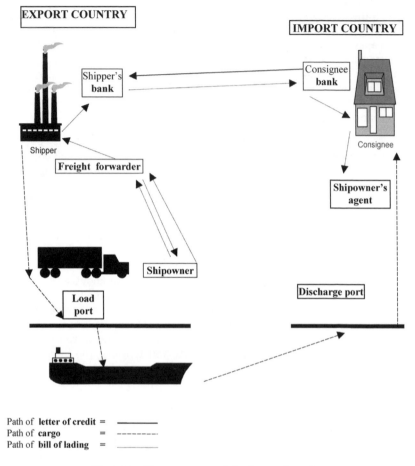

Fig 14.1   The movement of the letter of credit.

Problems with the B/L

A shipper will hope that a B/L states that the cargo received by the shipowner is in apparent good order and condition. When the shipowner is in agreement with this, the B/L is referred to as a clean B/L. However, should – on loading – the tally clerk or ship's officer note some defect, such as wet or stained cases, cartons missing, machinery rusty, etc, the bill is claused to this effect. Such Bs/L are referred to as dirty, unclean, foul or claused.

Although this is an obvious and necessary precaution for the shipowner to take, it may create problems for the shipper or exporter as this payment for the cargo by the letter of credit can usually only be made if the B/L is clean. If the B/L is dirty, there may be considerable delay in payment.

This, in turn, causes the shipper to ask the shipowner for clean Bs/L, even offering him a letter of indemnity by which he offers to accept the shipowner's liability for claims made against him for damaged cargo. Because the B/L is negotiable, such letters are illegal as the bill could be sold without the purchaser being aware of the existence of such a letter. Nevertheless, because of the financial problems that can arise for the shipper, they may still sometimes be accepted for this purpose. If the B/L is presented to the bank or consignee after the cargo is due at its destination, they are said to be stale – and payment may again be delayed.

Types of B/L

1 Shipped B/L As the name suggests, the bill is not signed and returned to the shipper until the cargo is actually loaded on board the ship that is to transport it to its destination. Many trades, banks and shippers insist on this type of bill.

2 Received for shipment B/L This type of bill can be issued by the shipping company as soon as it receives custody of the cargo at its transit shed, warehouse or inland collection depot. It has the advantage that the B/L can be issued sooner, as one of the problems of the modern liner trades is that although the berth-to-berth transit times for cargo have become much quicker, the same cannot always be said for the B/L. There is a possibility, therefore, of the cargo arriving before the B/L. However, many long-standing trade practices and contracts do not allow the received for shipment B/L. They are more common in the USA.

3 Through B/L
This B/L is used for multi-transport, which evidences a contract of carriage from one place to another in separate stages – of which at least one stage is sea transit, and by which the issuing sea carrier accepts responsibility for the sea carriage and acts as agent for the shipper in arranging carriage and in handling the goods to the subsequent carrier.

4 Combined transport B/L This is a negotiable document that evidences a combined transport contract, the taking in charge of the goods by the combined transport operator at a place of acceptance, and an undertaking by him to deliver the goods at a place of delivery against surrender of the document. A provision in the document that the goods are to be delivered to the order of a named person, or to the bearer, constitutes such an undertaking.
Note: There is an essential difference between a combined transport B/L and a through B/L. In the former, the issuer, in accepting full responsibility for the entire movement, acts as principal with respect to the shipper and other

carriers. In the latter, the issuer accepts responsibility only for his own segment of the movement (the liability of which would be limited to that contained in the Hague Rules or the Hague Visby Rules), then casts himself in the role of agent as between the shipper and other carriers. A further important difference is that in the case of through transport, more than one carrier is used (hence the expression multi-transport in the definition), whereas in the case of combined transport more than one type of carriage is used.

5 *Groupage B/L* In this, forwarding agents collect together items of cargo and despatch them as one consignment. The ship-owner issues a groupage B/L to the forwarding agent who will issue to the individual shippers a certificate of shipment. These are sometimes referred to as *house* B/L.

6 In 1979, the *common short form* of B/L was introduced. This is a standard B/L, but it has no printed carrier's logo − the carrier's name is simply typed on. In addition, it does not contain all the conditions of carriage, only a clause to the effect that the standard conditions apply. The advantages of this short form are that it is cheaper to produce and a shipper needs to keep only one bill in stock − not one for each of the shipping lines he uses.

Economic and operational problems of documentation

- *Too slow,* eg typical B/L:

Stages	B/L process	Time in days
1	Document consolidation	3–5
2	Create B/L	3–5
3	Present documents to bank	1–3
4	Examine documents	1–3
5	Correct discrepancies	2
	Total days in export country	10–18
6	Forward documents overseas	8–14
	Total days to consignee	18–32

- *Too expensive.* It is a labour-intensive process. A B/L produced as above could cost, say, $350 (USD) or a great deal more if it were necessary to reduce the time.
- *Too many.* A survey conducted a few years ago on containers moving from Europe to the USA showed that a typical container could require 2,000 documents. Of these, about one-third are official, with the remainder being operational. In 1995 in Korea, import and export

shipments could produce as many as 350 different paper documents. It is estimated that in any one day 2 million individual trade documents are produced at a cost of $8 billion (USD) per year.

- *Too many mistakes.* Another survey showed that 50 per cent of all documents contain errors. Errors increase both the time and the costs.

What can be done about these problems?

1 *Improve the conventional system* Much has been done to reduce the cost and time required for processing these documents.

In October 1960, a Committee of the Economic Commission for Europe (ECE) decided to set up a working party to consider the possible reduction, simplification and standardisation of trade documents. This working party started work in 1961.

By the mid-1960s, many organisations were producing ideas concerning *aligned documents* – this involves using documents of a standard size and a standard format. The advantage of using aligned documents is that after a master stencil has been made, the shipping note, B/L, insurance certificate, certificate of origin, etc can be run off by simply adjusting the position of masks over the master stencil.

In 1963, the ICS (International Chamber of Shipping) through its old Shipping Documentation Committee (now the Facilitation Committee) produced its first report on 'Standard Format for Bills of Lading'. This has had some modifications, and most modern Bs/L are now based on the ICS 1972 standard B/L.

The SITPRO (Simplification of Trade Procedures) Board was set up in 1970 to 'guide, stimulate and assist the rationalisation of international trade procedures and the documentation and information flows associated with them ... particularly in view of the widening use of computers and telecommunications links'. Its membership is drawn from a wide range of interests and includes shippers, carriers, forwarders, bankers, insurers and government representatives. Its working groups call on the specialist expertise of many commercial and official interests. Funds are provided by the Department of Trade through an annual grant, but the Board enjoys complete independence within its agreed terms of reference.

In 1975, FALPRO (the Special Program on Trade Facilitation in UNCTAD) was set up, which has greatly assisted in getting worldwide acceptance of the 1972 ICS standard B/L.

Some of the larger container companies that have international computer links can use these facilities for transmitting documentation. There is also a growing use of computer links with Customs for clearing documents, and in the future this type of link could become commonplace for all the parties concerned.

In 1980, the International Maritime Bureau (IMB) was set up to counter

SEA TRANSPORT

international maritime fraud, which about that time was estimated by UNCTAD to have reached a level of $200 million (USD) per annum.

2 *Introduce new documents* The advantage of a non-negotiable document is speed and lower cost, as it can be transmitted by computer or facsimile apparatus. Its disadvantage lies in whether or not banks will accept it.

In 1969, however, some British liner companies introduced non-negotiable liner waybills and in 1977 SITPRO and ICS introduced a standard non-negotiable liner waybill. The waybill's popularity has not been enormous, but the Carriage of Goods Act 1992 does redress one major problem by providing for consignees under waybills to be in the same position as if they were B/L consignees.

3 *Try to bypass the problem areas* There were at least two attempts in the 1980s to avoid the problems by creating a central registry, where the B/L once created was lodged. One was 'Seadocs' for tankers, and the First Bank of Chicago introduced an all-purpose variation but it seemed to have a shorter life than Seadocs.

4 *A radical new approach – paperless trading* EDI (electronic data interchange) has many obvious advantages such as speed, low cost and accuracy, and it integrates the documentary position with all the other operational activities. It seems inevitable that eventually this is the way that all documentation will proceed, and the only question is when (see Table 14.1).There are some who argue that such an EDI approach will increase the risk of fraud, but you could equally argue that the computer's ability to crosscheck data could easily eliminate many of the crude frauds perpetrated at the moment.

In September 1999, Bolero net went live. It claims to be the pioneer in creating a paperless international trading environment. Part of this system is SURF (Settlement Utility to Managing Risk and Finance), which acts as a documentary settlement system and automatically checks all documentary documents. In 2002, Bolero had 100 companies signed up to the system.

In March 2001, a system for electronic waybills was introduced – @Global Trader. At around this time, several similar systems were introduced by some of the large operators, eg www.ccweb.com by OOCL, cargosmart by APL, and www.intra.com by Maesk.

Since around 2000, the application of electronic documents has been widened through a change in European legislation, which allows a more extensive use of electronic signatures. Furthermore, the EC Commission is pushing ahead with its objective of developing a paperless electronic customs system within the expanding EU by 2007. Progress has been rather slow though. Although the technological barriers to reform the traditional paper bureaucracy have been tackled, the take-up commercially has not been dramatic.

Date	Development
	Table 14.1 The development of EDI
1968	LA and San Francisco clearing houses – Special Committee On Paperless Entries (SCOPE)
1975	Development of EDIFACT Electronic Data Interchange for Transport and Commerce by UN/ECE
1982	Hamburg – DAKOSY
1983	Le Havre – Automated Customs Clearance of Goods (ADEMAR)
1984	Felixstowe – FCP80
1984	Singapore – PORTNET – early 1990s TRADENET
1985	Rotterdam – International Transport Information Systems (INTIS)
1985	P&O – Data Interchange for Shipping (DISH) – INTIS Rotterdam
1986	Japan – SHIPNET – SEAGHA Antwerp
1987	ISO accepted UN/EDIFACT syntax
1988	Hong Kong – TRADELINK
1989	Australia – TRADEGATE
1993	Bremen BHT
1994	Gothenburg – EDIFACT – Korea KL-NET
1995	MARTRANS – an EU project to interconnect existing EDI port community systems and implementing new EDI systems in non-automated ports. However, since its inception the emphasis has shifted from maritime competitiveness to intermodal effectiveness, from European to international partnership and from EDI to the Information Highway
1997	MOSES – Modular and Scalable EDI system to provide an easy and cost-effective system for small and medium-size ports
1998	OOCL launch their internet B/L service
2000	Hamburg & Bremen implement EDIFACT B/L, so that customers can display and print out B/L. See www.bill-of-lading.de

The reasons for this are:

- The conservatism of international trade.
- The sheer complexity of international trade.
- The design of the current system.
- The price of technology at current states of evolution.
- The need for standards.

The CMI (Comité Maritime International) has established rules for electronic Bs/L.

The UNCITRAL Working Group on Electronic Commerce noted as part of its work in developing the UNCITRAL Model Law for Electronic Commerce of 1995 that the lack of uniformity in ocean Bs/L was a significant impediment to the development and acceptance of a fully electronic system for Bs/L. Upon their recommendation, the Commission requested the assistance of interested organisations in proposing rules to ensure uniformity. The result is the CMI proposal, which could be the first 'Bs/L' convention that actually takes up the trade and transport issues implicit in a B/L.

The first step in this effort to reach uniformity was to avoid getting bogged down in the long-running debate over what is or is not a B/L by using the term 'transport document' (which can be either negotiable or non-negotiable). Next, the exercise in semantics as to whether a B/L can ever be transmitted electronically was avoided by use of the term 'electronic record' (which can be either negotiable or non-negotiable).

The CMI's eCommerce drafting group had been challenged by the Commission to build rules for electronic records from the ground up, rather than mere 'functional equivalence', and they have succeeded in doing so. The proposed rules are 'stand alone' rules for the time when paper documents become the exception.

These rules would not conflict with the ICC's eUCP scheme, and should work in harmony with ICC's Incoterms. They would complement and support emerging systems, such as @GlobalTrade, for the transfer of electronic records. Yet these rules are sufficiently flexible that as 'documentary' practice evolves in the electronic age, they should meet the needs of systems that cannot yet be imagined.

5 *The use of the internet* At the end of 2001, it was estimated that in setting up typical liner documentation, the cost was estimated to be $295 (USD) by phone, $83 (USD) by e-mail, and $11 (USD) via web self-service.

Incoterms

Incoterms are a set of uniform rules that codify the interpretation of trade terms, defining the rights and obligations of both *buyer* and *seller* in an international transaction, thereby enabling an otherwise complex basis for a sale contract to be accomplished in three letters, eg FOB (free on board), CIF (cost, insurance & freight), etc.

Incoterms are drafted by the International Chamber of Commerce, and the latest set of rules were put into use on 1 January 2000.

Other documents There are, of course, many other documents involved in moving goods, such as:

- *The manifest.* This is a document prepared by the shipping company from the signed Bs/L and is a comprehensive list of all the cargo that is on board, complete with marks, amounts, shippers, etc.

It exists primarily for Customs, and it must be lodged with them within 14 days of the vessel sailing, showing the cargo exported, and within 24 hours of the arrival of a ship with imported cargo.

Copies of the manifest are sent to the ship and the agents at the ship's port of call so that they can be lodged with Customs there and enable the agent to know what cargo is arriving and to order the stevedores accordingly.

- *Certificates of origin and value.* These are prepared and translated where necessary. Some countries – such as Peru and Uruguay – require translations of the invoice to be certified by the importing country's consulate.

Ship's documents

This is a brief list of some of the more important documents that most ships should carry:

- Certificate of Registry. This is the vessel's identification certificate.
- Loadline certificate.
- Safety certificates – eg loadline certificate, safety radiotelegraphy certificate, cargo ship safety equipment certificate, cargo ship safety construction certificate. If it is a passenger ship, a passenger safety certificate is needed instead of the latter three.
- International tonnage certificates, eg ITC 69.
- Safe manning certificate.
- IOPPC international oil pollution prevention certificate. This is renewed every five years, but a ship must be surveyed annually by a certifying authority surveyor.
- Certificate of fitness (for the carriage of bulk chemical cargoes).
- Safety management certificate.
- Copy of document of compliance.
- International air pollution prevention certificate.
- ILO certificate, garbage pollution prevention certificate, international sewage pollution prevention certificate, ballast water management certificate.
- Articles – the official agreement between the owner of the vessel and the crew.
- Crew list, minimum safe manning document, certificates for master, officers and ratings, ILO Blue Card.
- Account of wages – a record of the seamen's earnings and expenditures.
- Official log – this is an official document that must be kept by the master of every British vessel, containing full details of lifeboat drills, draft of water entering and leaving port. A crew list and any births, deaths or marriages that take place on board, and any other data that

governments like to keep records of. After the voyage, this official record is kept by the state.

- Deck log – this is the important 'commercial' log from which times of arrival, delays, state of the weather, etc, are recorded.
- Engine log and radio log are records covering their respective areas of interest.
- Intact stability booklet.
- Depending on cargo: document of compliance with the special requirements for ships carrying dangerous goods; dangerous goods manifest or stowage plan; document for the authorisation to carry grain.
- A record of the surveys and tests to all ship's lifting gear.
- Anchor and cable certificate.
- Hull and machinery classification certificates; Suez and Panama Canal certificates – these give the Suez Canal tonnage and Panama Canal tonnage.
- Bill of health from the last port. Deratting or Deratting exemption certificate – to show that the ship is free from rats. It has to be renewed every six months.
- Receipts for the light dues paid for the current year. The lighthouses and buoys, etc around the UK coast are maintained by the light dues paid when ships enter a UK port. However, the dues have to be paid only a certain number of times each year, which is why the receipts should be kept.
- Charter party.
- Bs/L – if ready when the vessel sails.
- Manifest – if ready when the vessel sails.
- Oil record book.

Customs

As Customs are at the receiving end of a great number of documents, it is perhaps appropriate to discuss them briefly.

The functions of Customs are as follows:

1 To collect the appropriate duty on goods and to prevent evasion of payments. All ships arriving in the UK must lodge basic documents at a designated Customs office within three hours of arrival and then 'enter in' at the 'long room' at the Custom House within 24 hours of arrival.

   The introduction of containers has only been possible by the co-operation of Customs not only at the national level, but also at the international level through the Customs Co-operation Council (CCC), which has its headquarters in Brussels and has 52 member countries.

   To facilitate the international flow of trade, the 'Brussels Nomenclature' has been adopted. The Brussels Nomenclature is an internationally agreed tariff system used for the classification of all goods in international commerce.

It is worth noting that Customs duty in some developing countries may be high and a major source of foreign exchange revenue to the country. If this is the case, there is a danger of a high level of bureaucracy and delays at the port of entry. In some developing countries the transport delays caused by Customs may be weeks rather than hours.

2 To provide a record of imports and exports.

3 To act as agents for other organisations and government departments. For instance, in the UK when a ship 'enters in', Customs have to:

- Collect the light dues for Trinity House, which is the organisation responsible for maintaining the lighthouses around the English coast. They may also in some cases collect the pilotage dues and certain harbour dues.

  These dues are usually assessed on either GT or NT and, as proof of the ship's tonnage, the 'ship's register' must be produced. (The Ship's Certificate of Registry is completed by the Registrar of Shipping when the ship is first registered in the country concerned. This could be when the ship is built, sold to a new owner abroad, or transferred by the present owner to another flag. It is an official document giving precise details of the ship concerning tonnage and dimensions. It also contains the name and address of the owner and the name of the present master.)

- Inspect certificates to show that all the necessary precautions were taken, where legislation covers the safe carriage of certain cargoes.

- Make a return of passengers and any aliens among the crew to assist Immigration, and collect information on livestock for the Ministry of Agriculture and Fisheries.

- Ensure that all legislation concerning the crew has been complied with, before any British ship is finally cleared inwards. Also, before a ship leaves a port for sea the necessary certificates or proof must be shown to Customs to indicate that the ship is safe to do so, ie the ship's loadline certificate, safety radio certificate, safety equipment and construction certificates, or passenger certificate if it is a passenger ship. As various dues are affected by any deck cargo carried, a deck cargo certificate is also made out by the ship's agent to be presented when 'entering in'.

It is officially the master's duty to enter the ship in or clear the ship out from Customs, but he may delegate the task to the ship's agents. Over the last few years, this seems to have become the general practice.

15 PORTS

Seaports are areas where there are facilities for berthing or anchoring ships and where there is the equipment for the transfer of goods from ship to shore or ship to ship. To use more modern jargon, it is a ship/shore interface or a maritime intermodal interface. It is a major area of interest to those concerned with shipping, as it is the place:

- where most accidents happen to ship and crew;
- where cargo is damaged or stolen;
- where repairs are carried out;
- where most costs are incurred;
- where delays occur – which will usually involve a large unexpected cost;
- where surveys take place;
- where most shipping services are situated, eg agents, banking, broking, bunkers, etc;
- where industries are situated;
- where cargoes come from;
- where Customs and government policies are implemented.

A few definitions in relation to ports

- *Port*. A port is a town with a harbour and facilities for a ship/shore interface and also Customs facilities.
- *Harbour*. A harbour is a shelter, either natural or artificial, for ships.
- *Dock*. A dock is an artificially constructed shelter for shipping and, if tidal, it will perhaps have a set of locks at the entrance, so that ships within can remain afloat at all states of the tide.
- *Breakwater or mole*. This is a long solid structure, built on the seaward harbour side, for protection against weather, rough seas and swell.
- *Wharf*. This is a structure built along the shore where vessels can berth alongside.
- *Pier or jetty*. This is a structure built out from the shore or riverbank on masonry, steel or wooden piles for berthing ships. It is not a solid structure, and should not greatly impede the flow of tide or current. However, both these terms are often used with considerable variations.
- *Dolphin*. This is an isolated islet of piles or masonry to assist in the berthing or manoeuvring of ships.

- *Stevedore*. This is a person employed in moving the cargo on or off the ship. Again this is a term that has many local variations. For instance, in London it was the term for the men of the skilled team who stowed the cargo on board the ship, but after Lord Devlin's report the many traditional terms used in this area were abandoned in favour of the all-embracing word 'docker'.

- *Tides*. It is necessary to have some understanding of the basic facts concerning tides. The moon is the major tide-raising force, and because of this the spring tides (the tide with the maximum range) occurs approximately at new and full moon. Neap tides (the tide with the minimum range) occur about seven days later when the moon is in quadrature. Also, because of the moon the time from high water to high water is in theory about 12 hours 25 minutes. However, although the moon is the major tide-producing force, its effect will vary considerably from place to place depending on the size of the basin, the depth of water, the latitude, and numerous other factors. The greatest tidal range in the world is at the Bay of Fundy, where it exceeds 15 metres. In the Mediterranean, it seldom exceeds half a metre. Just to emphasise how it does vary from place to place, compare the following European ports:

	Spring range	Neap range
Avonmouth	12.2m	6.4m
London Bridge	6.7m	4.6m
Southampton	4m	1.8m
Le Havre	6.7m	3.7m
Antwerp	5.2m	4m
Hook of Holland	1.8m	1.2m

Note: (At Southampton and Le Havre there is a prolonged stand of tide at high water.)

Locks

Where there are significant tides it may be considered necessary to build enclosed docks, approached only through *locks*, because apart from the undesirability of the vessel going aground at low water there are problems of cargo-handling when the vessel is rising and falling 6–12 metres twice a day. Although these docks do have some advantages in that security is easier and that the depth can be increased by pumping in more water, they do have many disadvantages:

Fig 15.1 *(Opposite) The original Port of Tilbury was opened in about 1870 and would have occupied only the southern part of the map shown. Berths 39 and upwards were developed in the late 1960s as container and packaged timber berths. Northfleet Hope Riverside terminal was developed a few years later to cater for the ever-growing container ships that couldn't squeeze through the locks. An aerial photo (opposite below) gives a clear view of the entrance locks into the Port of Tilbury from the Thames. (Courtesy of Port of Tilbury)*

- they are expensive to construct, maintain and modernise;
- there are delays in moving through the locks, and possibly in waiting for the necessary tidal conditions;
- there is the possibility of a catastrophic delay and expense if the lock gate is damaged.

The size of the lock is often the factor that limits the size of ships that can enter many of the older docks, though forward-looking modern ports have built enormous ones. The largest lock in the world at the moment is at Le Havre; it was completed in December 1971 at a total cost of about £20 million and takes about 45 minutes for a large vessel to pass through.

Port development

Unlike ships, ports often have to last a long time – sometimes for centuries. They therefore have to adapt and change over the course of time. Many of the traditional British ports were developed and built well over a century ago, which means that many are now faced with a legacy of small antiquated docks. Many factors can cause ports to change, evolve or die:

- Changes in the inland transport infrastructure. For instance, the coming of the railways tended to make large ports like London and Liverpool bigger and small ports smaller. Road transport had the opposite effect, though the development of large container ships is again encouraging the growth of large regional ports.
- Changes in trade patterns, such as the UK joining the EU, had a very negative effect on Liverpool but a positive effect on Felixstowe.
- Changes in financial and logistical thinking. London at its peak was an enormous warehouse for Europe. Since the Second World War, the tendency is not to store 'things', but to use ports as industrial areas – such as in Rotterdam. More recently, the trend has been to develop 'value-added activities' and become a sophisticated marketing and distribution centre – such as Hamburg or Bremen.
- Changes in ship size with the need for 'more water' in the docks and approaches, and the associated need for faster cargo-handling and shorter turn-round times.

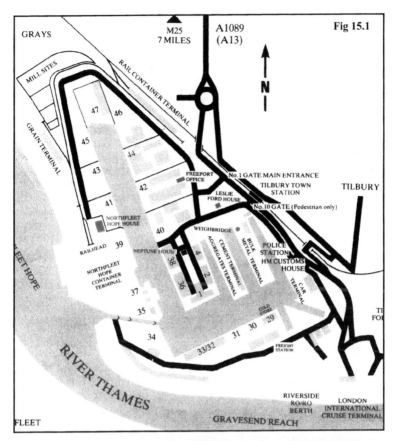

GRAYS

M25
7 MILES

A1089
(A13)

Fig 15.1

N

MILL SITES

RAIL CONTAINER TERMINAL

GRAIN TERMINAL

47 46

45

44

43

42

41

FREEPORT
OFFICE

No.1 GATE MAIN ENTRANCE

TILBURY TOWN
STATION

TILBURY

LESLIE
FORD HOUSE

No.10 GATE (Pedestrian only)

NORTHFLEET
HOPE HOUSE

40

WEIGHBRIDGE

RAILHEAD

39

NEPTUNE HOUSE

38

4

2

CEMENT TERMINAL

AGGREGATES TERMINAL

BULK METAL TERMINAL

POLICE
STATION

HM CUSTOMS
HOUSE

NORTHFLEET
HOPE
CONTAINER
TERMINAL

37

36

1

CAR TERMINAL

FLEET HOPE

35

34

33/32

31 30 29

COLD STORE

FREIGHT
STATION

TI
FO

RIVER THAMES

RIVERSIDE
RO/RO
BERTH

LONDON
INTERNATIONAL
CRUISE TERMINAL

FLEET

GRAVESEND REACH

The entrance locks into the Port of Tilbury.

277

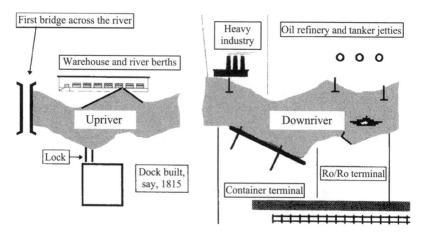

First bridge across the river

Warehouse and river berths

Upriver

Lock

Dock built, say, 1815

Heavy industry

Oil refinery and tanker jetties

Downriver

Container terminal

Ro/Ro terminal

Fig 15.2 A simple 'model' port. See Professor J Bird's Seaport and Seaport Terminals.

Fig 15.2 represents a simple 'model' port which shows how many estuarial ports have developed. Originally the ships approached as far upriver as possible and were usually forced to stop where the first bridge had been built. This was usually no problem as the bridge marked a main thoroughfare and a large trading city had probably developed there. If we take the case of London, the Romans built the bridge and developed the City of London and the ships would anchor or berth below the bridge and discharge. By the beginning of the nineteenth century, the river had become congested by ships and much of the cargo was being stolen – in fact, the London River Police was the City's first police force. To ease the congestion and increase security, various docks were built along the river. As ships got bigger with deeper drafts, the new docks and terminals moved downriver to the sea. By the 1870s, Tilbury docks in London had been built 35 miles downriver from the City. With the advent of containerisation and faster cargo-handling, more terminal space was needed as well as good access to inland transport systems (see Fig 15.2). In the 1970s, the port of London had plans to develop a new port system at the mouth of the Thames on Maplin sands, but this plan hit several problems – some environmental – so plans were shelved.

Some elements of the process indicated by the model in Fig 15.2 can in fact be observed in most ports. As the original port owned land in the old city centre, which in many cases has been considered highly desirable for development as high-rent offices, many ports have been able to fund their new projects by skilfully developing their redundant port sites. Good land management has therefore become an essential management function for many of the traditional port administrations. We can see good examples of this in London, New York, Copenhagen, Hamburg, Antwerp, etc. A summary of port development can be seen in Table 15.1.

Table 15.1   Port development – from a transport centre to a logistic platform

	First generation	Second generation	Third generation	Fourth generation
Period of development	Before 1960	After 1960s	After 1980s	After 1990s
Main cargo	Breakbulk (bb)	bb and bulk	Bulk and unitised. Larger ships, hence more space for cargo	Unitisation of a large % of the cargo
Attitude and strategy report development	Conservative. Changing point of transport mode	Expansionist. Transport, industrial and commercial centre	Commercially orientated. Integrated transport node and logistic centre	More sophisticated use of automation
Scope of activities	1) Ship/shore cargo interface	1) + 2) Cargo transformation. Industrial activities	1 + 2 + cargo and information distribution. Full logistic potential	Standardisation of information
Organisation characteristics	Independent activities. Informal relationships	Closer relationship to port and user. Loose relationship in port activities. Casual relationship with port and municipality	United and integrated relationships. Move to privatise	Globalisation of port communities. Greater environmental control
Production characteristics	Cargo flow. Low value added	Cargo flow and transformation. Combined services. Improved value added	Cargo/information flow and distribution. Multiple service package. High value added	Emphasis on quality of service and trained workforce
Decisive factors	Labour/capital	Capital	Technology/know-how	Information technology

(*Source: Based on Port Marketing and the Challenge of the 3rd Generation Port, UNCTAD Report 1990.*)

Classification of ports

Ports can be classified in many ways:

By function

A port can be:

1 a centre port (also sometimes referred to as a mega port or pivot port);
2 a feeder port – to feed and distribute cargo from 1;
3 an entrepot or transit port;
4 a domestic port, ie a natural outlet for surrounding hinterland;
5 a naval port;
6 a first, second- or third-generation port, etc;
7 an oil port;
8 a fishing port;
9 a Customs-free port (see below).

A port such as Rotterdam is many of these.

A Customs-free port (or zone) Dr Frankel distinguishes between several types of industrial free ports or zones, but essentially they are a small part of the national territory remaining under full sovereignty of the state though placed outside Customs limits. Goods are still subject to other laws, such as those involving the safety and sanitary aspects of goods.

The advantages of a free port are that it reduces the time and effort required in Customs formalities and avoids having large amounts of money deposited with the Customs for duty on goods that are only in transit, or being assembled in the area before being exported as part of a larger product. In 1986, TFB Helm estimated that 20 per cent of the world's trade was handled in the 478 free zones situated in more than 80 countries – compared with only 10 per cent in 1981. Hamburg is perhaps the most famous, being established as such in 1888. In 1984, six areas in the UK were allowed to be designated as free ports.

By geographic type

This classification is almost endless; therefore, only the more important types are considered here:

1 coastal submergence – New York and Southampton;
2 ryas (submerged estuaries) – Falmouth, Rio;
3 tidal estuaries – Bristol, London, Antwerp;
4 artificial harbours – Dover;
5 rivers (non-tidal) – Montreal.

The recognition of a geographic type may give us an insight into its operating advantages or disadvantages, eg a tidal estuarial port will probably require more expensive surveying and dredging than a closed dock system.

By size

A really satisfactory statistic for measuring the size or productivity of a port for comparative purposes does not seem to exist. The following, however, are some of the more popular ones:

1 The total weight of cargo handled in a year. This statistic gives a tremendous advantage to the oil ports where cargo is handled in thousands of tons per hour. In the early 1980s, Sullom Voe was the largest port in the UK — but how many people, even among the native British, know where it is! Table 15.2 gives some international comparisons, but here the situation is complicated in that some quote the tonnage in MT (metric tons), some in FT (freight tons), and some in RT (revenue tons). Table 15.2 shows that, on tonnage, Rotterdam is still in the lead — despite the fact that it had dropped 3.8 per cent over the previous five years.

Dover Harbour must be one of the world's most active ferry terminals. The terminals and ramps can be clearly seen, but note also the parking facilities and good road access. A good example of a successful artificial harbour.

Table 15.2 Major world ports' cargo traffic in million tons and number of ships in 2001

Port	Liquid	Dry bulk	Container	Other general	Total	TEUs (millions)	Ships (no)
Rotterdam	147	82.5	48.7	35.8	314	6.1	26,000
Singapore	114	13.7	171 (FT)	15 (FT)	313	15.6	146,265
Hong Kong	16.6	20.3	122	19	178	17.8	37,350
South Louisiana	85.5	147.3		28	252.8		4,351

(Source: ISL Bremen, October 2002.)

2 The total value of cargo handled. If this figure is used, Dover becomes the largest port in the UK. This is an almost impossible figure to assess globally.
3 The total number of ships that enter and leave the port each year. This enables ferry ports such as Dover and Southampton to exaggerate their importance. Singapore seems to be the largest if we use this statistic. Japanese ports also score well due to the large fishing fleets using many of their ports.
4 The number of berths available.
5 The size of the largest ship that can use the port's facilities. This would make Okinawa one of the largest ports in the world.

Relevance of size of ship Although the size of the largest ship that can use a port's facilities is not a very meaningful statistic when comparing the size of various ports, it is a very important criterion from the ship operator's point of view, and for those concerned with port planning and designing the ship of the future. The usual limiting figure and the one that is normally the most expensive and difficult to overcome is the draft or depth of water available. Because of this, it is perhaps necessary to explore this area in rather greater detail.

The approximate correlation between the ship's draft and her dwt tonnage is shown in Table 15.3. Not surprisingly, there are experimental designs for special 'reduced draft' large vessels.

Nor is it enough just to have sufficient water to float the ship. When large, fast ships get into shallow water they both slow down and squat (increase their draft at one or both ends). In 1961, the Permanent International Association of Navigation Congresses recommended that the depth of water in port approaches be at least the ship's draft plus 1.5–2.5 metres.

Finding ports with a sufficient depth of water to be able to accept loaded 200,000-ton dwt tankers is difficult. In 1970 (the early days of VLCCs) there were only eight ports in Europe that could accept such ships, and none on the east coast of North America. Energetic dredging operations have improved on this, and by 1975 there were 22 such ports in north-western

Table 15.3 Correlation between ship's draft and her dwt tonnage		
Dwt tonnage	Draft in feet	Draft in decimetres
10,000	26	79
20,000	30	91
50,000	38	116
100,000	48	146
200,000	60	183
300,000	72	219
500,000	90	274

Europe (of which nine are in the UK), 15 in the Mediterranean, 4 in North America, 16 in Japan, 4 in South America, 1 in South and East Africa, and 1 in Southeast Asia. Since this initial surge of improvement, the number of ports with sufficient depth of water has increased only gradually.

It is not only a question of finding sufficient depth of water at the port and in the port, but also in getting to the port – and many of the continental shelf areas of the world present real problems for the larger ship. This problem is aggravated at the moment by the fact that when much of the world was surveyed during the nineteenth century, the maximum draft that the surveyor could conceive possible was 6 fathoms – 11 metres. Depths greater than this did not always get the attention that many modern mariners would have wished.

Types of port ownership

Ports can also be classified as to their type of ownership or administration – in fact, over the last decade this has been one of the most debated topics concerning port efficiency. Before considering port ownership in any detail, though, there are one or two points that should be made:

- A ship is an entity, whereas a port is simply a collection of activities. This makes it more difficult to talk about ports in general. A little ship has many technical and operational features in common with a big ship, but it is sometimes difficult to see what a small fishing port in a developing country has in common with, say, Rotterdam.
- Most ships and ship operators are international in their design and ways of working, whereas ports tend to be more parochial in that they reflect more their local commercial attitudes and practices. The duties of the ship's captain are similar regardless of flag, whereas the duties of the port's harbourmaster can differ considerably between countries.

- Since the advent of intermodalism, ports now have to compete for cargo very much more than in the past – hence the great interest in increasing port efficiency and value-added activities over the last few years. (Value-added activities are described by UNCTAD as follows: 'The term *added value* signifies value newly added or created in the productive process of an enterprise. Loading and discharging are certainly value-adding activities, so are the industrial services of a port noted earlier. In a distribution centre, added value can take different forms such as cargo consolidation and deconsolidation – providing up-to-date information on the inventory and cargo movements; stuffing/unstuffing containers; crating; palletisation; shrink-wrapping; labelling; weighing; repacking etc.')
- Ports provide an economic multiplier for a region, and many ports now do economic impact studies to determine which aspects of their work should be encouraged. It should also be remembered that ports are not only 'gateways' for cargo, but also obvious sites for industry, banks, agents, storage depots and distribution centres. They are also large employers of labour.
- Ports are also an important part of a nation's transport infrastructure and must be part of a nation's transport planning. These latter two points are why any national government or local government will wish to have some input into the general port strategic planning.

Traditionally, British textbooks classified port ownership under the following headings:

1 State ownership This heading can cover everything from absolute political supervision to state ownership of majority shares.

2 Autonomous public trusts Many UK ports used to have this type of administration before they were privatised in the late 1980s. Such a trust is a quasi-governmental organisation set up by an Act of Parliament. It is non-profit-making and offers a unified functional administration over a functionally defined area. It may suffer from insufficiency of funds and may be burdened with unnecessary restrictions.

3 Municipal ownership Examples such as at Rotterdam, Hamburg, Kobe and Yokohama. This has as one of its major advantages complete co-operation on all the local needs of the port. The municipality may also agree to subsidise the port, for by offering competitive port charges and encouraging trade, the overall prosperity of the region can be greatly increased. One of its major disadvantages is a natural unwillingness to co-operate in any national plan. The term can be confusing as the expression 'municipal' can have different significance in different countries.

4 Private ownership ports The UK, which encouraged most of its ports to move to private ownership in the 1980s, is one of the few countries to have adopted this approach in its extreme. In 1983, ABP (19 UK ports) was privatised, with most employees owning at least 1,000 shares. Since then, labour productivity increased by 40 per cent. Privatisation also caused a reallocation of port property which was put to new use – doubling its capital value and stimulating local economies. In the late 1980s and early 1990s, most UK ports were privatised.

In many modern ports such a classification as this might be considered simplistic as the ownership might in fact consist of a combination of two or three of the above. A few years ago a well-known consultant sent a questionnaire to ports, asking which type of ownership they should be classified under. Antwerp's reply was 'we don't know'. This is not surprising as one of the most common growing forms of port ownership/operation is the *landlord* port. In this type, the state or the city own the land and the port's sea approaches and lease out the terminals to private stevedoring firms to operate. There are several variations to this approach.

Port Kelang's *privatisation* started in 1985 when the government gave a 21-year contract to Port Kelang's container terminal as a private consortium. Since then, repair, maintenance and administration costs have been halved – container tonnage increased 75 per cent and wages increased 85 per cent.

The quest for greater efficiency in ports

As the main motive behind management and administration changes is the quest for greater efficiency, perhaps it is worth considering what is entailed

Valetta on the island of Malta is an excellent natural harbour, well-placed on the trade routes through the Mediterranean.

by this. If *efficiency* is defined as the optimum use of resources within an acceptable context of safety, we have a reasonable starting point.

To optimise we have to be able to quantify, so the first step should be to define what *can* be quantified on a comparable basis. The comparable basis is necessary as there is no absolute measure of commercial efficiency, only that A is better than B or that A is better this year than last year.

At the moment, most forms of financial comparability are not possible. Different ways of depreciating port assets, different methods of allocating capital costs, different taxation systems, different forms of 'financial assistance', etc make comparing profitability a waste of time. Similar difficulties apply to cargo-handling costs, with the extra difficulty that actual costs are a matter of confidential negotiation with each client. However, we can try to produce an aggregated benchmark norm.

A basic starting point would therefore seem to be to identify what can be precisely measured with the minimum of confusion. Apart from perhaps port dues, there is little that can be measured on a whole-port basis. Therefore, most comparable data must concentrate on a terminal basis.

Productivity As regards productivity, one of the most commonly used statistics is *berth occupancy ratio*. However, as a useful comparable statistic it is of limited value. There are many reasons for this, but the two main ones are:

1 In many terminals with a long quay wall, there is no determined number of berths.
2 The time actually measured varies from port to port.

Therefore, it would be better to look at things from a different perspective:

- Consider each crane or 'cargo-handling gateway' and measure the number of boxes moved per crane in both the total ship time on the berth, and the working ship time on the berth. This gives a gross and net productivity level.
- The number of people employed on the terminal concerned with cargo-handling can also be measured, as can the equipment (eg straddle carriers, fork lifts etc). Therefore the annual number of boxes per person and per piece of equipment per annum can be measured.
- The ratio of berth length to the number of cranes is also a useful indicator.
- The dwell time of a container on the terminal is important, but not too easy to measure to get a meaningful result. However, the time for a driver arriving at the gate to drop/pick up cargo and return back through the gate is measurable and a useful indicator. Also, we can consider the length of time per day that the gate is in operation.
- Further delays lost by strikes should be recorded – say, average days lost per month over the last five years. These are recorded by the various strike P&I clubs that exist – they are also given in *Lloyd's List*.

Safety The safety of cargo through ports is seldom covered or mentioned by the ports for obvious reasons. Global average statistics are produced and published by the major P&I clubs, and these do provide some guidance as regards a norm. For instance, the UK P&I club shows that for the years 1987–90 the average for major cargo claims (ie claims over $100,000 (USD)) are:

> 23% due to bad stowage
>
> 8% due to bad handling
>
> 2% due to bad fraud
>
> 1% failure to collect cargo

Statistical data in relation to productivity In most cases, the following statistics are calculated as averages of random samples of at least 50 ports taken on a worldwide basis. Where no figures are given, this indicates that research in that area is not complete.

1 All port non-cargo-handling disbursements – charges per NT in $ (USD): Dry cargo vessels average 2 USD per NT, SD 1.5 (ship handling 57% of total)
  Tankers average 1.5 USD per NT, SD 0.97 (ship handling 55.5% of total)
2 Total terminal cargo-handling charge per TEU = average 136.8 USD, SD 56.5
3 Waiting time = total time in port – berth time (see port time other than berth time)
4 a) Berth length/number of cranes = 350 metres where v/l capacity < 1,500 TEUs
  b) Berth length/number of cranes = 130 metres where v/l capacity > 1,500 TEUs
5 Total working time on berth/total time on berth. There is no average for this, but a higher figure indicates higher productivity
6 Number of TEUs/terminal area in square metres – seems to vary between 0.53 and 2.1
7 Average vehicle turn-round time on the terminal when receiving/delivering containers. For an efficient port, the average should lie between about 20 and 30 minutes

Statistical data in relation to port safety Suggested comparable statistics that could be collected in relation to safety – perhaps as average figures over five years – are:

1 Percentage of cargo value lost through cargo damage over 5 years
2 Percentage of boxes handled that are damaged
3 Percentage of cargo lost or stolen
4 Percentage number of port workers who suffer from industrial injuries

All the above data is recorded by different organisations, and so could be uncovered by any diligent researcher.

Environmental safety

After discussions with environmental experts, I am of the opinion that environmental safety, like profit, can only be self-compared – eg is water quality improving or worsening each year?

There are, however, certain aspects – such as the percentage losses of environmentally dangerous commodities (eg bulk fertiliser) at a terminal – that could be measured and compared.

Time spent in port (cargo-handling)

Statistics for this are given in Tables 15.4 and 15.5.

Look at the figures in Table 15.4. For all bulks in sample:

Mean loading speed 365 tph

Mean discharge speed 218 tph

Correlation between loading speed and cargo dwt is 0.85
Correlation between discharging speed and cargo dwt is 0.78

These correlation figures indicate that larger vessels go to larger ports where the cargo-handling speed is faster.

UNCTAD Port Development gives the figures shown in Table 15.5 and the following text:

Conventional breakbulk

Handling speed per hatch 10–40 tph
Loading speed on average about half discharge speed
Cranes about twice as fast as derricks

Table 15.4 Bulk cargo-handling speeds (tons per hour)

Commodity	Average of sample		Best of sample
	Load	Discharge	
Grain	167	108	316
Ore	618	482	1,705
Coal	678	352	1,342
Phosphorus	183	120	340
Scrap	96	49.5	174

Note: Sample of 50 load ports and 50 discharge ports, selected at random from the Bimco Journal.

Table 15.5	Bulk cargo-handling speeds given by UNCTAD Port Development
Ship loaders	1,000–7000 tph
Grabs	180–2,000 tph
Slurry	6,000–8,000 tph
Pneumatic	200 tph
Bucket elevators	1,000–5,000 tph

Note: Weighing accuracy between 1 and 2 per cent.

Containers
Loading/discharge speed the same
Speed in boxes per hour 10–50 (30 average for good port)

Tankers
72 hours allowed for load + discharge time
Discharge time usually slightly longer than loading

Port time other than berth time

The National Ports Council Report 1978 states that for UK ports 'port time is 6.5% longer than berth time'. However, if all the ships that loaded or discharged at Bombay are considered for the years 1983–7, then the average excess of port time over berth time was about 40 per cent. It would, though, only be fair to state that the situation has greatly improved since then.

Ship catastrophes and delays

The global probability of a delay or problem due to a mechanical failure, collision, damage, fire, etc has been estimated at .00012 per day (analysis of one month's casualty data reported in *Lloyd's List* in the mid-1970s).

Pilotage and mooring time delays

This will obviously vary for each port depending on the length of pilotage, tide, currents, weather, locks, etc. Table 15.6 shows the pilotage times for large powerful vessels arriving and leaving 18 randomly selected ports on the world's major trade routes.

Weather delays

The weather can affect port time in several ways: gales and fog can reduce or halt movement within a port, and gales may also prevent cargo-handling at berths with large cranes – as at container terminals and at exposed berths.

Table 15.6 Pilotage time	
Hours	No of ports
0	0
0.5	4
1	5
2	2
3	2
4	2
5	1
8	1
22	1

Note: Of these pilotage movements, more than 80 per cent were under four hours.

The weather can be one of the few causes of stoppages at a tanker terminal. With some cargoes – particularly the traditional general cargoes and bulk cargoes such as sugar – rain can stop all cargo work.

Climates do of course vary widely between ports throughout the world, and at any one port the climate will of course change with the seasons. However, by consulting the Admiralty pilot books and the Admiralty seasonal climatological charts for 16 major ports positioned evenly over the major trade routes, the figures given in Table 15.7 should give some indication of the meteorological problems to be expected in port over the course of a year's worldwide trading.

Port delays as a result of congestion

Port congestion arises when port capacity is insufficient to cope with the traffic arriving at the port. It is not a new problem and can occur at any port if there is a sudden upsurge in demand or a hold-up in the port such as a strike. After the oil price rise in 1973, many of the OPEC countries spent their increased revenues on extra imports and this caused severe congestion in

Table 15.7 The effects of the weather on port time		
Weather type	Range in days per annum that phenomenon experienced	Percentage time (average for all 16 ports)
Gales	0–30	5
Fog	0–45	1
Rain	0–169	5

PORTS

Table 15.8   Port delays as a result of congestion

Year	Average delay (in days)
1971	2.2
1972	2.3
1973	4.0
1974	4.8
1975	14.3
1976	40.4

many cases. In 1976 for example, ships carrying cement to Nigeria waited over 200 days at Apapa/Lagos.

In April 1976, a conference of experts organised by UNCTAD gave the figures shown in Table 15.8 for the average waiting time for 30 ports that are regularly subject to port congestion.

Extending Table 15.8 for the delay at the 30 worst ports for a further 10 years following 1976, based on the port data given in *Lloyd's List*, gives an average of days delayed as follows:

1979	17.5
1983	8.9
1986	4.5

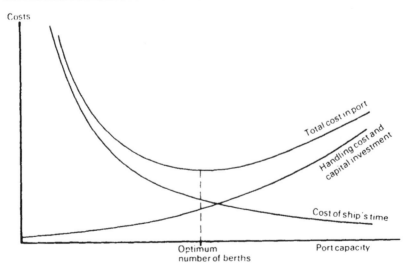

Fig 15.3   Conventional breakbulk general cargo berth.

291

The above extension to Table 15.8 shows that the problem has declined, but still flares up from time to time during periods of sudden increases in local demand. Also since the 1976 period, the half-dozen or so ports that are most seriously affected by congestion have developed various queue reporting systems.

It is very important to clearly identify the cause of the delay. If, for instance, the delay was caused by slow Customs clearance, but this was not recognised and new berths were built, then it would only aggravate the situation.

Because of the severe nature of some of these congestions in the early 1970s, UNCTAD in 1975 set up a small group to analyse the situation. Bimco, who were represented on the UNCTAD working group, summarised the 10 major causes of congestion in one of their 1976 *Bulletins* as follows, and although this assessment is now nearly 30 years old, the summary is still valid:

1 Planning

(A) Investment in new berths without assuring that back-up areas, port access and operating capabilities such as trained manpower, cargo-handling equipment and warehousing space (either within or outside the port area) are able to service these new berths.

(B) Inadequacy of inland transport, both in capacity and efficiency, in relation to trucks, wagons, highways and port access routes.

(C) Late completion of port and transport development projects, so that expected capacity is not available on time.

(D) Failure to keep traffic forecasts updated to reflect changes in the pace of major economic developments.

(E) Improvements by rebuilding wharves without providing for the accommodation of expanding traffic volumes during construction.

(F) Failure of port management and planning authorities to make adequate plans in time for port developments.

(G) Inflexibility in development plans to allow for later changes in modes of traffic flows.

(H) Low appeal of port and shipping problems in the public mind, leading to lesser priorities being accorded to port investment.

(I) Political and social interference that have a bearing on the decision-making processes.

2 Management

(A) Lack of continuity in senior port management positions.

(B) Senior port management chosen without regard for the qualifications required by the job and the adequate provision for upgrading knowledge.

(C) Too little training for other staff, particularly of the middle management and operating levels.

(D) Lack of direct authority of management to effect remedial actions.

3 Labour

(A) Poor labour relations, leading to inefficient restrictive practices.

(B) Problems caused by too much or too little labour, according to circumstances.

(C) Inefficient deployment of labour.

(D) Failure to adapt working practices to local circumstances, such as climates.

(E) Lack of training of dockworkers, especially in the use of sophisticated equipment.

4 Co-ordination

(A) Lack of co-operation between different private and governmental organisations working in the port area.

(B) Inadequate consultation between the port authority and users of the port in respect of operations and development.

5 Traffic

(A) Irregular traffic due to erratic import and export policies, especially with regard to bulk purchasing and the granting of import licences.

(B) Short-term traffic variations due to unrationalised shipping schedules, leading to ship bunching.

(C) Too many ships operating on certain routes, and consequently calling for small tonnages and making inefficient use of berths.

(D) Inefficient distribution of cargo between hatches, thus preventing intensive working of the ship.

(E) Cargo stowed at port of loading without regard to efficiency of discharge.

(F) Forms of packaging and cargo presentation unsuitable for efficient handling at the port.

The photo shows bagged grain being handled using a fairly sophisticated bag transporter. (Courtesy of Fairplay)

(G) Consignees without adequate financial resources or physical facilities to take cargo.

(H) Ships spending longer than necessary at berth for reasons such as slack in their schedules.

6 Operations

(A) Inappropriate policies that lead to transit facilities being used for long-term storage where space is inadequate, thus reducing berth throughput.

(B) Lack of inland or port warehousing facilities, causing cargo to have to remain too long in the port transit facilities.

(C) Necessity to handle bulk cargoes at general-cargo berths.

(D) Lack of reserve capacity to deal with surges of demand on ports.

(E) Pilferage and smuggling resulting in tight controls that impede a free and efficient movement.

(F) Lack of finance for modern handling equipment.

(G) Inefficient mix of handling equipment due to circumstances beyond the control of port management.

7 Maintenance

Inadequate maintenance policies that result in a large proportion of equipment being out of service due to:

(A) Absence of preventative and running maintenance.

(B) Lack of qualified maintenance personnel.

(C) Lack of adequate stocks of spare parts.

(D) Insufficient standardisation of equipment types.

8 Clearance procedures and documentation

(A) Late arriving documents.

(B) Faulty documents.

(C) Outmoded documentation requirements and processing methods.

(D) Outmoded clearance facilities for vessel and cargo.

(E) Importers allowed to order shipments without sufficient funds to take delivery on arrival.

9 Dynamic effects

(A) Changes in ship types, especially on an experimental basis, with inadequate prior consultation, leading to temporary inefficiency.

(B) Teething troubles with new cargo-handling methods.

(C) Emergency diversion and transhipment of cargo destined for another port, which can bring temporary peaks in quantities of cargoes that a port has to handle.

(D) Periods of exceptionally bad weather.

10 Function and location of the port

(A) Impossibility of improving back-up land access in ports because adjacent lands have been occupied by urban developments.

(B) Activities carried out in the port area, not related directly to cargo-handling, which may conflict with higher port throughput (eg Customs controls, inspection procedures, etc.).

(C) Special difficulties that may occur with traffic of landlocked countries.

(D) Ports may be serving a regional trade, and traffic may be dislocated by decisions of neighbouring countries.

In the *long term* the cure for congestion is of course to rectify the cause. In the *short term*, though, there are some immediate alternatives that can be tried:

- Use other ports nearby.
- Use different types of ships – for instance, Ro/Ro ships have helped considerably to reduce congestion at some ports in the last few years.
- Use alternative transport systems, ie air.
- Pass immediate legislation to give better control on the flow of traffic entering the country.

Security delays

Ports, just like airports and any other large goods storage depot, have a variety of security problems, including the obvious ones of theft and terrorism. The solution will depend on the extent and sophistication of the local problem. The solution will obviously cost money, though some ports are able to use the local police force at no direct cost to them. What is sometimes overlooked, however, is that most forms of security will take time, cause delays, and involve a further layer of bureaucracy with all its related complications. Note also the additional requirements of the ISPS code that came into force in July 2004.

Number of berths needed in ports

Ideally, the ship operator would like to see empty berths in ports to ensure there are no delays for his ship when it arrives. The port operator, on the other hand, would like to reduce his capital outlay, have only one berth, and a queue of ships so that the berth is always in use and earning! However, in the long run it will be to the advantage of both of them to keep the total costs to a minimum. Hence for any given conditions it is theoretically possible to determine the optimum number of berths. The optimum shown in the graph (Fig 15.3) is an optimum for the total costs and would only be true in a situation where the ship and the port were part of an integrated cost structure – as, say, where an oil company owns both ships and port. In practice, it is seldom easy to establish the given conditions as ports suffer from the old transport problem of *peaks* – ie one day the port is empty, and the next there is a queue waiting. Furthermore, as there is now usually

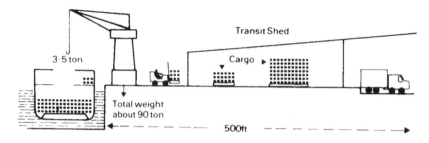

Fig 15.4 Conventional breakbulk general cargo berth.

competition between ports, most have adopted the dictum that 'the berth must wait for the ship, not the ship for the berth'.

The problem can be analysed quantitatively in different ways:

1 *By the application of queuing theory* This is rather a dated method now, as this theory was introduced between 1910 and 1920 by the Danish statistician Erlang for queuing problems at telephone exchanges, and the same theory can be used wherever a queuing situation occurs. This theory has severe limitations for a modern port, as it assumes that ships arrive in a random fashion. In reality, in most ports liner ships arrive to fixed schedules, as do many other ships. Also, some ships on certain trades may arrive in 'waves' due to seasonal or other demand considerations. Queuing theory also assumes that all berths are interchangeable and it can only cope with individual berths – it cannot cope with a long berth that might take, say, three big ships or four small ones. It assumes that the queue is on a first-come, first-served basis and does not allow for priority or queuing systems.

2 *Simulations* This is a sound method and has few of the problems posed by queuing theory. There are two types of simulation:

- *Computer simulations.* These can be expensive as a 'good' one needs to be tailor-made for 'your' port. Depending on the cost, some assumptions will have to be made.
- *Physical manual simulations.* These have the advantage that they are simple, cheap and everyone understands them.

3 *Analyse arrival and departure data on a well-organised spreadsheet* The same spreadsheet of data can do a great deal more than just analyse the queuing problem. It can also analyse many of the other significant port operational problems.

Comparing the various types of berth

The set-up shown in Fig 15.4 is labour-intensive, in that some 20 men per shift are required for the ship-crane-transit shed movement for each hatch of the ship working. It is also relatively slow as, for general cargo, this system

The number 2 container terminal at Marsaxlokk freeport in Malta. (Courtesy of Malta Maritime Authority)

would probably move only about 20 to 30 tons an hour per hatch working. Many ports also work only two eight-hour shifts a day plus Saturday mornings.

Berths designed to transfer palletised cargo

These are very similar to conventional general cargo berths, and in fact usually are general cargo berths with the cranes removed and the quay resurfaced to facilitate the smooth running of the fork-lift trucks, which now handle the cargo directly from the ship's hold to the transit shed through openings in the ship's side or via ramps. One or more mobile cranes may be available to be used if necessary.

This relatively small increase in mechanisation can reduce the labour force by a third, and yet can treble the cargo-handling speed.

The area required per berth by both the above methods is about 1 acre, though ideally the palletised berth may require better lorry-handling facilities because of the greater number of lorries that need to be handled per shift if the greater flow of cargo is to be maintained.

297

The container berth

One of the first obvious differences is that of size. The OCL berth 39 at Tilbury was probably both one of the first container terminals to be built in the UK and also one of the smallest – being only just over 12 acres (about 5 hectares). At the OCL berth at Tilbury the containers had to be stacked five high, whereas the ideal would be to have enough space to avoid stacking at all. As already mentioned, at many ports the terminal is not divided up into individual berths, but ships can be berthed alongside a long straight terminal which allows for a variety of permutations. It is therefore better to consider the space and length of berth and area per gantry crane. From a sample of 20 modern container terminals from ports around the world, we can see that a typical container terminal might have:

> 7.4 hectares per gantry crane, with a standard deviation of 3 hectares
> *and*
> 170 metres of berth length per gantry crane, with a standard deviation of 60 metres

Reception facilities at the entrance to the terminal should include a weighbridge, and also some arrangement to assist the person receiving the container – to give it as complete an inspection as possible and to check on obvious external damage to the container.

Special facilities for refrigerated containers have to be available; these are usually under cover, to avoid the extreme external temperature fluctuations.

Containers may weigh anything up to 30 tons and have to be positioned with great precision. To load and discharge them quickly requires expensive cranes. The modern 'portainer' crane with an outreach of 120 feet is also very heavy and may weigh up to 450 tons. To take this weight, specially constructed quays are necessary and these are very expensive. Labour requirements are in the region of 12 to 15 men per shift (there are a few terminals that have reached a high degree of cargo-handling automation, so labour requirements will be less), and at many container berths three shifts may be worked a day. Working individual ships, 50 containers (approximately 500 tons – assuming an average of 10 tons per TEU) can be handled per hour per crane, though it is unlikely to be able to sustain this throughput over a long period. In comparing a conventional and a container berth, the throughput of cargo per acre remains very similar.

A roll-on/roll-off berth

This is one of the simplest types of berths to construct. About 7 acres of land are required for car or lorry parking space, and the only sophisticated apparatus needed is an adjustable loading ramp. Some of these berths also have a portable crane.

The ferry terminal at Rosslare with two ferries in position. The car parks and ramps can be clearly seen and in the foreground the rails can be seen leading to the passenger station on the terminal.

Labour requirements are minimal, though as each of the vehicles may have a driver and passengers, some terminal facilities to cater for their needs will be required. Cargo-handling speeds are also very high.

Specialist oil berths

These tend to be long jetties stretching from the shore into the deep water. When some of the jetties at Milford Haven were built they were over 3,000 feet long and the 1970 cost for such a jetty was over £5 million. Because of the economies of using large tankers, large storage space near to the berth is necessary. To avoid any secondary transport of crude oil, the position of a tanker terminal and a refinery is usually a common project.

Associated with an oil terminal we would expect to find oil reception facilities and also environmental protection equipment against oil spills such as 'booms', etc.

Other specialist berths

With the growth of the carriage of cargo in bulk and the subsequent increase in the size of ship concerned, specialist berths have been constructed. These have specific-handling equipment to discharge the cargo rapidly and with the minimum labour requirements (eg ores, grain, sugar, coal, sulphur, wine, etc).

Alternatives to formal port systems

For general cargo

Theoretically, barge-carrying ships such as the LASH system could dispense with much of the traditional general cargo port set-up. The ship could steam round in circles dropping off 'floating containers' and collecting others while passing. It has also been suggested that heavy-lift helicopters could load and discharge the ship while it was steaming along the coast!

Bulk (other than oil)

The first SBM (single buoy mooring) for loading slurry was installed at Waipip in New Zealand and loaded its first ship (50,000 dwt) in June 1971. It is 1½ miles offshore and can load at over 1,000 tons an hour.

A development that is in use for bulk cargoes – and sometimes referred to as logistic outsourcing – is the floating terminal. For example, as reported in *Lloyd's List* in October 1998, the port of Bahrain, which uses a self-unloading Panamax vessel, the *Bulk Gulf*, lightens the 170,000 Capesize vessels laden with iron ore pellets some 40 nm out at sea. The *Bulk Gulf* is fitted with four

A sulphur terminal with piles of sulphur clearly visible in the centre of the picture. Ideally, such mounds of sulphur should be well away from habitation areas and terminals handling foodstuffs as wind-blown sulphur particles can travel considerable distances.

cranes, which guarantees fast operation and reliability. The choice between a floating terminal or a floating crane tends to be dependent on the various constraints involved, eg whether shallow barges are necessary, the volume of throughput, the average weather profile, etc. Floating terminals will usually work out more economically, with higher volumes of cargo throughput. Another advantage of such a floating terminal is that it does not necessarily have to be a capital investment, but could be chartered on a variety of contracts for short or long periods.

Bulk (oil)

There are now numerous SBMs and SPMs all over the world, though they probably peaked in the early 1980s. (In 1983, there were about 250. In 1998, there were around 180 ports that had SBM or SPM facilities.) Since then, many of their functions have been taken over by floating storage terminals and floating production, storage and offloading units.

The Sky Wing (300,000 dwt) and the Okinoshima Maru (258,079 dwt) discharging at the Keiyo sea berth. This is a huge floating man-made islet designed for the handling of oil – it is 470 metres long and 54 metres wide. It lies seven kilometres offshore from Sodegaura in Chiba-ken, north-east of Tokyo. The Keiyo sea berth is linked to four oil refineries and handles 2.5 million kilolitres of oil per year. More than 100 oil tankers use the sea berth facility during the course of a year. (Courtesy of the Japanese Ship Owners Association)

FSOs (floating storage terminals) have been in operation since 1972 and FPSOs (floating production, storage and offloading units, or 'floaters') are now becoming increasingly popular and more versatile. One of the first FPSOs was a tanker converted for use at Shell's Castellon field in offshore Spain in 1977. Deadweight tonnage of 'floaters' ranges from 52,000 to 285,000.

With the growth of offshore oil fields and their development there has grown up a sophisticated technology associated with floaters. For instance, in 1998 we were told that in the North Sea there were five STL (submerged turret loading) systems in operation. With this system, a buoy is moored to the seabed. The buoy is then pulled into and secured in a mating cone in the bottom of the floater, thus mooring the vessel and establishing a means of oil transfer.

Port labour

In the port, the ship operator is concerned with those involved with the cargo-handling, ie the docker and the tally clerk — and these make up the largest percentage of those who work in the docks.

The ship operator wants a quick and efficient turn-round for his ship and a good turnout for the cargo. Port labour is the most likely cause for his possible frustration.

Labour difficulties in ports have been very serious ones in British industry: working days lost per 1,000 employees averaged 1,941 annually for the period 1965–9, compared with 1,639 for motor vehicle manufacturing, and 166 for all industries. Since the 1970s, though, the growth of Ro/Ro freight traffic at ports such as Dover has reduced the effectiveness of national strike action; and since the government repealed the Dockworkers (Regulation of Employment) Act (1946) in the early 1990s, UK ports have changed from being the most strike-prone to perhaps being the most strike-free ports in Europe.

Problems for port labour

- The life of a dock is much longer than the vehicles it serves. Therefore many of them tend to be old-fashioned, with poor working facilities and amenities.
- The 1970s and early 1980s were a period of change throughout the UK port industry — from a labour-intensive industry to a capital-intensive industry. This meant that the labour force required diminished. (In 1964, there were 64,000 registered dockworkers in the UK, but by the end of 1973 they had been reduced to 32,000, and by the end of 1982 the figure was only 15,000.) It is hoped that in the UK, the ports' labour position has now largely stabilised. This reduction in labour cost the industry dearly in redundancy payments, but it is hoped that those remaining in

Table 15.9 Employment in the port of Rotterdam in 1989 (percentages)	
Stevedores	15
Shipping	7.5
Inland transport	13.8
Storage and distribution	3.2
Agents and brokers	12.7
Navigation-related services	10.2
The rest	37.6

the industry with a job have a *better* job. This problem of over-staffing of ports due to mechanisation, etc has been universal. Even ports such as Singapore, which must have grown more than any other port during the 1980s and increased its productivity fivefold during this period, has had to reduce its workforce from 10,500 in the early 1980s to just over 7,000 in the early 1990s. In Rotterdam, the number of stevedores employed in general cargo-handling was 4,228 in 1982, but this had dropped to 2,150 stevedores by 1989 (see also Table 15.9).

- Ports are physically vast, and in London the port area is spread along some 70-odd miles of the Thames. This makes good communications difficult.
- The large fluctuation in demand for labour obviously creates problems for an employer who wants to give good service to the shipowner and offer continuous regular employment to the docker. One way round this problem is for the docker to become versatile and be prepared to switch from stevedore to maintenance man, depending on the demand. This flexibility has been largely achieved in UK ports, but in many ports around the world it is still a problem.

A brief history of dock labour

Until the Second World War, dock labour was almost universally casual – ie at the commencement of each shift the contractor would offer employment to those who offered themselves for work. When work was available there was no problem, but during the 1930s when work was scarce, discrimination and unfair practices as to who was chosen when work *was* available gave rise to greater bitterness than the simple lack of work.

During the war the labour had to be made less casual, and it was put on a permanent basis after the war, in 1947, when the National Dock Labour Board was formed. This drew up a register of dockworkers, and only registered dockworkers could be employed.

During the early 1960s Lord Devlin was set the task of investigating the problems that beset dock labour and in 1965 his final report appeared. In this report he lists casual labour, restrictive practices and the system of piecework payments as being among the major causes of labour unrest in the docks. The number of different piecework rates had by this time grown into thousands, and dockers either were reluctant to work cargoes where the rates were low, or wasted time in disputes over the rate for a new cargo that they were called upon to handle.

In 1967, in what was referred to as Devlin Stage 1, casual labour was abolished and the dockers were guaranteed a weekly wage – though this was paid to them by the Dock Labour Board. Employers also had to be registered and, of course, pay the money for the dockers' salaries into the pool. This reduced the number of employers in the London enclosed docks from over one hundred to eight.

The final stage, Devlin Stage 2, was introduced port by port around the country. Each man had to work for a particular employer and gradually many of the old restrictive practices disappeared. The details, however, varied from port to port. In London, Stage 2 was introduced in September 1970 and here piecework rates were abolished altogether and the dockers were given a fixed weekly wage. Other ports have kept some form of financial incentive, but this has been greatly simplified. The final step, as already mentioned, was when the Dockworkers (Regulation of Employment) Act 1946 was repealed in the early 1990s.

A further important development that was started in the early 1960s, and has since been growing in impetus, has been training. Not only are training schemes being devised for the dockers, where skill and safety are obviously necessary, but also for good leadership among both the union officials and the management.

It might be possible to make a variety of derogatory inferences about dockers from some of the preceding statements, but they would almost certainly be untrue. British dockers in general – and London dockers in particular – have been, and are, very good at their job.

Although the dock labour situation in the UK has mainly been discussed here, the same basic problems and the same social evolution have an almost universal application. For instance, New York decasualised in 1954, New Zealand in 1965, Australia and Sweden in 1967, and Dublin in 1971, but casual labour can still be found employed in many ports around the world.

Port management and administration

There are three main functions particular to port operation, ie:

1 Maintaining the fabric of the port (port engineer).
2 Moving the ships in and out of the port (harbourmaster).
3 Collecting and moving the cargo on and off the ship (cargo super-intendent).

How these various functions are organised into specific working units will vary greatly from port to port depending on its size, history and the division of responsibility. In addition, what is involved in maintaining, say, the approaches to the port can vary considerably. In some countries this is done by a government agency, while in London, for example, it is done by the PLA.

In the UK, the main historical trend since the Harbours Act in 1964 has been to reorganise ports on principal estuaries into larger units and to reduce the size of management boards (which in many cases had become extraordinarily large) and to move management from the city centre to the dockside where they can be in contact with problems and situations as they develop. During the 1980s and 1990s, many of the UK ports were privatised, and this has helped to streamline their administration.

The port's need for a *computerised information system* can also be considered in three parts:

1 Business: payment of salaries, accountancy, its investment portfolio, preparing strategic plans, etc.
2 Specific operations: cargo-handling, statistics, maintenance, etc.
3 Community needs such as inventory control, cargo clearance and communications, etc.

Port charges

These are very important, as some 50 per cent of ocean transportation costs can be made up of port costs.

In his report on British ports (1962), Lord Rochdale stated: 'There has been a tendency, not only in this country, to treat various branches of the transport industry as some form of public service to which, for one reason or another, sound financial principles need not be applied. As far as major ports are concerned, we entirely reject the concept of public service in so far as this might be held to limit the responsibility for conducting their financial affairs on the basis of sound economic and accounting principles. In other words, we see no reason why the major ports should not be treated for this purpose as commercial undertakings.'

The pricing policy of ports is one that national authorities usually monitor, as do regional authorities such as the EU. With the advent of intermodalism, which has brought growing competition between ports, the analysis of port-pricing policy has become a popular study for academics. In practice, though, I suspect that ports, like supermarkets, watch their major competitors and try to not charge more.

According to a report made by the National Ports Council in 1969, many Continental countries – such as Germany, Belgium, the Netherlands and France – do offer very extensive subsidies to their ports. Even though this was some time ago, British ports are still convinced that their Continental rivals do receive considerable 'financial aid' in some form or other. However, it is very difficult to prove or establish that one port is helped more, or needs more help, than another.

These Continental ports are competing for a very large Continental hinterland and the ports in this case can be tremendous foreign currency earners. These possibilities do not really apply to ports in the UK, though London has undoubtedly lost trade to Rotterdam with its lower charges. The National Ports Council is now defunct, but the literature and surveys that this body completed were among some of the best documentary work on British ports.

The National Ports Council proposed standard nomenclature of main port charges:

1 Conservancy charge This charge is made for the upkeep of the approach channel and waterways. (On most of the Continent, this charge is met by the taxpayer.)

2 Dock charge This is to cover the cost of locks, other entrance charges and berth charges.

3 Wharfage This is dues paid by the cargo for passing over dock estate.

4 Handling charge In most cases, this will be the largest single item.

5 Storage charge This will be levied if the cargo is not collected within a specified time.

6 Passenger charge

7 Other charges This is for services and facilities offered.

With the advent of containers, there has been a move to simplify these charges. For instance, at some ports, container-ship operators are charged a standard rate per container, laden or empty, which is inclusive of dock and conservancy charges, port rates and all normal handling charges from time of receipt or discharge until time of shipment or loading to land transport. In short, the first five of the above charges are made as a single charge. (See also Chapter 8.)

Ship canals

Ship canals serve two main functions:

1 To reduce the length of important trade routes such as the Suez, Panama, Kiel and Corinth Canals:

	Via Suez	Via Cape of Good Hope	Via Panama
London to Kuwait	6,500	11,300	
London to Yokohama	11,150	14,470	12,520
London to Melbourne	11,060	11,900	12,950
London to Auckland	12,670	13,480	11,380

2 To provide access for ships to inland areas such as the St Lawrence Seaway, the North Sea Canal and the Manchester Ship Canal.

The Suez Canal

This joins the Mediterranean (Port Said) with the Gulf of Suez (Suez). The Canal is about 100 miles long (no locks). The maximum ship dimensions usually allowed are 64 metres breadth and 16 metres draft, though if present plans are completed it should be able to accept fully laden VLCCs.

The ships go through the Canal in convoys – with one convoy usually waiting in the Bitter Lakes for the other to pass. The average time for transit is about 15 hours.

The Suez Canal was opened in 1869, having taken 10 years to build. It was closed from 1967 to 1975. In the year 2000, an average of around 40 ships a day passed through the Canal (80 is the maximum capacity per day). About 9 per cent more transits are southbound rather than northbound. The percentage share of the total number of ships transiting laden are: tankers 14 per cent, bulk carriers 22 per cent, general cargo 14.5 per cent, containers 35 per cent. In ballast the figures are: tankers 63 per cent, bulk carriers 5 per cent, general cargo 9 per cent, containers 2 per cent.

The Panama Canal

The Canal crosses the isthmus of Panama from north-west to south-east and joins the Caribbean Sea (Cristobal) to the Pacific Ocean (Balboa). It was opened in 1914. It is 45 miles long, and the locks have to lift ships some 85 feet. The average time of transit is eight to ten hours. The maximum ship dimensions usually allowed are 274.3 metres length, 32.3 metres breadth, and 11.28 metres draft. In 2000, an average of about 35 ships passed through the Canal each day. The most popular ship types using the Canal are bulk carriers (about 50 per cent) and container ships (about 24 per cent).

The ownership of the Canal was transferred from the USA to Panama on 31 December 1999.

New, larger locks are proposed for the Canal in 2025.

A pusher tug and oil barge in lock 3 on the Welland canal, which joins Lake Ontario to Lake Erie. As vessels using the Seaway have to pass under bridges, their air draft (height above the water) is often asked for in charters to this area.

Kiel Canal

This Canal, completed at the end of the nineteenth century, cuts across the base of Schleswig–Holstein, linking the Baltic to the North Sea. Its length is 53 miles and the average transit time is about seven hours. It has locks at each end, and the maximum ship dimensions allowed are 315 metres length, 40 metres breadth, and 9 metres draft.

In the year 2000, the average number of ships per day was 36 westbound and 35 eastbound – with the most popular type being general dry cargo vessels.

St Lawrence Seaway

When the Seaway was opened in 1959 it opened up a vast new hinterland to ocean-going ships. The distance, for instance, from the Belle Isle Straits at the mouth of the St Lawrence to Chicago is some 2,250 miles, with 17 locks in the whole system.

The maximum draft allowed is just under 8 metres, and the maximum length of ship allowed is 220 metres. Its use is seasonal because of the ice. Over 80 per cent of the cargo carried down the Seaway is bulk cargo (iron ore, wheat and coal). The maximum air draft is about 35 metres. During the open season in 2000, transits of the Welland Canal varied between 10 to 39 a day.

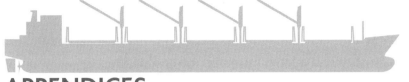

APPENDICES

(From a paper given by Dr Giziakis and Dr P Rogers in July 1980.)

The database was the entire world fleet of tankers of between 6,000 and 550,000 dwt and the world fleet of bulk carriers between 10,000 and 170,000 dwt.

Tankers

GRT = 3,394.3 + 0.483 dwt
dwt = −6,207.5 + 2.06 GRT
NRT = 5,462 + 0.839 GRT
Capacity = −197 + 1.19 dwt

Bulk carriers

Consumption at 14 knots in tons/day = 19.15 + 0.00034 dwt
GRT = 3,174 + 0.496 dwt
TPI = 46.8 + 0.00163 dwt
dwt = −6,280 + 2.0 GRT
NRT = −298 + 0.68 GRT

Appendix B: Voyage estimate using Excel

	A	B	C	D	E	F	G	H
1								
2		Distance	Speed	Time	FO pd	FO used	mdo pd	mdo used
3	Distance to loadport	4,558	14.5	=B3/C3/24	=34*C3^3/14.5^3	=D3*E3	2.00	=D3*G3
4	Port time loadport			4.00	0	=D4*E4	1.00	=D4*G4
5	Distance to canal	1,212	14.5	=B5/C5/24	=34*C5^3/14.5^3	=D5*E5	2.00	=D5*G5
6	Canal time			1.00	30	=D6*E6	2.00	=D6*G6
7	Distance to disport	4,150	14.5	=B7/C7/24	=34*C7^3/14.5^3	=D7*E7	2.00	=D7*G7
8	Port time disport			7.00	0	=D8*E8	1.00	=D8*G8
9	Extra time allowance			0.49				
10	Total	=Sum (B3:B7)		=Sum (D3:D9)		=Sum (F3:F8)		=Sum (H3:H8)
11							mdo cost	132
12	FO cost (per ton) loadport	97						
13	FO cost next bunker port	99						
14	Freight rate per ton	14						
15	Maximise cargo or bunkers	*See below						
16		Tonnes			27,849			
17	Loadline dwt (if dwt cargo)	26,000			679			
18	Bunkers	700						
19	Stores	200						
20	Constant	100						
21	Cargo	=B17−(B18+B19+B20)						
22								

Excel spreadsheet continued

	A	B	C	D	E	F	G	H
		Distance	Speed	Time	FO pd	FO used	mdo pd	mdo used
1								
2								
23	Cost of fuel oil	=F10*97						
24	Cost of mdo	=H10*H12						
25	DRC	=D10*G25				DRC cpd	3,000	
26	Leaving previous port	1,000						
27	Loadport costs	10,000						
28	Canal costs	50,000						
29	Disport costs	11,000						
30	Total Costs	=Sum(B23:B29)						
31								
32	Total freight	=B21*B14						
33	Commission							
34	Total Earnings	=B32 – B32* (B3/100)						
35								
36	Total voyage profit	=B34 – B30						
37	Profit per day	=B36/D10						

*B15 = IF ((B13 – B12) > B14 'max bunkers', 'max cargo'

A spreadsheet may not be the most elegant way to compute a voyage estimate, but it is a process the majority are familiar with. The advantage over a dedicated program is that you are in control over any assumptions – for instance, the formula used in column E to estimate the fuel consumption is fairly crude and should be adjusted for each specific ship. (see Chapter 3).
The table above indicates the formulae needed to be inserted in the worksheet which, when completed, should appear as on page 190.

Excel spreadsheet continued

	A	B Distance	C Speed	D Time	E FO pd	F FO used	G mdo pd	H mdo used
1								
2								
3	Distance to loadport	4,558	14.5	13.10	34	445.32	2.00	26.20
4	Port time loadport			4.00	0	0.00	1.00	4.00
5	Distance to canal	1,212	14.5	3.48	34	118.41	2.00	6.97
6	Canal time			1.00	30	30.00	2.00	2.00
7	Distance to disport	4,150	14.5	11.93	34	405.46	2.00	23.85
8	Port time disport			7.00	0	0.00	1.00	7.00
9	Extra time allowance			0.49				
10	Total	9,920		41.00		999.20		70.01
11								
12	FO cost (per ton) loadport	97					mdo cost	132
13	FO cost next bunker port	99						
14	Freight rate per ton	14						
15	Maximise cargo or bunkers	max cargo						
16		Tonnes						
17	Loadline dwt (if dwt cargo)	26,000						
18	Bunkers	700						
19	Stores	200						
20	Constant	100						
21	Cargo	25,000						

Excel spreadsheet continued

	A	B Distance	C Speed	D Time	E FO pd	F FO used	G mdo pd	H mdo used
1								
2								
22								
23	Cost of fuel oil	96,922						
24	Cost of mdo	9,242						
25	DRC	122,987				DRC cpd	3,000	
26	Leaving previous port	1,000						
27	Loadport costs	10,000						
28	Canal costs	50,000						
29	Disport costs	11,000						
30	Total Costs	301,151						
31								
32	Total freight	350,000						
33	Commission	6						
34	Total earnings	329,000						
35								
36	Total voyage profit	27,849						
37	Profit per day	679						

Appendix C: Distances along the world's major trade routes

London to:	Panama 4,720
	New York 3,200
	Montreal 3,135
	Gibraltar 1,301
	Monrovia 3,225
	Cape Town 6,150
	Recife 4,115
	Rio de Janeiro 5,200
	Buenos Aires 6,330
	Cape Horn 7,510

Tokyo to:	Sydney 4,348
	Valparaiso 9,298
	Honolulu 3,413

Gibraltar to:	Marseilles 690
	Naples 980
	Piraeus 1,481
	Port Said 1,913
	Panama 4,340
	New York 3,145
	Buenos Aires 5,365
	Cape Town 5,190
	Rio de Janeiro 4,235
	St Vincent 1,540

Suez to:	Kuwait 3,199
	Colombo 3,394
	Calcutta 4,604
	Bombay 2,959
	Sydney 8,233
	Tokyo 7,853

San Francisco to:	Tokyo 4,554
	Vladivostock 4,566
	Hong Kong 6,050
	Bangkok 8,061
	Manila 7,540

New York to:	Panama 1,972
	New Orleans 1,707
	Montreal 1,516
	St John 537
	Hong Kong 11,230
	Madeira 3,735
	Montevideo 5,750
	Monrovia 4,089

Panama to:	San Francisco 3,245
	Vancouver 4,022
	Yokohama 7,680
	Wellington 6,500
	Hong Kong 9,194
	Sydney 7,680
	Montreal 3,200

Cape Town to:	Buenos Aires 3,718
	Rio de Janeiro 3,718
	New York 6,800
	Colombo 4,395
	Bombay 4,630
	Kuwait 5,170
	Tokyo 8,338

SEA TRANSPORT INDEX